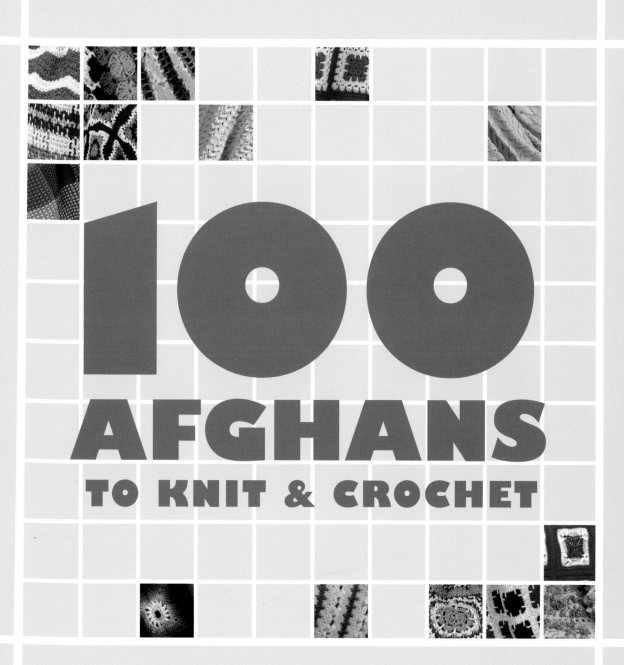

100 AFGHANS
TO KNIT & CROCHET

Jean Leinhauser & Rita Weiss

Sterling Publishing Co., Inc.
New York

This book is dedicated to Janie Herrin without whose talents,
it would have never been possible.

Library of Congress Cataloging-in-Publication Data

10 9 8 7 6 5 4 3 2 1

Published by Sterling Publishing Co., Inc.
387 Park Avenue South, New York, NY 10016
© 2005 by The Creative Partners, LLC™
Distributed in Canada by Sterling Publishing
^c/o Canadian Manda Group, 165 Dufferin Street
Toronto, Ontario, Canada M6K 3H6
Distributed in Australia by Capricorn Link (Australia) Pty. Ltd.
P.O. Box 704, Windsor, NSW 2756, Australia

Printed in China
All rights reserved

Sterling ISBN 1-4027-2314-8

For information about custom editions, special sales, premium and
corporate purchases, please contact Sterling Special Sales
Department at 800-805-5489 or specialsales@sterlingpub.com.

INTRODUCTION

What project do knitters and crocheters like to make above all others?

Why, afghans of course!

Afghans are fun to make and great to give, and—probably best of all—they don't have to fit anybody!

An afghan made for a special person will be a continuing reminder of the giver and the loving wishes that were worked into the stitches.

Afghans not only provide warmth and comfort but are magnificent decorative accents for any room. A gift of an afghan can commemorate a special occasion: a birth, a marriage, a wedding anniversary—or can be made and given just for fun. A toddler will cherish his very own afghan, and one made for a first-year college student will be a welcome connection to home.

Whether you make an elaborate knitted cable stitch version, or crochet a colorful one in squares, you will have created a permanent record of your talents.

In this book we've assembled a collection that runs the gamut from sweet and simple to elaborate and elegant. No matter what type of afghan you're looking for, you are sure to find it here: an elegant aran, a lacy pineapple, a bright and cheery child's afghan, a unique one made from scraps, a fascinating ripple, dimensional shells, a mile-a-minute are among the choices. We think you'll have fun choosing your favorites from this large collection of 100 wonderful designs

And once a much-loved afghan finally becomes old and worn, it can continue giving comfort as a snuggly bed for the family dog or cat!

We had a great time collecting the projects for this book, and hope that you will share our pleasure.

Rita Weiss   *Jean Leinhauser*

CONTENTS

TURTLE SHELLS
#1
8

WHITE STARS
#6
18

EARTH TONES
#11
28

PRETTY LACE
#16
39

SINGING THE BLUES
#21
48

CABLES & CHECKS
#2
10

NURSERY TIME
#7
21

LUMBERJACK
#12
31

BLUEBERRY PIE
#17
40

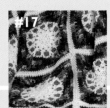
BRANCHES & BERRIES
#22
50

DANCING DAISIES
#3
12

CURLED TIPS DAISY
#8
22

AUTUMN GLORY
#13
32

CLASSIC STYLE
#18
42

FRINGED FOR BABY
#23
54

BEAUTIFUL BLUES
#4
14

QUICK CABLE
#9
24

RIPPLE ROMANCE
#14
35

SAND CASTLE
#19
44

SCRAP SENSATION
#24
56

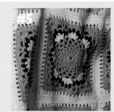
LILAC LACE
#5
16

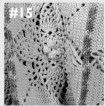
COUNTRY ROSES
#10
26

MONET PINEAPPLE
#15
36

SHADED PANELS
#20
46

SWEET SCALLOPS
#25
59

#26

REFLECTIONS ON THE GO
60

#27

IN THE PINK
62

#28

PRETTY PLAID
64

#29

SAILING ALONG
66

#30

COTTON CANDY
68

#31

ARAN ISLE
70

#32

DEEP PURPLE
72

#33

WAVES
75

#34

POPCORN & LACE
76

#35

COMING UP ROSY
78

#36

JEWEL RIPPLE
81

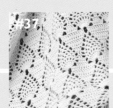

#37

PINEAPPLE THROW
82

#38

AMERICANA
84

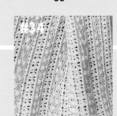

#39

LEMONADE SKIES
86

#40

EVENING SHADOWS
88

#41

TIFFANY ROSE
90

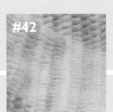

#42

PRETTY PUFFS
93

#43

FILET RUFFLES
94

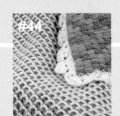

#44

TWO SIDES TO THE STORY
96

#45

SUMMER SUNSHINE
98

#46

STARRY NIGHT
100

#47

SAGE WHEEL
102

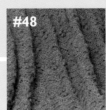

#48

ROSE RIPPLE
104

#49

DREAM PANELS
106

#50

ROSY RUFFLES
108

#51

RICH CABLES
110

#52

CHEVRONS & DIAMONDS
113

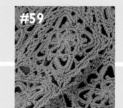

#53

MARVELOUS MAUVE
116

#54

JUST PEACHY
118

#55

VINEYARD VIEW
120

#57

COZY MILE-A-MINUTE
124

#58

LOVELY LACE
126

#59

RENAISSANCE BEAUTY
128

POLKA DOT COUNTRY
122

#60

CLUSTER WHEEL
130

#61

CHOO-CHOO
132

#62

BOLD PLAID
134

#63

#64

AFGHANS IN A JIFFY
137

#65

GRANNY GOES STRAIGHT
138

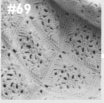

#66

CATHEDRAL WINDOWS
140

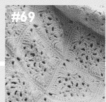

#67

IMPRESSIONS
142

#68

CAPTAIN'S WHEEL
146

#69

MERRY SUNSHINE
148

#70

SHIP AHOY
150

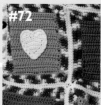

#72

COUNTRY HEARTS
154

#73

STAINED GLASS
157

#74

RAINBOW RIB
160

JACOB'S LADDER
152

RIPPLE AT DAWN
162

BABY CLOUDS
164

TROPICAL DAISY
174

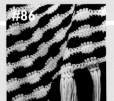
SOPHISTICATED SUMMER
186

CABLED CLASSIC
196

VICTORIAN ROSES
209

TWILIGHT WAVE
166

SNOW TREES
176

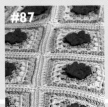
FLOWER POWER
188

EMBOSSED FLORAL
198

BRIGHT AND BOLD
212

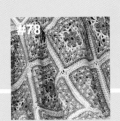
GARDEN PATH
168

ROSE GARDEN
179

A WALK IN THE WOODS
190

SUMMER NIGHT
PATCHWORK
200

BABY STRIPES
214

CURLY O'S
170

SOFT SHADES
182

DAISIES WON'T
TELL LAPGHAN
192

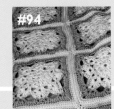
SOFT AND SWEET
204

CROSS OVER THROW
216

SWEET HEARTS
172

BLUE IS FOR BOYS
184

MESH'IN AROUND
194

LONG STITCH RIPPLE
206

FLORAL ACCENT
218

GENERAL DIRECTIONS . . . PAGE 220

INDEX . . . PAGE 223

TURTLE SHELLS

Designed by Janie Herrin

SIZE
45" x 60"

MATERIALS
Worsted weight yarn,
  32 oz burgundy
  8 oz green
  8 oz buff

Note: *Photographed model made with Red Heart® Super Saver® #376 Burgandy, #389 Hunter Green, and #334 Buff*

Size H (5mm) crochet hook
  (or size required for gauge)

GAUGE
7 dc = 2"
1 square = 7 $\frac{1}{2}$" x 7 $\frac{1}{2}$"

INSTRUCTIONS

Square (make 48)

With burgundy, ch 5, join with sl st to form a ring.

Rnd 1: Ch 3 (equals first dc), work 15 dc in ring, join with sl st in 3rd st of beg ch-3: 16 dc.

Rnd 2: Work beg shell in joining, (skip next dc, shell in next dc) around, skip last dc, join in top of beg ch-3: 8 shells.

Rnd 3: Sl st in next dc and in ch-2 sp of next shell; work beg shell in same sp; (ch 4, sc in ch-2 sp of next shell, ch 4, shell in next shell) around, end ch 4, join as before in beg ch-3; finish off burgundy.

Rnd 4: Join buff with sl st in any corner ch-2 sp; in same sp work beg shell; *dc in next 2 dc, ch 4, Cl in next sc, ch 4, dc in next 2 dc, shell in next ch-2 corner sp; rep from * around, ending join with sl st in top of beg dc; finish off buff.

Rnd 5: Join green with sc in any corner ch-2 sp, ch 2, sc in same sp; *sc in next 4 dc, working in front of ch-4 sp, work 3 tr in ch-4 lp on Rnd 3, sc in top of Cl, working in front of next ch-4 sp, 3 tr in next ch-4 lp on Rnd 3, sc in next 4 dc, (sc, ch 2, sc) in corner sp; rep from * around , join in beg sc; finish off green.

Rnd 6: Join burgundy with sl st in any corner ch-2 sp, work beg shell; dc in each st around, working shell in each rem corner ch-2 sp, join in beg dc.

Rnd 7: Ch 1, sc in each st around, working 3 sc in each corner sp; finish off, weave in ends.

Joining

To join, hold two squares with right sides tog and sew with overcast st along one side, carefully matching sts and corners, and working in outer lps only. In same manner join squares into 8 rows of 6 squares each.

Border

Rnd 1: Hold piece with right side facing you; join burgundy with a sc in center sc of 3-sc corner group in upper right corner; 2 sc in same sc; sc in each st and joining around, working 3 sc in every outer corner; join, finish off.

Fringe

Following Fringe instructions on page 221, cut strands 15" long from each color.

Using one strand of each color, work single knot fringe across each short end, placing a knot in each outer corner and spacing knots evenly about 3 sts apart across.

#2 CABLES & CHECKS

Designed by Michele Thompson for Coats and Clark

SIZE

53" x 70"

MATERIALS

Worsted weight yarn,
  56 oz off white (A)
  23 oz rose (B)
  23 oz blue (C)

Note: Photographed model made with Red Heart® Super Saver® #313 Aran (A), #374 Country Rose (B) and #382 Country Blue (C)

Size J (6mm) crochet hook (or size required for gauge)

GAUGE

8 sts = 3" in check patt

16 rows = 4" in check patt

20 sts = 7" in cable patt

INSTRUCTIONS

With B, ch 153.

Row 1 (right side): Sc in 2nd ch from hook and in each ch across: 152 sc; ch 1, turn.

Row 2: Sc in each st across changing to A in last st; ch 1, turn.

Note: Carry color not in use loosely up side of work.

Row 3: Sc in first sc; Ldc in ch 2 rows below next st; (sc in next sc, Ldc in ch 2 rows below next st) 3 times; *sc in next 2 sc, (Ldc in each ch 2 rows below next 4 sts, sc in next 2 sc) 3 times**; (Ldc in ch 2 rows below next st, sc in next sc) 4 times, Ldc in ch 2 rows below next st; rep from * to last 8 sts, end at **; (Ldc in ch 2 rows below next st, sc in next sc) 4 times: 88 Ldc and 64 sc; ch 1, turn.

Long dc (Ldc): YO, insert hook in specified st, YO and draw up a lp to height of working row, (YO and draw through 2 lps on hook) twice (skip st behind ldc): Ldc made.

Double Triple Crochet (dtr): YO hook 3 times, insert hook in specified st and draw up a lp (5 lps now onhook); (YO and draw through 2 lps) 4 times: dtr made.

Work around post: Insert hook from front to back to front around post of specified st.

Row 4: Rep Row 2 changing to C in last st.

Row 5: Sc in first 2 sc, (Ldc in sc 2 rows below next st, sc in next sc) 3 times; *Ldc in each sc 2 rows below next 2 sts, (sc in next 4 sc, Ldc in each sc 2 rows below next 2 sts) 3 times**; (sc in next sc, Ldc in sc 2 rows below next st) 4 times, sc in next sc; rep from * to last 8 sts, end at **; (sc in next sc, Ldc in sc 2 rows below next st) 3 times, sc in last 2 sc: 62 Ldc and 90 sc; ch 1, turn.

Row 6: Rep Row 2 changing to A in last st.

Row 7: Sc in first sc, Ldc in sc 2 rows below next st; (sc in next sc, Ldc in sc 2 rows below next st) 3 times; **sc in next 2 sc; *skip next 2 sts, (dtr around post of next Ldc 3 rows below next st) twice, (dtr around post of Ldc 3 rows below skipped st) twice (skip 4 sc behind 4 dtr): cable made; sc in next 2 sc; rep from * twice more***; (Ldc in sc 2 rows below next st, sc in next sc) 4 times, Ldc in sc 2 rows below next st; rep from ** to last 8 sts, end at ***; (Ldc in sc 2 rows below next st, sc in next sc) 4 times: 60 dtr, 28 Ldc and 64 sc; ch 1, turn.

Row 8: Rep Row 2 changing to B in last st.

Row 9: With B, rep Row 5.

Row 10: Rep Row 2.

Row 11: With A, sc in first sc, Ldc in sc 2 rows below next st; (sc in next sc, Ldc in sc 2 rows below next st) 3 times, *sc in next 2 sc, (dtr around post of each of next 4 dtr 3 rows below (skip 4 sc behind 4 dtr), sc in next 2 sc) 3 times**; (Ldc in sc 2 rows below next st, sc in next sc) 4 times, Ldc in sc 2 rows below next st; rep from * to last 8 sts, end at **; (Ldc in sc 2 rows below next st, sc in next sc) 4 times: 60 dtr, 28 Ldc and 64 sc; ch 1, turn.

Row 12: Rep Row 4.

Rep Rows 5 through 12 for patt, working cable as dtr around the post of dtr instead of Ldc on Row 7 until about 70" from beg, end by working Row 11. Finish off and weave in ends.

Finishing

With right side facing and A, work 1 row sc across lower edge in rem 1ps of beg ch. Finish off and weave in ends.

Fringe

Following Single Knot Fringe Instructions on page 221, cut strands of A 10" long and knot 2 strands in each st opposite each A Ldc and cable on top and bottom edges. Trim fringe.

#3 DANCING DAISIES

Designed by Nazanin S. Fard

SIZE
36" x 54"

MATERIALS
Worsted weight yarn
  400 yds yellow (A)
  1200 yds white (B)
  1200 yds sage green (C)

Note: Photographed model made with Plymouth Encore #1382(A), #208(B), and #9401(C)

Size G (4mm) crochet hook, or size required for gauge

GAUGE
16 dc = 4"

INSTRUCTIONS

Note: The afghan is worked in strips. Each strip consists of 13 daisies and the afghan is 6 strips wide.

First Daisy (make one for each strip)

With A ch 6, join with a sl st to form a ring.

Rnd 1: Ch 1, (sc in ring, ch 9) 12 times, join with sl st in beg sc: 12 ch-9 sps; finish off, weave in ends.

Rnd 2: Join B with sl st in any ch-9 sp, (2 sc, hdc, 3 dc, 2tr, 3 dc, hdc, 2 sc) in same sp and in each ch-9 sp around: 12 petals made; finish off, weave in ends.

Second and following 11 daisies (make 12 for each strip)

Work same as first daisy to end of Rnd 1.

Rnd 2: Join B with sl st in any ch-9 sp, in same sp work (2 sc, hdc, 3 dc, tr, sl st between the 2 tr on a petal of previous daisy, tr, 3 dc, hdc, 2 sc) 3 times joining each time to next petal on previous daisy; *in next ch-9 sp, work (2 sc, hdc, 3 dc 2 tr, 3 dc, hdc, 2 sc); rep from * around: 12 petals, 3 joined to prev daisy; finish off, weave in ends. On following daisies, join to previous daisy on opposite side from previous joining, leaving 3 petals unattached between each set of 3 joined petals as shown. (End daisies on each strip will have 9 petals still free.)

Border for first strip

Rnd 1: Join C with sl st between the 2 tr in top daisy's end petal at top; **ch 9 for corner, sl st between 2 tr on next petal; * (ch 5, sl st between the 2 tr on next petal) twice; ch 5, sl st between the 2 tr on next daisy; rep from * to end of one side of strip, ch 9, sl st between 2 tr on next petal; (ch 5, sl st between the 2 tr on next petal) twice**; rep between **, join.

Rnd 2: Sl st into next ch-9 sp, ch 3 (counts as a dc), 5 dc in same ch-5 sp, ch-5, 6 dc in same ch-sp for corner; * [4 dc in next ch-5 sp, ch 3, 4 dc in same ch-sp], rep between [] to end of one side of strip; (6 dc, ch 5, 6 dc) in ch-9 sp, (4 dc in next ch-5 sp, ch 3, 4 dc in same ch-sp) twice, (6 dc, ch 5, 6 dc) in ch-9 sp; repeat from * around, join; finish off, weave in ends.

Border for all other strips

Rep Rnd 1 same as first border.

Rnd 2: Sl st into next ch-9 sp, ch 3 (counts as a dc), 5 dc in same ch-sp, ch 3, sl st into corresponding ch-sp on previous strip, ch 3, 6 dc in same ch-9 sp; * [4 dc in next ch-5 sp, ch 1, sl st into corresponding ch-5 sp of prev strip, ch 1, 4 dc in same ch-5 sp]; rep between [] to end of one side of strip, (6 dc, ch 3, sl st into corresponding ch-9 sp of previous strip, 6 dc) in ch-9 sp, follow instructions for Rnd 2 of first border for the rest of the round. Finish off, weave in all ends.

#4 BEAUTIFUL BLUES

Designed by Janie Herrin

SIZE
47" x 52"

MATERIALS
Bulky weight yarn,
   42 oz blue and white mix

Worsted weight yarn,
   6 oz blue

Note: Photographed model made with Lion Brand® Homespun® #355 Delft and Lion Brand® Wool-Ease® #116 Delft

Size K (6.5mm) crochet hook
   (or size required for gauge)

GAUGE
10 sc = 4"

10 sc rows = 4"

INSTRUCTIONS

With bulky yarn, ch 113 loosely.

Row 1: Sc in 2nd ch from hook and in each rem ch: 112 sc; ch 3 (counts as first dc of next row), turn.

Row 2 (right side): Dc in next sc; *sk next sc, dc in next 3 sc, YO, insert hook in skipped sc and pull up a lp to height of a dc, (YO and draw through 2 lps) twice; rep from * across to last 2 sc, dc in last 2 sc; ch 1, turn.

Row 3: Sc in each st; ch 3, turn.

Rep Rows 2 and 3 alternately until piece measures about 50", ending by working a Row 3. At end of last row, ch 1 instead of 3, turn.

Border

Rnd 1: 3 sc in first sc for corner; sc across to last sc, 3 sc in last sc for 2nd corner; work even in sc around outer edges of afghan, working 3 sc in each rem outer corner; join with a sl st to beg sc; finish off bulky yarn.

Rnd 2: Working now with two strands of worsted weight held tog, join yarn with sl st in center sc of any 3-sc corner group, ch 1, 3 sc in same st; work sc in each sc around, working 3 sc in center st of each 3-sc corner group; join in beg sc.

Rnd 3: Ch 1, sc in each sc around, working 3 sc in center st of each 3-sc corner group; join in beg sc.

Rnd 4: Ch 2; working now from left to right, sk next sc, ch 1; * reverse hdc in next sc to right, ch 1, sk next sc to right; rep from * around, join in first ch of beg ch-2; finish off, weave in ends.

#5 LILAC LACE

Designed by Janie Herrin

SIZE
55" x 66" before border

MATERIALS
Worsted weight yarn,
   28 oz lilac
   7 oz purple
   28 oz off white

Note: Photographed model made with Bernat® Berella® 4, #01317 Lilac, #08724 Velvet Night, and #08940 Natural

Size H (5mm) crochet hook
   (or size required for gauge)

GAUGE
7 dc = 2"

Square = 11" x 11"

INSTRUCTIONS

Square (make 30)

With lilac, ch 6, join with sl st to form a ring.

Rnd 1: Ch 3 (equals first dc), 15 dc in ring, join in 3rd ch of beg ch-3: 16 dc.

Rnd 2: Ch 1, sc in same ch, (ch 2, sc in next dc) around, ch 1, sc in beg sc to form last lp:16 ch-2 lps.

Rnd 3: Ch 1, reaching back with hook, sc in same sp made with ch-1 and sc, (ch 2, sc in next sp) around, ch 1, sc in beg sc as before.

Rnd 4: Ch 1, sc in same sp, (ch 3, sc in next sp) around, ch 1, hdc in beg sc to form last lp.

Rnd 5: Ch 1, sc in same sp, (ch 4, sc in next sp) around, ch 2, hdc in beg sc as before.

Rnd 6: Rep Rnd 5; at end of rnd, ch 4, join in beg sc, finish off: 16 ch-4 lps.

Rnd 7: Join off white with sl st in any ch-4 lp, ch 3, (2 dc, ch 2, 3 dc) in same sp; *ch 1, sc in next lp, ch 1, in next lp work (3 dc, ch 2, 3 dc): shell made; rep from * around, end with last ch 1, join in 3rd ch of beg ch-3, finish off: 8 shells.

Rnd 8: Join purple with sc in center sp of any shell; *ch 3, skip next dc, sc in next dc, ch 3, sc in ch-1 sp; sc in sc and in next ch-1 sp, ch 3, skip next dc, sc in next dc; ch 3, sc in center sp of shell; rep from * around, end with ch 3, join in beg sc; finish off.

Rnd 9: Join lilac with sc in center sc of any 3-sc group; *(ch 3, sc in next ch-3 lp) 4 times, ch 3, skip next sc, sc in next sc; rep from * around, end with ch 3, join.

Rnd 10: Sl st in next sp, work beg V-st; *ch 2, skip next lp, in next lp work (3 dc, ch 2, 3 dc) for corner; ch 2, skip next lp, V-st in next lp, ch 1, skip next lp, (dc, hdc, sc) in next lp; 3 sc in next lp, (sc, hdc, dc) in next lp, ch 1, skip next lp, V-st in next lp; rep from * around, end with ch 1, join in 3rd ch of beg ch-5.

Rnd 11: Ch 3, dc in sp of V-st and in next dc; *2 dc in next sp, dc in next 3 dc, in ch-2 sp of corner work (2 dc, ch 2, 2 dc); dc in next 3 dc, 2 dc in ch-2 sp, dc in next dc, dc in sp of V-st and in next dc; in ch-1 sp work (dc, hdc), sc in next 9 sts, (hdc, dc) in ch-1 sp, dc in next dc, dc in sp of V-st and in next dc; rep from * around, end last rep with (hdc, dc) in last sp, sl st in beg dc; finish off.

Rnd 12: Join white with sl st in any corner ch-2 sp, ch 3, (dc, ch 2, 2 dc) in same sp; *(ch 1, skip next st, dc in next st) 16 times; ch 1, in corner ch-2 sp work (2 dc, ch 2, 2 dc); rep from * around, end with ch 1, join in beg dc.

Rnd 13: Ch 2, hdc in next dc and in each dc and in each ch-1 sp around. working 3 hdc in corner sps; end with sl st in beg ch 2; finish off. Weave in ends.

Joining

Hold two squares with right sides tog; with off white, sew with overcast st along one side edge, carefully matching sts and corner lps. Join squares in 6 rows of 5 squares each.

Border

Rnd 1: Hold piece with right side facing you; join off white with sc in upper right corner sp; 2 sc in same place (corner made); sc in each st and joining around, adjusting sts to keep work flat, working 3 sc in each rem outer corner sp; join in beg sc.

Rnd 2: Sc in next sc; *ch 3, sk 2 sc, sc in next sc; rep from * around; join in beg sc.

Rnd 3: Sl st into next ch-3 sp; (sc, hdc, dc, hdc, sc) in same sp, sc in next sc; * (sc, hdc, dc, hdc, sc) in next sp, sc in next sc; rep from * around, join in beg sc. Finish off.

#6 WHITE STARS

Designed by Katherine Eng for Coats and Clark

SIZE
43" x 65"

MATERIALS
Worsted weight yarn,
  42 oz white

Note: *Photographed model made with Red Heart® Super Saver® #316 Soft White*

Size H (5mm) crochet hook
  (or size required for gauge)

GAUGE
Rnds 1 through 2 = 2 $1/4$"

Square = 7 $1/2$" x 7 $1/2$"

INSTRUCTIONS

Square (make 40)

Ch 4; join with a sl st to form a ring.

Rnd 1: Ch 1, 8 sc in ring; join with sl st in first sc.

Rnd 2: Ch 1, sc in first sc, (ch 4, sc in next sc) 7 times; ch 1, dc in first sc to form last sp.

Rnd 3: Ch 1, (sc, ch 3, sc) in this last sp on Rnd 2, ch 2, *(sc, ch 3, sc) in next ch-4 sp, ch 2; rep from * 6 times more; join with sl st in first sc.

Rnd 4: (Sl st, ch 1, sc) in first ch-3 sp; shell in ch-2 sp; *sc in ch-3 sp, shell in ch-2 sp; rep from * 6 times more; join as before.

Rnd 5: Ch 3, sl st in same sc as joining; *sc in next 2 dc, (2 sc, ch 2, 2 sc) in ch-3 sp, sc in next 2 dc, sl st in next sc; sc in next 2 dc, (2 sc, ch 2, 2 sc) in next ch-3 sp, sc in next 2 dc**; (sl st, ch 3, sl st) in next sc rep from * 2 times more, then; rep from * to ** once; join with sl st in joining sl st.

Rnd 6: (Sl st, ch 4, 2 tr, ch 3, 3 tr) in first ch-3 sp; *ch 2, sl st in next ch-2 sp, ch 2, (dc, ch 1, dc) in next sl st, ch 2, sl st in next ch-2 sp, ch 2**; (3 tr, ch 3, 3 tr) in next ch-3 sp rep from * 2 times more, then; rep from * to ** once; join with sl st in top of ch-4.

Rnd 7: Ch 1, sc in same ch as joining; *sc in next 2 tr, (2 sc, ch 2, 2 sc) in ch-3 sp, sc in next 3 tr, 2 sc in ch-2 sp; ch 1, skip sl st, 2 sc in next ch-2 sp, sc in next dc, sc in ch-1 sp; sc in next dc, 2 sc in ch-2 sp, ch 1, skip sl st, 2 sc in next ch-2 sp**; sc in next tr rep from * 2 times more; then rep from * to ** once; join with sl st in first sc.

Rnd 8: Sl st in next sc, ch 3, skip next sc, hdc in next sc, ch 1, skip next sc; *(hdc, ch 2, hdc) in ch-2 sp, ch 1, skip next sc**, (hdc in next sc or ch-1 sp, ch 1, skip next sc) 11 times; rep from * 2 times more; rep from * to ** once; (hdc in next sc or ch-1 sp, ch 1, skip next sc) 9 times; join with sl st in 2nd ch of ch-3.

Rnd 9: Ch 1, (2 sc in next ch-1 sp) twice; *(sc, ch 3, sc) in corner ch-2 sp**, (2 sc in next ch-1 sp) 12 times; rep from * 2 times more; rep from * to ** once; (2 sc in next ch-1 sp) 10 times; join with sl st in first sc. Finish off and weave in ends.

Joining

Hold two squares with right sides tog and sew tog with overcast sts, carefully matching sts and corners. Join in 8 rows of 5 squares each.

Continued on next page.

Edging

Rnd 1: With right side facing, join with sl st in corner ch-3 sp before a long side; ch 1; *(sc, ch 2, sc) in corner sp, work 227 sc evenly spaced across long side; (sc, ch 2, sc) in corner ch-3 sp, work 143 sc evenly spaced across short side; rep from * once more; join with sl st in first sc: 229 sc across each long side between ch-2 sps and 145 sc across each short side between ch-2 sps; turn.

Rnd 2 (wrong side): Ch 1, *sc in next sc, ch 1, skip next sc; rep from * to corner; (sc, ch 3, sc) in next corner ch-2 sp, ch 1, skip next sc; rep from * around; join as before; turn.

Rnd 3 (right side): Ch 1, sc in ch-1 sp, sc in sc; *(sc, ch 3, sc) in corner ch-3 sp, sc in each ch-1 sp and in each sc to next corner; rep from * around; join; do not turn.

Rnd 4 (right side): Ch 1, sc in same sc as joining; **skip next 2 sc, corner shell in corner ch-3 sp; skip next 2 sc, sc in next sc; *skip next 2 sc, shell in next sc, skip next 2 sc***, sc in next sc; rep from * to next corner; rep from ** around, end at ***; join; turn.

Rnd 5 (wrong side): Ch 5 (counts as dc and ch-2); *sc in next ch-3 sp, ch 2, dc in sc, ch 2; rep from * to corner shell; skip first dc, sc in next dc, ch 2, (sc, ch 2, sc) in corner ch-3 sp; ch 2, skip next dc, sc in next dc**, ch 2, dc in next sc, ch 2; rep from * around, end at **; hdc in 3rd ch of ch-5 to form last sp; turn.

Rnd 6 (right side): Ch 1, sc in first sc; **skip next ch-2 sp, corner shell in next ch-2 sp, skip next ch-2 sp, sc in next sc, *shell in next dc***, sc in next sc; rep from * to next corner; rep from ** around, end at ***; join with sl st in first sc; do not turn.

Rnd 7 (right side): Ch 1, sc in first sc; **ch 2, skip next 2 dc of corner shell, (sc, ch 2, sc) in next dc, (sc, ch 3, sc) in corner ch-3 sp; (sc, ch 2, sc) in next dc, ch 2, skip next 2 dc, sc in next sc, *ch 2, (sc, ch 2, sc) in next ch-3 sp, ch 2***, sc in next sc; rep from * to next corner; rep from ** around, end at ***; join as before. Finish off and weave in ends.

Flower (make 54)

Rnd 1: Ch 2; 6 sc in 2nd ch from hook.

Rnd 2: (Sl st, ch 3, dc, ch 3, sl st) in first sc, *(sl st, ch 3, dc, ch 3, sl st) in next sc; rep from * around; join with sl st in first sl st. Finish off, leaving a long end for sewing. Sew a flower at the corner of each square or intersection of squares as shown in photo.

#7 NURSERY TIME

SIZE
30" x 36"

MATERIALS
Sport weight yarn,
    20 oz multi-color

Note: *Photographed model made with Lion Brand® Babysoft® #250 Nursery Print*

Size J (6mm) crochet hook (or
    size required for gauge)

GAUGE
13 dc = 4" with 2 strands of
    yarn:

8 dc rows = 4"

STITCH GUIDE
Long dc (Ldc): YO, insert hook in specified st, YO and draw up a long lp, (YO and draw through 2 lps on hook) twice: Ldc made.

INSTRUCTIONS
(use 2 strands throughout)

Ch 121.

Row 1 (wrong side): Dc in 4th ch from hook (3 skipped chs count as first dc), dc in each ch across: 119 dc; ch 3 (counts as dc on next row, now and throughout), turn.

Row 2 (right side): Skip first dc; *dc in next 3 dc, Ldc in dc 3 sts back on previous row (same st as first dc of 3 dc just worked); rep from * across; dc in 3rd ch of ch-3: 39 Ldc and 119 dc; ch 3, turn.

Row 3 (wrong side): Skip first dc; *skip next Ldc, dc in next 3 dc, Ldc on right side in skipped Ldc; rep from * across; dc in 3rd ch of ch-3; ch 3, turn.

Row 4 (right side): Skip first dc; *skip next Ldc, dc in next 3 dc; rep from * across; dc in 3rd ch of ch-3: 119 dc; ch 3, turn.

Row 5 (wrong side): Skip first dc, dc in each dc across, dc in 3rd ch of ch-3; ch 3, turn.

Rows 6 through 53: Rep Rows 2 through 5 twelve times more.

Rows 54 through 56: Rep Rows 2 through 4 once. At end of Row 56, do not ch 3 and turn. Finish off and weave in ends.

Edging Loops
With right side facing, join with sl st in edge of last dc on Row 1; *ch 25, sl st in edge of next st along right-hand edge; rep from * across. Finish off and weave in ends. With right side facing, join with sl st in last st on Row 56, work edging loops along left-hand edge same as before. Finish off and weave in ends.

#8 CURLED TIPS DAISY

Designed by Bonnie Pierce

SIZE
35" x 49"

MATERIALS
Worsted weight yarn,
  3 ¹/₂ oz medium gold
  8 oz dark gold
  16 oz brown

Note: Photographed model made with Red Heart® Classic™ Honey Gold #645 and Red Heart® Super Saver® #321 Gold and #336 Warm Brown

Size F (3.75mm) crochet hook
  (or size required for gauge)

Size G (4mm) crochet hook

GAUGE
Square = 7" x 7"

INSTRUCTIONS

Square (make 35)

With smaller hook and dk gold, ch 4, join with a sl st to form a ring.

Rnd 1: Ch 1, 8 sc in ring, join with sl st in beg sc; finish off dk gold.

Rnd 2: Join med gold with sl st in in front lp only of any sc; working entire rnd in front lps only, *ch 9, sl st in 2nd ch from hook, sc in next 7 chs, sl st in same st on working rnd, sl st in next st; rep from * 7 times more, join with sl st in first sc; finish off: 8 petals made.

Rnd 3: With larger hook, join brown with sl st in back lp only of any sc in Rnd 1, ch 1; in same lp work (sc, ch 3, sc); (sc, ch 3, sc) in back lp of each rem sc in Rnd 1: 8 ch-3 sps, join in beg sc.

Rnd 4: Sl st in next ch- 3 sp, ch 3, 3 dc in same sp, 4 dc in next ch-3 sp, ch 2; *(4 dc in next ch-3 sp) twice, ch 2; rep from * twice more, join with sl st in 3rd ch of beg ch-3.

Rnd 5: Ch 1, sc in joining; * twist next petal to left so that wrong side is facing you, sl st in back ridge of 2nd sc from tip of petal, skip st behind petal, sc in next 4 sc; twist next petal to left, sl st in back ridge of 2nd sc from tip of petal, skip next st, sc in next sc; in corner ch-2 sp work 3 sc, sc in next sc; rep from from * to * three times more, join with sl st in first sc.

Rnd 6: Ch 3, dc in next 8 sts (including sl sts); in corner work *(2 dc, ch 2, 2 dc), dc in next 10 sts; rep from * twice more, (2 dc, ch 2, 2 dc) in next st for corner, dc in next st, join with sl st in 3rd ch of beg ch-3; finish off brown.

Rnd 7: Join dk gold with sl st in any corner, ch 5, dc in same corner; *(skip 2 sts, work V-st) 4 times, skip 2 sts , in corner work (dc, ch 2, dc, ch 2, dc); rep from * twice more, (skip 2 sts, work V-st) 4 times, skip 2 sts, end (dc, ch 2) in beg corner; join with sl st in 3rd ch of beg ch-5.

Rnd 8: Ch 1; *3 sc in corner dc, 2 sc in ch-2 sp, sc in next 2 sts, (sc in next ch-1 sp and in next 2 sts) 4 times, 2 sc in next ch-2 sp; rep from * 3 times more: 84 sc; join, finish off dk gold.

Rnd 9: Join brown with sl st in center st of any corner, 3 sc in joining; (sc in each st to next corner, 3 sc in corner) two times; sc in each st to beg corner, join; finish off, leaving an 18" yarn end for sewing. Weave in all other yarn ends.

Joining

To join, hold two squares with right sides tog and with brown, sew along one side edge with overcast st, working in outer lps only, carefully matching sts and corners. Join in 7 rows of 5 squares each.

Edging

Rnd 1: With right side facing, join brown in upper right outer corner with sc, 2 sc in same st for corner; sc evenly around, working 3 sc in each outer corner and adjusting sts to keep work flat, join in beg sc.

Rnd 2: Sl st in next sc, ch 1, 3 sc in same st; sc in each sc around, working 3 sc in center st of each corner.

Rnd 3: Work reverse sc in each st around, working 2 sts in center st of each corner; join, finish off; weave in all ends.

#9 QUICK CABLE

SIZE
60 1/2" x 67"

MATERIALS
Worsted weight yarn,
   85 oz dark green

Note: *Photographed model made
with Red Heart® Super Saver®
#633 Dk Sage. 36"*

36" Size 13 (9mm) circular
   knitting needle (or size
   required for gauge)

Cable needle

GAUGE
12 sts = 4" in patt with two
   strands of yarn held tog

16 rows = 4"

PATTERN

Note: Slip all sts as if to purl with yarn held on wrong side of fabric.

Row 1 (right side): K3, P2; *sl 1, K2, sl 1, P4; rep from * to last 9 sts; sl 1, K2, sl 1, P2, K3.

Row 2: K5; *sl 1, K2, sl 1, K4; rep from * to last 9 sts; sl 1, K2, sl 1, K5.

Row 3: K5; *T4B, K4; rep from * to last 9 sts, T4B, K5.

Row 4: K3, P3; *K2, P6; rep from * to last 8 sts, K2, P3, K3.

Rows 5, 7, and 9: Knit.

Rows 6, 8 and 10: Rep Row 4.

INSTRUCTIONS

Note: Afghan is worked with 2 strands of yarn held tog throughout.

Lower Border

CO 160 sts; do not join, work back and forth in rows.

Rows 1 through 4: Knit.

Row 5 (wrong side): K6; *K in front and back of next st, K6; rep from * across: 182 sts.

Body

Work Rows 1 through 10 of pattern until piece measures about 66" from beg, ending by working a Row 3.

Upper Border

Row 1 (wrong side): K6; *K2tog, K6; rep from * across: 160 sts.

Rows 2 through 5: Knit.

BO and weave in ends.

#1 COUNTRY ROSES

Designed by Janie Herrin

SIZE
57 1/2" x 69" before border

MATERIALS
Worsted weight yarn,
 49 oz lt rose
 14 oz dk rose
 11 oz white

Note: *Photographed model made with Bernat® Berella® "4" #08815 Lt Antique Rose, #01505 Dark Country Rose, and #08942 White*

Size H (5mm) crochet hook
 (or size required for gauge)

GAUGE
7 dc = 2"

Square = 11 1/2" x 11 1/2"

INSTRUCTIONS

Square (make 30)

With lt rose, ch 8, join to form a ring.

Rnd 1: Ch 3 (equals first dc), 23 dc in ring, join in 3rd ch of beg ch-3: 24 dc.

Rnd 2: Ch 1, sc in same st, ch 3; *skip 2 dc, sc in next dc, ch 3; rep from * around, join in beg sc: 8 ch-3 lps.

Rnd 3: Sl st in next ch-3 lp, ch 1, in same lp and in each lp around work (sc, hdc, dc, tr, dc, hdc, sc), join with sl st in beg sc: 8 petals made.

Rnd 4: Sl st to next tr, ch 3, (dc, ch 2, 2 dc) in same st for first corner; *ch 5, sc in tr at center of next petal, ch 5, in next tr work (2 dc, ch 2, 2 dc); rep from * around, end with last ch 5, join in 3rd ch of beg ch-3: 8 ch-5 lps and 4 corner sps.

Rnd 5: Ch 1, sc in same st and in next dc; *3 sc in ch-2 sp, sc in next 2 dc, 5 sc in ch-

5 sp, sc in sc, 5 sc in next ch-5 sp, sc in next 2 dc; rep from * around, end with 5 sc in last ch-5 sp, join in beg sc; finish off.

Rnd 6: Join white with sl st in center sc of any corner 3-sc group, ch 3, (dc, ch 2, 2 dc) in same st; *(ch 1, skip next sc, dc in next sc) 8 times; ch 1, skip next sc, in next sc work (2 dc, ch 2, 2 dc): corner made; rep from * around, end with last ch 1, join in beg dc.

Rnd 7: Ch 4 (equals first dc plus ch-1); *skip next dc, work corner as before in ch-2 sp, ch 1, skip next dc; (dc in next dc, ch 1) 10 times; rep from * around, ending ch 1, join in 3rd ch of beg ch 4; finish off.

Rnd 8: Join dk rose with sc in any corner sp, ch 2, sc in same sp; *sc in next 2 dc, sc in ch-1 sp and in next dc; (Lsc in next ch-1 sp 2 rows below, sc in next dc) 9 times, sc in next sp and in next 2 dc; in corner sp work (sc, ch 2, sc); rep from * around, end with sl st in beg sc: 36 Lsc.

Rnd 9: Sl st in ch-2 sp, ch 3, (dc, ch 2, 2 dc) in same sp; *ch 1, (skip next st, dc in next st, ch 1) 13 times, skip next st, work corner in ch-2 sp; rep from * around, ch 1, join in beg dc; finish off.

Rnd 10: Join lt rose with sl st in any corner sp, ch 3, (dc, ch 2, 2 dc) in same sp, dc in each dc and in each ch-1 sp around, working (2 dc, ch 2, 2 dc) in each rem corner sp, end with sl st in 3rd ch of beg ch-3.

Rnd 11: Ch 4 (equals first dc plus ch 1); *skip next dc, work corner in ch-2 sp, ch 1; (skip next dc, dc in next dc, ch 1) 17 times; rep from * around ending with last ch 1, join in 3rd ch of beg ch-4.

Rnd 12: Ch 1, sc in same st, sc in each ch-1 sp and in each dc around working 3 sc in each corner sp, end with sl st in beg sc; finish off. Weave in ends.

Joining

To join, hold two squares with right sides tog, and with lt rose, sew tog with overcast st, carefully matching sts and corners. Join squares in 6 rows of 5 squares each.

Border

Rnd 1: Hold afghan with right side facing you and join lt rose with sc in upper right corner; 2 sc in same st; sc in each st and joining around, carefully matching sts and adjusting to keep work flat, and working 3 sc in each rem outer corner sp; join with sc in beg sc.

Rnd 2: *Ch 3, sk 2 sc, sc in next sc; rep from * around, join.

Rnd 3: *In next ch-3 sp work (sc, hdc, dc, tr, dc, hdc, sc); rep from * around, join in beg sc; finish off.

#11 EARTH TONES

Designed by Patons Design Staff

SIZE
44" x 63"

MATERIALS
Worsted weight yarn,
   24 1/2 oz variegated (MC)
   7 oz off white (A)
   7 oz dk taupe (B)
   7 oz lt beige (C)
   7 oz med taupe (D)

Note: *Phtographed model made with Patons® Décor #1621 Woodbine Variegated (MC), #1602 Aran (A), #1633 Chocolate Taupe (B), #1630 Pale Taupe (C), and #1632 Rich Taupe (D)*

36" Size 7 (4.5mm) circular
   knitting needle (or size
   required for gauge)

GAUGE
21 1/2 sts = 4" in patt
38 rows = 4" in patt

INSTRUCTIONS

Bottom Section

With D, cast on 211 sts, do not join, work back and forth in rows.

Row 1 (wrong side): Knit.

Row 2: Kl, K2tog, knit to last 3 sts, K2tog, Kl.

Rows 3 through 10: Rep Rows 1 and 2 in sequence 4 times.

Row 11: Rep Row 1: 201 sts. Cut D; attach C.

Row 12: With C, Kl, K2tog, knit to last 3 sts, K2tog, Kl: 199 sts.

Row 13: Knit.

Row 14: Kl, K2tog, K6, (Ml, K20) 9 times, M1, K7, K2tog, Kl: 207 sts.

Row 15: Purl.

Row 16: Kl, K2tog, knit to last 3 sts, K2tog, KI.

Row 17: Purl.

Row 18: Rep Row 16.

Row 19: Rep Row 17: 203 sts.

Row 20: K 1, K2tog, knit to last 3 sts, K2tog, K1: 201 sts.

Row 21: Knit.Cut C; attach MC.

Middle Section

Note: Sl all sts as to purl.

Row 1: With MC, knit.

Row 2: (P13, M1P) 15 times, P3, M1P, P3: 217 sts. Drop MC; attach A.

**Row 3: With A, K1, *sl 1, K1; rep from * across.

Row 4: K1,* yf, sl 1, yb, K1; rep from * across. Cut A.

Row 5: With MC, knit.

Row 6: Purl.

Row 7: K2, *sl 1, K1; rep from * to last st, K1.

Row 8: K2, *yf, sl 1, yb, K1; rep from * to last st, K1.

Row 9: Knit.

Row 10: Purl. Drop MC; attach B.

Row 11: With B, Kl, *sl 1, Kl; rep from * across.

Row 12: Kl, *yf, sl 1, yb, Kl; rep from * across. Cut B.

Row 13: With MC, knit.

Row 14: Purl.

Row 15: K2, *sl 1, Kl; rep from * to last st, Kl.

Row 16: K2, *yf, sl 1, yb, Kl; rep from * to last st, Kl.

Continued on next page.

Row 17: Knit.

Row 18: Purl.

Rep Center Section Rows 3 through 18 until piece measures about 61" long, ending by working a Row 4, 8 or 12.

Top Section

Row 1: With MC, knit.

Row 2: (P12, P2tog) 15 times, P2tog, P5: 201 sts. Cut MC; attach C.

Rows 3 and 4: With C, knit.

Row 5: Kl, M1, knit to last st, M1, Kl.

Row 6: Purl.

Rows 7 through 10: Rep Rows 5 and 6 in sequence twice more: 207 sts.

Row 11: Kl, Ml, K7, (K2tog, K19) 9 times, K2tog, K7, Ml, Kl, 199 sts.

Row 12: Knit. Cut C; attach D.

Row 13: With D, Kl, M1, knit to last st, M 1, Kl.

Rep Rows 12 and 13 five times more: 211 sts at end of last row. BO as to knit.

Weave in all yarn ends.

Side Borders

With right side of work facing and C, pick up and knit 290 sts along one side edge.

Row 1: Knit.

Row 2: Kl, Ml, knit to last st, Ml, Kl.

Row 3: Purl.

Rows 4 through 7: Rep Rows 2 and 3 in sequence twice more: 296 sts.

Row 8: Kl, Ml, K6, (K2tog, K18) 14 times, K2tog, K6, M1, Kl: 283 sts.

Row 9: Knit. Cut C; attach D.

Row 10: With D, Kl, M1, knit to last st, Ml, Kl.

Rep Rows 9 and 10 five times more: 295 sts. BO as to knit. Bringing slanted edges together to form corner, sew corner seams and weave in ends.

Rep Side Border on opposite side edge.

INSTRUCTIONS

Note: Afghan is made using 21 Main Squares (Sq 1) and 21 complementary Squares (Sq 2) and is joined alternating both squares.

Square One (make 21)

With Color B, ch 4; join with sl st to form a ring.

Rnd 1: Ch 1, 12 sc in ring; join with sl st in beg sc.

Rnd 2: Work beg Pc; * † ch 1, turn, Pc in next st, (ch 10, sl st in 9th ch from hook, ch 1): lp made; turn, skip next st, † Pc in next st; rep from * 2 times more, then rep from † to † once, join top of beg Pc: 8 Pc and 4 lps.

Rnd 3: Sl st to next ch-1 sp, ch 3, 2 dc in same sp; in next sp work [2 dc to right of lp, work lp, (to work lp, ch 10, sl st in 9th ch from hook, ch 1), 2 dc to left of loop]; * 3 dc in next ch-1 sp, in next sp work (2 dc to right of lp, work lp, 2 dc to left of lp); rep from * 2 times more; join in 3rd ch of beg ch-3, finish off.

Rnd 4: Join Color A in any corner sp to right of lp; ch 3, dc in same sp, work lp, 2 dc in same sp to left of lp; * † dc in next dc, (ch 1, skip next dc, dc in next dc) 3 times, † 2 dc in next sp to right of next lp, work lp, 2 dc in same sp to left of lp; rep from * 2 times more, then rep from † to † once; join, finish off.

Rnd 5: Join Color C in any corner sp to right of lp, ch 3, dc in same sp, work lp, 2 dc in same sp to left of lp; * † dc in next 3 dc, (working in front of ch-1, FPdtr in skipped st on Rnd 3, dc in next dc) 3 times; dc in next 2 dc; † in corner sp work (2 dc to right of lp, work lp, 2 dc in same sp to left of lp); rep from * 2 times more, then rep from † to † once; join in beg ch-3.

Rnd 6: Ch 3, dc in next st; * † in next corner sp work (2 dc to right of lp, ch 2, 2 dc to left of lp), dc in next 2 dc; † (ch 1, skip next st, dc in next st) 6 times, dc in next st; rep from * 2 times more, then rep from † to † once, end with (ch 1, skip next st, dc in next st) 5 times, ch 1, join in beg ch-3, finish off.

Starting with any corner, braid corner lps as follows: (pull lp of Rnd 3 through loop of Rnd 2, pull lp of Rnd 4 through lp of Rnd 3, pull lp of Rnd 5 through lp of Rnd 4); rep for all rem corners.

Rnd 7: Working over both lps at the same time, join Color A with sl st in any corner lp of Rnd 5 and in ch-2 sp of Rnd 6, ch 3, (dc, ch 2, 2 dc) in same sp (beg corner made); * † dc in next 4 dc, (FPdtr in skipped st on rnd 5, dc in next dc) 6 times, dc in next 3 dc †; 2 dc in next corner lp of Rnd 5 and in ch-2 sp of Rnd 6, ch 2, 2 dc in same sp, (corner made); rep from * 2 times more, then rep from † to † once; join with sl st in beg ch-3.

Continued on next page.

Rnd 8: Ch 1, sc in same sp and in next dc; * 3 sc in ch-2 corner sp, sc in each st across to next corner; rep from * around, ending with sl st in beg sc; finish off. Weave in ends.

Square Two (make 21)

With Color A, ch 4; join with sl st to form a ring.

Rnd 1: Ch 3, in ring work: 2 dc, work lp as on Square One; (3 dc, work loop) 3 times; join with sl st in 3rd ch of beg ch-3.

Rnd 2: Ch 3, dc in each of next 2 dc; * † in corner sp work (2 dc to right of lp, work lp, 2 dc to left of lp) †, dc in each of next 3 dc; rep from * 2 times more, then rep from † to † once, join.

Rnd 3: Ch 4 (counts as first dc plus ch 1), skip next dc, dc in next dc, ch 1, skip next dc, dc in next dc, in corner sp work (2 dc to right of lp, work lp, 2 dc to left of lp); * dc in next dc, (ch 1, skip next dc, dc in next dc) 3 times, in next sp work (2 dc to right of lp, work lp, 2 dc to left of lp); rep from * around ending with dc in next dc, ch 1; join with slip st to 3rd ch of beg ch-4, finish off.

Rnds 4 through 8: Rep Rnds 4 through 8 of Square One.

Joining

Arrange blocks in 7 rows of 6 squares each, alternating blocks in a checkerboard pattern. To join, hold squares with right sides tog and use Color A to sew squares tog with overcast sts through outer lps only of each square, matching sts and corners. Join in rows; then join rows, always alternating colors.

Edging

Rnd 1: With right side facing, join Color A with sl st in center sc of any corner 3-sc group, ch 3, (dc, ch 2, 2 dc) in same st, dc in next sc and in each sc and joining around, working (2 dc, ch 2, 2 dc) in each corner sc; join, finish off.

Rnd 2: Join Color B with sc in any dc, sc in each dc around working 3 sc in each corner sp, join in beg sc; finish off.

Rnd 3: Join Color A with sc in any corner st, ch 2, sc in same st, ch 2; *skip next sc, sc in next sc, ch 2; rep from * around working (sc, ch 2, sc) in each corner sc, join, finish off.

INSTRUCTIONS

Square (make 24)

Rnd 1: With lt blue, ch 2, 8 sc in 2nd ch from hook, join with sl st in beg sc.

Rnd 2: Ch 1, turn; (sc, ch 3, sc) in joining, CL in next sc; *(sc, ch 3, sc) in next sc, CL in next sc; rep from * 2 times more, join in beg sc: 4 CL, 4 ch-3 sps.

Rnd 3: Sl st in next sp, ch 1, turn, 2 sc in same sp; *dc in next sc, sc in CL, dc in next sc, 3 sc in ch-3 sp; rep from * around ending with sc in beg sp, join.

Rnd 4: Work (beg V-st, ch 2, V-st) in same sp; *skip 2 sts, V-st in next st, skip 2 sts, in next st work (V-st, ch 2, V-st); rep from * around ending with sl st in 3rd ch of beg ch-5.

Rnd 5: Sl st to corner ch-2 sp, in same sp work (beg V-st, ch 2, V-st); *skip next V-st, 6 tr in next V-st, skip next V-st, in corner ch-2 sp work (V-st, ch 2, V-st); rep from * around ending with sl st in 3rd ch of beg ch-5.

Rnd 6: Sl st to corner ch-2 sp, in same sp work (beg V-st, ch 2, V-st); *ch 3, skip next V-st, (dc in next tr, ch 1) 5 times; dc in next tr, ch 3, skip V-st, in next ch-2 corner sp work (V-st, ch 2, V-st); rep from * around ending with last ch 3, join in 3rd ch of beg ch-5.

Rnd 7: Sl st in ch-2 sp of V-st, work beg V-st in same sp; *in corner ch-2 sp work (V-st, ch 2, V-st), V-st in ch-2 sp of next V-st, ch 3, skip ch-3 sp; (sc in next ch-1 sp, ch 3) 5 times, V-st in ch-2 sp of next V-st; rep from * around ending with last ch 3, join to 3rd ch of beg ch 5.

Rnd 8: Sl st in ch-2 sp of V-st, ch 3 (equals first dc), 2 dc in same sp, 3 dc in sp of next V-st; *in corner ch-2 sp work (2 dc, ch 2, 2 dc); (3 dc in ch-2 sp of next V-st) twice, ch 3, skip next ch-3 sp; (sc in next ch-3 sp, ch 3) 4 times, (3 dc in sp of next V-st) twice; rep from * around ending with last ch 3, join to beg dc.

Rnd 9: Ch 3, dc in same st and in each of next 7 dc; *work (2 dc, ch 2, dc) in ch-2 sp, dc in each of next 7 dc, 2 dc in next dc, ch 3, skip ch-3 sp, (sc in next ch-3 sp, ch 3) 3 times, skip next ch-3 sp, 2 dc in next dc, dc in each of next 7 dc; rep from * around ending with last ch 3, join.

Rnd 10: Ch 3, dc in same st and in each on next 10 dc; *work corner in sp, dc in each of next 10 dc, 2 dc in next dc, ch 3, skip ch-3 sp, (sc in next ch-3 sp, ch 3) twice, skip next ch-3 sp, 2 dc in next dc, dc in each of next 10 dc; rep from * around ending with last ch 3, join.

Continued on next page.

Rnd 11: Ch 3, dc in same st and in each of next 13 dc; *work (2 dc, ch 2, 2 dc) in ch-2 sp, dc in each of next 13 dc, 2 dc in next dc, ch 3, skip ch-3 sp, sc in next ch-3 sp; ch 3, skip next ch-3 sp, 2 dc in next dc, dc in each of next 13 dc; rep from * around ending with last ch-3, join; finish off.

Rnd 12: Join multicolor yarn with sc in any corner ch-2 sp, 2 sc in same sp; *sc in each of next 16 dc, 2 sc in next dc, ch 3, skip next 2 ch-3 sps, 2 sc in next dc, sc in each of next 16 dc, 3 sc in sp; rep from * around ending with sl st in beg sc; finish off. Weave in ends.

Joining

To join, hold 2 squares with right sides tog and sew tog along one side with multicolor yarn and overcast st, carefully matching sts and corners. Join squares in 6 rows of 4 squares.

Border

Rnd 1: Hold afghan with right side facing you; join multicolor with sc in at upper right outer corner; *ch 3, sk 2 sc, sc in next sc; rep from * around, join with sl st in beg sc.

Rnd 2: Sl st in next ch-3 sp; in same sp work (ch 3, 2 dc, ch 3, 3 dc); *sc in next ch-3 sp, in next ch-3 sp work (3 dc, ch 3, 3 dc): shell made; rep from * around, join in 3rd ch of beg ch-3.

Rnd 3: Sl st in next 2 dc and into ch-3 sp; (ch 3, 2 dc, ch 3, 3 dc) in same sp; *tr in next sc, (3 dc, ch 3, 3 dc) in ch-3 sp of next shell; rep from * around, join in 3rd ch of beg ch-3. Finish off multicolor yarn.

Rnd 4: Join lt blue yarn with sc in any tr of Rnd 3; *(4 dc, ch 3, 4 dc) in ch-3 sp of next shell, sc in next tr; rep from * around, join in beg sc; finish off.

#16 PRETTY LACE

SIZE
49" x 60"

MATERIALS
Worsted Weight Yarn,
    31 oz pink

Note: Photographed model made with Red Heart® Super Saver® #372 Rose Pink

36" Size 10 (6mm) circular
    knitting needle (or size
    required for gauge)

GAUGE
19 sts = 4" in patt

20 rows = 4"

PATTERN
Row 1 (right side): Knit.

Row 2: K4, purl to last 4 sts;
K4.

Row 3: K4; *K2, YO, P1,
P3tog, P1, YO; rep from * to
last 6 sts; K6.

Row 4: K4, purl to last 4 sts,
K4.

INSTRUCTIONS.

CO 234 sts. Do not join; work back and
forth in rows.

Lower Border
Rows 1 through 5: Knit.

Body
Rep Rows 1 through 4 of Pattern until
piece measures approx 59" from CO row,
ending by working Row 4.

Upper Border
Rows 1 through 5: Knit.

BO.

#17 BLUEBERRY PIE

Designed by Janie Herrin

SIZE
48" x 72"

MATERIALS
Worsted weight yarn,
  32 oz white (A)
  8 oz lavender (B)
  4 oz blue multi-color(C)

Note: Photographed model made with Red Heart® Super Saver® #311 White(A), #358 Lavender (B), #943 Blueberry Pie (C)

Size H (5mm) crochet hook,
  (or size required for gauge)

GAUGE
7 dc = 2"

Square = 12" x 12"

INSTRUCTIONS

Square (make 24)

Rnd 1: With Color A, ch 2, work 6 sc in 2nd ch from hook, join with sl st in beg sc: 6 sc.

Rnd 2: Ch 1, sc in same st, ch 1, (sc in next sc, ch 1) around, join in beg sc: 6 ch-1 sps.

Rnd 3: Ch 1, sc in same st, (ch 1, sc in next ch-1 sp, ch 1, sc in next sc) around, end with ch 1, sc in last ch-1 sp, ch 1, join in beg sc: 12 ch-1 sps.

Rnd 4: Sl st in ch-1 sp, work beg CL, ch 2, (CL in next sp, ch 2) around, join to top of beg CL: 12 CL.

Rnd 5: Sl st in ch-2 sp, ch 1, in same sp work (sc, ch 2, sc), ch 2; *(sc, ch 2, sc) in next sp, ch 2; rep from * around, join in beg sc; finish off Color A: 24 ch-2 sps.

Rnd 6: Join Color B with sl st in any ch-2 sp between clusters, work beg shell, (skip next ch-2 sp, shell in next ch-2 sp between clusters) around, sk last ch-2 sp, join to beg dc; finish off Color B: 12 shells.

Beg Cluster(beg CL): Ch 2, holding back last lp of each st on hook, work 2 dc in same sp, YO, draw through all 3 lps on hook: beg CL made.

Cluster(CL): Holding back last lp of each st on hook, work 3 dc in sp indicated, YO, draw through all 4 lps on hook: CL made.

V-st: (dc, ch 1, dc) in sp indicated.

Beg Shell: ch 3, in same sp work (dc, ch 2, 2 dc).

Shell: (2 dc, ch 2, 2 dc) in sp indicated.

Rnd 7: Join Color A with sc in ch-2 sp of any shell, 2 sc in same sp; *working in front of Rnd 6, work V-st in ch-2 sp on Rnd 5, 3 sc in ch-2 sp of next shell; rep from * around, end with last V-st, join in beg sc: 36 sc, 12 V-sts; finish off Color A.

Rnd 8: Join Color C with sl st in ch-1 sp of any V-st, ch 4 (equals first tr), in same sp work (tr, ch 3, 2 tr for first corner); *dc in next 3 sc, 3 hdc in ch-1 sp of V-st, sc in next 3 sc; 3 hdc in ch-1 sp of next V-st, dc in next 3 sc, in ch-1 sp of V-st work (2 tr, ch 3, 2 tr); rep from * around, end with dc in last 3 sc, join in 4th ch of beg ch-4. 16 tr, 24 dc, 12 hdc, 12 sc.

Rnd 9: Ch 3, dc in each st around, working (2 tr, ch 2, 2 tr) in each corner sp; end with sl st in 3rd ch of beg ch-3.

Rnd 10: Ch 4 (equals first dc plus ch 1), skip next tr, dc in next tr; *ch 1, (2 dc, ch 2, 2 dc) in ch-2 sp (corner made), (ch 1, skip next st, dc in next st) across; rep from *around, end with last ch 1, join to 3rd ch of beg ch-4: 48 ch-1 sps, 4 corner sps.

Rnd 11: Ch 3, dc in each ch-1 sp and in each dc around, working corner in ch-2 corner sps, end with sl st in 3rd ch of beg ch-3; finish off Color C: 124 dc.

Rnd 12: Join Color A with sl st in any corner sp, ch 2, 2 hdc in same sp; hdc in each dc around, working 3 hdc in each rem corner, end with sl st in beg ch-2; finish off. Weave in ends.

Joining

To join, hold two squares with right sides tog and with Color A, sew with overcast st along one side, carefully matching sts and corners, and working in outer lps only. In same manner join into 6 rows of 4 squares each.

Edging

Hold afghan with right side facing you and join Color A in upper right corner sp, ch 1, 3 sc in same sp; work sc around outer edges, working 3 sc in each corner sp; join, finish off.

Fringe

Cut strands of Color C l8" long; work single knot fringe (see page 221) across both short ends of afghan.

#18 CLASSIC STYLE

Designed by Mary Jane Protus for Coats and Clark

SIZE

50" x 70" before fringe

MATERIALS

Worsted weight yarn,
 44 oz black (A)
 22 oz white (B)

Note: *Photographed model made with Red Heart® Super Saver® #312 Black and #311 White*

Size I (5.5mm) crochet hook
 (or size required for gauge)

GAUGE

12 dc = 4"

Rows 8 through 23 = 6 ³/4"

INSTRUCTIONS

With A, ch 212.

Row 1 (right side): Sc in 2nd ch from hook and in each ch across: 211 sc; ch 3, turn.

Row 2: Skip first sc; puff st in next sc; *ch 1, skip next sc, puff st in next sc; rep from * to last sc; dc in last sc: 105 puff sts; ch 1, turn.

Row 3: Sc in first dc; *sc in puff st, sc in ch-1 sp; rep from * to last 2 sts; sc in puff st, sc in 3rd ch of beg ch-3: 211 sc; ch 3, turn.

Rows 4 through 7: Rep Rows 2 and 3 two times more changing to B in last sc on Row 7.

Row 8: With B, skip first sc, dc in each sc across: 211 dc (turning ch-3 counts as dc); ch 1, turn.

Row 9: Sc in each dc across, sc in 3rd ch of beg ch-3; ch 3, turn.

Row 10: Rep Row 8 changing to A in last dc.

Row 11: With A, sc in first dc, FPtrtr, skip dc behind FPtrtr; *sc in next 3 dc, FPtrtr, skip dc behind FPtrtr; rep from * to last st; sc in 3rd ch of beg ch-3; ch 3, turn.

Rows 12 and 13: Rep Rows 2 and 3 changing to B in last st on Row 13.

Rows 14 through 16: Rep Rows 8 through 10.

Row 17: Rep Row 11.

Rows 18 through 23: Rep Rows 2 and 3 three times more, changing to B in last st on Row 23.

Rep Rows 8 through 23 six times more. Finish off and weave in ends.

Fringe

Following Single Knot Fringe instructions on page 221, cut strands 12" long and knot 4 strands in edge of each dc or puff st row, matching row colors.

#19 SAND CASTLE

Designed by Janie Herrin

SIZE
42" x 56" before border

MATERIALS
Worsted weight yarn,
   16 oz gold (A)
   24 oz off white (B)
   8 oz coffee (C)

Note: Photographed model made with Red Heart® Super Saver® #321 Gold (A), #323 Aran(B), and #365 Coffee(C)

Size H (5mm) crochet hook,
   or size required for gauge

GAUGE
7 dc = 2"

Square = 7" x 7"

INSTRUCTIONS

Square (make 48)

With Color A, ch 6, join to form a ring.

Rnd 1: Work beg V-st, (V-st in ring) 7 times, join with sl st in 3rd ch of beg ch-5: 8 V-sts.

Rnd 2: Sl st in next ch-2 sp, in same sp work (beg V-st, V-st); *V-st in next ch-2 sp, 2 V-sts in next ch-2 sp; rep from * around, ending with sl st in 3rd ch of beg ch-5.

Rnd 3: Sl st in next ch-2 sp, beg V-st in same sp; *2 tr in next dc, ch 2, 2 tr in next dc, work V-st in next 3 ch-2 sps; rep from * around, ending with sl st in 3rd ch of beg ch-5; finish off Color A.

Rnd 4: Join Color B with sl st in any corner ch-2 sp, ch 3, 2 dc in same sp; *ch 1, skip next tr, dc in next tr; ch 1, dc in next ch-2 sp, ch 1, 3 dc in next ch-2 sp, ch 1, dc in next ch-2 sp, ch 1, skip next dc, dc in next tr, ch 1, work 5 dc in corner ch-2 sp; rep from * around ending with 2 dc in same sp as beg dc, join; ch 3, pull up a long lp and drop yarn, do not cut.

Rnd 5: Join Color C with sl st in center dc of any 5-dc group, ch 3, in same st work (2 dc, ch 2, 3 dc); *(ch 1, dc in next sp) 3 times, ch 1, skip next dc, dc in next dc, (ch 1, dc in next sp) 3 times; ch 1, skip 2 dc, in center dc of 5-dc group work (3 dc, ch 2, 3 dc); rep from * around, ending with sl st in beg ch-3; finish off Color C.

Rnd 6: Insert hook in long lp from Rnd 4, tighten yarn, sc in ch-2 corner sp, sc in each dc and in each ch-1 sp around, working 3 sc in corner sps, end with 2 sc in beg corner, join; finish off. Weave in ends.

Joining

To join, hold two squares with right sides tog and with Color B, sew tog through outer lps only with overcast st. In same manner join squares in 8 rows of 6 squares each. Weave in ends.

Border

Rnd 1: With right side of work facing you, join Color B with sc in sp at upper right corner, 2 sc in same sp; work sc evenly around outer edge of afghan, adjusting sts as needed to keep work flat, and working 3 sc in each rem outer corner sp; join with sl st to beg sc; finish off Color B.

Rnd 2: Join Color C with sl st in center sc of any 3-sc corner group; ch 3, 2 dc in same sc; *ch 1, sk next sc, 3 dc in next sc; rep from * around, join in 3rd ch of beg ch-3; finish off Color C.

Rnd 3: Join Color B with sc in same st; ch 4, sk next dc, sc in next dc; *sc in next dc, ch 4, sk next dc, sc in next dc; rep from * around, join, finish off Color B.

#20 SHADED PANELS

Designed by Mary Jane Protus for Coats and Clark

SIZE
51" x 62"

MATERIALS
Worsted weight yarn,
   9 oz lt green (A)
   11 oz med green (B)
   12 oz dk green (C)
   15 oz white (D)

Note: *Photographed model made with Red Heart® Super Saver® #661 Frosty Green (A), #631 Light Sage (B), #633 Dark Sage (C) and #316 Soft White (D)*

Size J (6mm) crochet hook (or size required for gauge)

GAUGE
2 shells = 4 3/4"

Panel = 10 1/4" wide

INSTRUCTIONS

Panel (make 5)

First Half

With A, ch 265.

Row 1 (right side): Work beg $\frac{1}{2}$ shell; (*skip next 4 chs, sc in next ch, skip next 4 chs**, shell in next ch) 25 times; rep from * to ** once; work end $\frac{1}{2}$ shell in last ch, changing to B in last tr: 25 shells and two $\frac{1}{2}$ shells; ch 1, turn. Finish off A and weave in ends.

Row 2: With B, sc in first tr; *ch 3, Crtr, ch 3, skip next 3 tr, sc in next tr; rep from * across working last sc in last ch: 26 Crtr; ch 1, turn.

Row 3: Sc in sc; *shell in ch-1 sp of Crtr, sc in sc; rep from * across changing to C in last sc: 26 shells; ch 4, turn. Finish off B and weave in ends.

Row 4: With C, tr in sc; (*ch 3, skip next 3 tr, sc in next tr, ch 3**, Crtr) 25 times; rep from * to ** once; 2 tr in last sc: 25 Crtr; ch 4, turn.

Row 5: 3 tr in first tr, sc in next sc; *shell in ch-1 sp of Crtr, sc in next sc; rep from *

across to ch-4; 4 tr in top of ch-4 changing to D in last tr: 25 shells and two $\frac{1}{2}$ shells; ch 1, turn. Finish off C and weave in ends.

Rows 6 through 8: With D only, rep Rows 2 through 4. Finish off and weave in ends.

Second Half

Row 1: With right side facing and working across beg ch on First Half, join A with sl st in free lp of ch at base of end $\frac{1}{2}$ shell on Row 1; ch 4, 3 tr in same st; (*skip 4 chs, sc in free lp of next ch at base of sc on Row 1, skip 4 chs**, shell in free lp of next ch at base of shell) 25 times; rep from * to ** once; 4 tr in free lp of ch at base of beg $\frac{1}{2}$ shell on Row 1, changing to B in last tr: 25 shells; ch 1, turn. Finish off A and weave in ends.

Rows 2 through 8: Work same as Rows 2 through 8 on First Half.

Finishing

Whip stitch Row 8 on panels together.

Edging

Rnd 1: With right side facing, join D with sl st in any corner; ch 1, work 1 rnd sc evenly around, taking care to keep work flat and working 3 sc at outer corners; join with sl st in first sc. Finish off and weave in ends.

Rnd 2: With C, rep Rnd 1. Finish off and weave in ends.

#21 SINGING THE BLUES

Designed by Janie Herrin

SIZE

37" x 63"

MATERIALS

Worsted weight yarn,
  14 oz dk blue
  12 oz med blue
  12 oz lt blue

Note: *Photographed model made with Bernat® Berella® "4" #01141 Rich Periwinkle, #01142 True Periwinkle, and #01143 Soft Periwinkle*

Size H (5mm) crochet hook
  (or size required for gauge)

GAUGE

7 dc= 2"

INSTRUCTIONS

With dk blue, ch 130.

Row 1 (right side): Dc in 4th ch from hook and in next 3 chs; *shell in next ch, dc in next 5 chs, skip 2 chs, dc in next 5 chs; rep from * across to last 6 chs, shell in next ch, dc in last 5 chs; ch 3 (equals first dc of next row), turn.

Row 2: Dec over next 2 dc, dc in 3 dc; *sk next dc, shell in shell, sk next dc, dc in 5 dc; skip 2 dc, dc in 5 dc; rep from * across, ending last rep with skip next dc, shell in shell, skip next dc, dc in 3 dc, dec over 2 dc, dc in 3rd ch of beg ch-3, changing to med blue in last st; ch 3 with new color, turn.

Row 3: Dec over next 2 dc, 2 dc; *long dcCL in skipped st 2 rows below, skip 2 dc, shell in shell; skip 2 dc, long dc CL in skipped st 2 rows below, dc in 4 dc, skip 2 dc, dc in 4 dc; rep from * across, ending last rep with long dc CL in skipped st 2 rows below, dc in 2 dc, dec over next 2 dc, dc in 3rd ch of turning ch; ch 3, turn.

Row 4: Rep Row 2, changing to lt blue in last st; ch 3, with new color, turn.

Row 5: Rep Row 3.

Continue to rep Rows 2 and 3, working two rows of each color, in sequence of dk blue, med blue and lt blue, until piece measures about 62" long, ending by working a Row 2; at end of last row, ch 1, turn.

Edging

Rnd 1: 3 sc in first st, sc in 4 dc, sk next dc, 3 sc in ch-2 sp of shell, skip next 2 dc, sc in 5 dc; *skip 2 dc, sc in 5 dc, sk next dc, 3 sc in ch-2 sp of shell, sk next dc, sc in 5 dc; rep from * across, ending last rep with sc in 4 sc, 3 sc for corner in last sc; working across long side edge, 2 sc in sides of rows, adjusting sts to keep work flat; at end of side, 3 sc in last st for corner; working in unused lps of beg ch, sc in each lp across, working 3 sc in peaks and 1 sc in valleys, 3 sc in last st for corner; work up long side as before, end with sl st in beg sc. Finish off, weave in all ends.

#22 BRANCHES & BERRIES

SIZE
49" x 63"

MATERIALS
Worsted weight yarn,
  62 oz cranberry

*Note: Photographed model made
with TLC Essentials #2915
Cranberry*

Size I (5.5mm) crochet hook
  (or size required for gauge)

GAUGE
12 sc = 4"

16 sc rows = 4"

STITCH GUIDE

Large Puff st (LPst): (YO, insert hook in specified st, YO and draw up a lp) 5 times, YO and draw through all 11 lps on hook: LPst made; push st to right side.

Small Puff st (SPst): (YO, insert hook in specified st, YO and draw up a lp) 3 times, YO and draw through all 7 lps on hook: SPst made; push st to right side.

Front post dc (FPdc): YO, insert hook from front to back to front around post of sc or FPdc one row below next st on previous row (unless another st is specified), YO and draw up a lp, (YO and draw through 2 lps on hook) twice (skip st behind FPdc): FPdc made.

Front post dc decrease (FPdc dec): (YO, insert hook from front to back to front around post of next FPdc, YO and draw up a lp, YO and draw through 2 lps on hook) 3 times, YO and draw through all 4 lps on hook (skip st behind FPdc dec): FPdc dec made.

INSTRUCTIONS

Ch 144.

Row 1 (right side): Sc in 2nd ch from hook and in each ch across: 143 sc; ch 1, turn.

Row 2: Sc in first 4 sc, LPst in next sc, sc in next 5 sc, LPst in next sc; (sc in next 25 sc, LPst in next sc, sc in next 5 sc, LPst in next sc) 4 times, sc in last 4 sc: 10 LPsts and 133 sc; ch 1, turn.

Row 3: Sc in first sc, FPdc; (sc in next 5 sts, FPdc) twice, *sc in next 19 sc, FPdc, (sc in next 5 sts, FPdc) twice; rep from * to last sc; sc in last sc: 15 FPdc and 128 sc; ch 1, turn.

Row 4: Sc in each st across; ch 1, turn.

Row 5: Rep Row 3

Row 6: Sc in first 23 sts, SPst in next sc, (sc in next 31 sts, SPst in next sc) 3 times, sc in last 23 sts: 4 SPsts and 139 sc; ch 1, turn.

Row 7: Rep Row 3.

Row 8: Sc in first 4 sts, LPst in next sc, sc in next 5 sts, LPst in next sc, (sc in next 8 sts, SPst in next sc, sc in next 7 sts, SPst in next sc, sc in next 8 sts, LPst in next sc, sc in next 5 sts, LPst in next sc) 4 times, sc in last 4 sts: 10 LPsts, 8 SPsts and 125 sc; ch 1, turn.

Row 9: Sc in first sc, FPdc, (sc in next 5 sts, FPdc) twice; *sc in next 9 sts, FPdc around SPst 2 rows below next st of prev row, sc in next 9 sts, (FPdc, sc in next 5 sts) twice, FPdc; rep from * to last sc; sc in last sc: 19 FPdc and 124 sc; ch 1, turn.

Row 10: Sc in first 17 sts, SPst in next sc, sc in next 11 sts, SPst in next sc, (sc in next 19 sts, SPst in next sc, sc in next 11 sts, SPst in next sc) 3 times, sc in last 17 sts: 8 SPsts and 135 sc; ch 1, turn.

Row 11: Sc in first sc, FPdc; (sc in next 5 sts, FPdc) twice, *sc in next 6 sts, FPdc around first SPst 2 rows below previous row, (**Note:** *Top of FPdc slants toward center of this section*) sc in next 2 sc, FPdc, sc in next 2 sc, FPdc around next SPst 2 rows below prev row, sc in next 6 sts, FPdc, (sc in next 5 sts, FPdc) twice; rep from * to last sc; sc in last sc: 27 FPdc and 116 sc; ch 1, turn.

Row 12: Rep Row 4.

Continued on next page.

Row 13: Sc in first sc, FPdc; (sc in next 5 sts, FPdc) twice, *sc in next 4 sc, FPdc around first SPst 2 rows below prev row, sc in next 2 sc, FPdc, (sc in next sc, FPdc) twice, sc in next 2 sc, FPdc around next SPst 2 rows below prev row, sc in next 4 sc, FPdc, (sc in next 5 sts, FPdc) twice; rep from * to last sc; sc in last sc: 35 FPdc and 108 sc; ch 1, turn.

Row 14: Rep Row 2.

Row 15: Sc in first sc, FPdc; (sc in next 5 sts, FPdc) twice, *sc in next 5 sts, FPdc, sc in next 2 sc, FPdc 3 times (skip 3 sc behind 3 FPdc), sc in next 2 sc, FPdc, sc in next 5 sts, FPdc, (sc in next 5 sts, FPdc) twice; rep from * to last sc; sc in last sc: 35 FPdc and 108 sc; ch 1, turn.

Row 16: Rep Row 4.

Row 17: Sc in first sc, FPdc; (sc in next 5 sts, FPdc) twice, *sc in next 6 sts, FPdc, sc in next 2 sc; FPdc dec; sc in next 2 sc, FPdc, sc in next 6 sts, FPdc, (sc in next 5 sts, FPdc) twice; rep from * to last sc; sc in last sc: 4 FPdc dec, 23 FPdc and 116 sc; ch 1, turn.

Row 18: Rep Row 4.

Row 19: Sc in first sc, FPdc; (sc in next 5 sts, FPdc) twice, *sc in next 7 sts, FPdc, sc in next sc, FPdc around FPdc dec, sc in next sc, FPdc, sc in next 7 sts, FPdc, (sc in next 5 sts, FPdc) twice; rep from * to last sc; sc in last sc: 27 FPdc and 116 sc; ch 1, turn.

Row 20: Rep Row 2.

Row 21: Sc in first sc, FPdc; (sc in next 5 sts, FPdc) twice, *sc in next 8 sts, FPdc 3 times skipping 3 sc behind 3 FPdc, sc in next 8 sts, FPdc, (sc in next 5 sts, FPdc) twice; rep from * to last sc; sc in last sc: 27 FPdc and 116 sc; ch 1, turn.

Row 22: Rep Row 4.

Row 23: Sc in first sc, FPdc, (sc in next 5 sts, FPdc) twice; *sc in next 9 sts, FPdc dec, sc in next 9 sts, FPdc, (sc in next 5 sts, FPdc) twice; rep from * to last sc; sc in last sc: 4 FPdc dec, 15 FPdc and 124 sc; ch 1, turn.

Row 24: Rep Row 4.

Row 25: Rep Row 5.

Row 26: Rep Row 2.

Row 27: Rep Row 5.

Rows 28 through 243: Rep Rows 4 through 27 nine times more. At end of Row 243, ch 1, turn to work down long edge.

Edging

Rnd 1: With right side facing, work 183 sc evenly down side edge, taking care to keep work flat (work about 3 sc per every 4 rows); 3 sc in first st of lower edge, 141 sc across lower edge, 3 sc in last st of lower edge, sc evenly up next side as before, 3 sc in first sc of top edge, 141 sc across top edge, 3 sc in last sc of top edge; join with sl st in first sc; ch 4, turn.

Rnd 2: Skip next sc; **(dc, ch 1, dc, ch 1, dc) in center sc of 3-sc corner group, ch 1, skip next sc, *dc in next sc, ch 1, skip next sc; rep from * to next 3-sc corner group; rep from ** around; join with sl st in 3rd ch of turning ch-4; ch 1, turn.

Rnd 3: Sc in same st as joining, sc in each ch-1 sp and in each dc around and work 3 sc in center dc of each corner; join with sl st in back lp of first sc; turn.

Rnd 4: *Ch 2, sl st in 2nd ch from hook, sl st in front lp of next 3 sts; rep from * around; join with sl st in joining sl st. Finish off and weave in ends.

Finishing

With right side facing, beg at lower edge, holding hook above and yarn under fabric, work surface chain embroidery up each vertical row of large puff stitches to top of throw following diagrams. Draw ends through to wrong side and weave in.

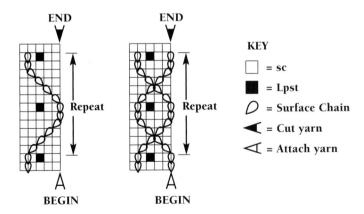

KEY

☐ = sc

■ = Lpst

𝒟 = Surface Chain

◄ = Cut yarn

◁ = Attach yarn

#23 FRINGED FOR BABY

SIZE
35" x 43"

MATERIALS
Bulky weight yarn,
    12 oz mint green (A)
    12 oz lt pink (B)

Note: Photographed model made with Lion Brand® Jiffy® #156 Mint and #101 Lt Pink

Size K (6.5mm) crochet hook
    (or size required for gauge)

GAUGE
8 sts = 3" in patt

PATTERN STITCH

Row 1 (right side): Dc in 4th ch from hook (counts as 2 dc); * dc in each of next 6 chs, ch 1, skip next ch, dc in next ch; rep from * across, ending dc in last 7 chs, ch 4, turn.

Row 2: Skip first 2 dc; * dc in next 5 dc, ch 1, skip next dc, dc in ch-1 sp, ch 1, skip next dc; rep from * across, ending dc in next 5 dc, ch 1, skip next dc, dc in top of turning ch, ch 3, turn.

Row 3: Skip first dc; *dc in ch-1 sp, ch 1, skip next dc, dc in next 3 dc; ch 1, skip next dc, dc in ch-1 sp, dc in next dc; rep from * across, ending last rep with dc in 4th, then 3rd ch of turning ch, ch 3, turn.

Row 4: Skip first dc, dc in next dc; * dc in next ch-1 sp, ch 1, skip next dc, dc in next dc; ch 1, skip next dc, dc in next ch-1 sp, dc in next 3 dc; rep from * across, ending dc in ch-1 sp, ch 1, skip next dc, dc in next dc; ch 1, skip next dc, dc in ch-1 sp, dc in last dc and in top of ch-3; ch 5, turn.

Row 5: Skip first dc, dc in next 2 dc, dc in ch-1 sp; * ch 1, skip next dc, dc in ch-1 sp, dc in next 5 dc, dc in ch-1 sp; rep from *across, ending ch 1, skip next dc, dc in ch-1 sp, dc in next 2 dc, dc in top of ch-5; ch 3, turn.

Row 6: Skip first dc, dc in next 2 dc; * ch 1, skip next dc, dc in ch-1 sp, ch 1, skip next dc, dc in next 5 dc; rep from * across, ending ch 1, skip next dc, dc in ch-1 sp, ch 1, skip next dc, dc in last 2 dc, dc in ch-3; ch 3, turn.

Row 7: Skip first dc, dc in next dc; * ch 1, skip 1 dc, dc in ch-1 sp, dc in next dc, dc in ch-1 sp, ch 1, skip 1 dc, dc in next 3 dc; rep from * across, ending ch 1, skip 1 dc, dc in ch-1 sp, dc in next dc, dc in ch-1 sp, ch 1, skip 1 dc, dc in last dc and in turning ch; ch 4, turn.

Row 8: Skip first 2 dc; * dc in ch-1 sp, dc in next 3 dc, dc in ch-1 sp, ch 1, skip 1 dc, dc in next dc, ch 1, skip 1 dc; rep from * across, ending dc in ch-1 sp, dc in next 3 dc, dc in ch-1 sp, ch 1, skip 1 dc, dc in turning ch; ch 3, turn.

Row 9: Skip 1 dc, dc in ch-1 sp; * dc in next 5 dc, dc in ch-1 sp, ch 1, skip 1 dc, dc in ch-1 sp; rep from * across, ending dc in next 5 dc, dc in 4th, then 3rd ch of turning ch; ch 4, turn.

Rep Rows 2 through 9 for pattern.

INSTRUCTIONS

Body

With A, ch 91.

Work Rows 2 through 9 in pattern and alternate colors, working 8 rows with A and 8 rows with B. Work until four A stripes are completed, then finish off. Weave in ends.

Border

Hold piece with right side facing. Attach A in any outer corner and work 2 rnds of dc, spacing sts to keep work flat and working 3 dc in each outer corner. Finish off.

Fringe

Following Fringe instructions on page 221, cut strands 10" long and use 2 strands in each knot. Work single knot fringe in every 3rd st of first row of each color strip. Trim as desired.

#24 SCRAP SENSATION

Designed by Janie Herrin

SIZE
43" x 55"

MATERIALS
Worsted weight yarn,
  8 oz black and a variety of
  different colored scrap yarn

Size I (5.5mm) crocohet hook
  (or size required for gauge)

GAUGE
Square = 8" x 8"

INSTRUCTIONS

First Strip

Square A

With first color, ch 5, join to form ring.

Rnd 1: Ch 3 (equals first dc), 15 dc in ring, join: 16 dc; finish off.

Rnd 2: Join new color with sl st around post of any dc, ch 3, FPdc in each dc around, join; finish off.

Rnd 3: Join new color with sl st between any 2 FPdc, ch 3, BPdc in next st, (dc in sp before next FPdc, BPdc in next st) around, join: 16 dc, 16 BPdc; finish off.

Rnd 4: Join new color with sl st in any dc, ch 3, 4 dc in same st *ch 1, skip next st, 2 hdc in next st, ch 1, skip next st, 2 sc in next st, ch 1, skip next st, 2 hdc in next st, ch 1, skip next st, 5 dc in next st; rep from * around, ending with last ch 1, join: 20 dc, 16 hdc, 8 sc; finish off.

Rnd 5: Join new color with sl st in center dc of any 5-dc group, ch 3, 6 dc in same st; *ch 5, skip 2 hdc, sc in each of next 2 sc, ch 5, skip 2 hdc, 7 dc in center dc of next 5-dc group; rep from * around, end with last ch 5, join: 28 dc, 8 sc, 8 ch-5 lps; finish off.

Rnd 6: Join new color with sl st in center dc of any 7-dc group, work beg corner; *ch 1, skip next 3 dc, working behind ch-5 lp, tr in next 2 dc on Rnd 4 and in next ch-1 sp, ch 1, tr in next sc on Rnd 5, ch 1, tr in next sc, ch 1; working behind next ch-5 lp, skip next ch-1 sp, tr in next ch-1 sp on Rnd 4 and in each of next 2 dc, ch 1, work corner in center dc of next 7-dc group; rep from * around, end with last ch 1, join: 4 corners, 32 tr, 20 ch-1 sps; finish off.

Rnd 7: Join new color with sl st in any corner ch-2 sp, work beg corner; *ch 1, 3 dc in next ch-1 sp, ch 1; working behind next ch-1 sp, 3 tr in ch-5 lp on Rnd 5, ch 1, skip next 2 tr; working behind next ch-1 sp, 3 tr in next ch-5 lp on Rnd 5, ch 1, skip next 3 tr, 3 dc in next ch-1 sp, ch 1, work corner in corner ch-2 sp; rep from * around, end with last ch 1, join: 48 dc, 24 tr, 20 ch-1 sps, 4 ch-2 sps; finish off.

Rnd 8: Join new color with sl st in any corner ch-2 sp, work beg corner; *(ch 1, 3 dc in next ch-1 sp) twice, ch 1, skip next 3 tr; working in front of next ch-1 sp, tr in ch-1 sp bet trs on Rnd 6, working behind tr just made, dc in ch-1 sp on Rnd 7, tr in same sp as last tr on Rnd 6, ch 1, skip 3 tr, (3 dc in next ch-1 sp, ch 1) twice, work corner in corner ch-2 sp; rep from * around, end with last ch 1, join: 76 dc, 8 tr, 24 ch-1 sps, 4 ch-2 sps; finish off.

Continued on next page.

Square B

Work Rnds 1 through 7 same as Square A

Rnd 8: Join new color with sl st in any corner ch-2 sp, ch 3, 2 dc in same sp, ch 1; with wrong sides facing, sc in corner sp of Square A, ch 1, 3 dc in same sp as last 3 dc made (corner joined), sc in next ch-1 sp of Square A, 3 dc in next ch-1 sp on working sq; continue in pattern working sc joinings across to next corner, join next corner same as before, work in pattern around rem sides, end with sl st in beg dc: one side joining made; finish off.

Work Square B 4 more times, joining to each previous square in same manner to make one strip of 6 squares.

Strip Edging

Rnd 1: With right side facing, join black with sl st in any corner ch-2 sp, work beg corner; *(ch 1, 3 dc in next sp) across to next corner, ch 1, work corner in corner sp; rep from * around strip, end with sc in first dc to equal last ch-1 sp.

Rnd 2: Ch 1, sc in same sp; *ch 5, in corner sp work (sc, ch 7, sc), (ch 5, sc in next sp) across to next corner; rep from * around, end with last ch 5, join in beg sc; finish off.

Second Strip

Make and join 6 squares same as first strip.

Second Strip Edging

Rnd 1: Work same as first strip.

Rnd 2: Work same as first strip omitting center ch and replacing with sc in corresponding lps of first strip: 2 strips joined.

Third and Fourth Strips

Work same as Second Strip, including edging.

Border

When all strips are joined, hold piece with right side facing. Join black with sc in any outer corner sp, 6 sc in same sp, 5 sc in each lp around, working 7 sc in rem corner lps, end with sl st in beg sc; finish off.

#25 SWEET SCALLOPS

SIZE
48" x 63".

MATERIALS
Worsted weight yarn,
 34 oz lt beige

Note: Photographed model made with Red Heart® Super Saver® #330 Linen

36" Size 10 (6mm) circular
 knitting needle (or size
 required for gauge)

GAUGE
14 sts = 3" in patt

20 rows = 4"

PATTERN
Row 1 (right side): K1; *YO, K3, P2, P3tog, P2, K3, YO, K1; rep from * across.

Row 2: P1; * P4, K5, P5; rep from * across.

Row 3: K1; *YO, K4, P1, P3tog, P1, K4, YO, K1; rep from * across.

Row 4: P1; * P5, K3, P6; rep from * across.

Row 5: K1; *YO, K5, P3tog, K5, YO, K1; rep from * across.

Row 6: P1; *P6, K1, P7; rep from * across.

INSTRUCTIONS

CO 225 sts; do not join, work back and forth in rows.

Work Rows 1 through 6 of pattern, then rep Rows 1 through 6 until piece measures about 63" from beg, ending by working a Row 5. BO loosely as to knit.

#26 REFLECTIONS ON THE GO

Designed by Janie Herrin

SIZE
45" x 60" before edging

MATERIALS.
Worsted weight yarn,
  6 oz aran (MC)
  6 oz dark green (A)
  6 oz navy (B)
  6 oz purple (C)
  6 oz burgundy (D)

Note: *Photographed model made with TLC® Essentials™ #2676 Forest Green (A), and #2855 Navy (Color B), and Red Heart® Super Saver® #4313 Aran Fleck (MC), #356 Amethyst (C), and #376 Burgandy (D)*

Size H (5mm) crochet hook
  (or size required for gauge)

GAUGE
7 dc = 2"

Square = 5 " x 5"

INSTRUCTIONS

Square

Square A (make 27)

With Color A, ch 5, join with sl st to form a ring.

Rnd 1: Ch 3 (counts as first dc of rnd), 15 dc in ring, join with sl st in 3rd ch of beg ch-3: 16 dc.

Rnd 2: Ch 3, in same st as joining work (2 dc, ch 2, 3 dc) for corner; ch 1, skip next 3 dc; *in next dc, work (3 dc, ch 2, 3 dc) for corner; ch 1, skip next 3 dc; rep from * 2 times more, join with sl st in 3rd ch of beg ch-3.

Rnd 3: Ch 3 (counts as a dc), dc in each of next 2 dc; *(2 dc, ch 2, 2 dc) for corner in next ch-2 sp, dc in each dc and ch-1 sp to next corner; rep from * around ending dc in last ch-1 sp, join in beg ch-3, finish off.

Rnd 4: Join MC with sl st in any corner ch-2 sp, (ch 3, dc, ch 2, 2 dc) in same sp; * † dc in each of next 2 dc, FPtr around post of first dc of 3-dc group in Rnd 2

Front Post tr (FPtr): YO twice, insert hook from front to back to front around post (vertical bar) of st indicated, YO and pull up a lp, (YO and draw through first 2 lps on hook) 3 times: FPtr made.

below, skip dc behind FPtr, dc in each of next 5 dc, FPtr around post of third dc of 3-dc group in Rnd 2, skip dc behind FPtr, dc in each of next 2-dc, † work (2 dc, ch 2, 2 dc) in ch-2 corner sp; rep from * 2 times more then rep from † to † once, join in beg ch-3, finish off.

Square B (make 27)

Using Color B through Rnd 3 instead of Color A, work same as Square A.

Square C (make 27)

Using Color C through Rnd 3 instead of Color A, work same as Square A.

Square D (make 27)

Using Color D through Rnd 3 instead of Color A, work same as Square A.

Joining

Color Sequence

Row 1: (A, B, C, D); rep once, end with A

Row 2: (D, A, B, C); rep once, end with D

Row 3: (C, D, A, B); rep once, end with C

Row 4: (B, C, D, A); rep once, end with B

Rep Color Sequence 2 times more.

Using preceding color sequence and always working in the same direction, join squares forming 12 horizontal strips of 9 squares each as follows: holding two squares with right sides tog, join MC in corner sp at right, and sl st through outer lps only, care-fully matching sts, ending with sl st in next corner sp, ch 1; pick up two more squares in color sequence and with right sides facing, join as before; continue until first 2 horizontal rows are joined in one direction. Add rem rows then join vertically in same manner.

Border

Rnd 1: Hold piece with right side facing you; join MC with sc in any outer corner ch-2 sp, 2 sc in same sp, sc in each dc and FPtr around, working one sc in each joining where two squares meet and working 3 sc in each outer corner ch-2 sp; join in beg sc, finish off.

Rnd 2: Join Color C with sl st in center sc of any corner 3-sc group, ch 3, (dc, ch 2, 2 dc) in same st, dc in each sc around working FPtr around post of corresponding FPtr on square below, (skip sc behind FPtr), and working (2 dc, ch 2, 2 dc) in center sc of corner 3-sc groups; join in beg ch-3, finish off.

Rnd 3: Join MC with sc in any corner ch-2 sp, 2 sc in same sp, sc in each dc and FPtr around working 3 sc in each corner ch-2 sp; join in beg sc, finish off.

Rnd 4: With Color B, rep Rnd 2, working FPtr sts around those made in Rnd 2 of edging; finish off.

Rnd 5: Rep Rnd 3, finish off. Weave in rem yarn ends.

#27 IN THE PINK

Designed by Patons Design Staff

SIZE
41" x 54"

MATERIALS
Worsted weight yarn,
   35 oz lt pink (MC)
   10 ¹/₂ oz med pink (A)

Note: *Photographed model made with Patons® Décor #1645 Pale Country Pink (MC) and #1646 Dark Country Pink (A)*

Size 9 (5.5mm) knitting needles (or size required for gauge)

Cable needle

GAUGE
17 sts = 4" in stockinette st
   (knit one row, purl one row)

24 rows = 4" in stockinette st

INSTRUCTIONS

Strip A (make 4)

With MC, CO 50 sts.

Row 1 (right side): K1, *YO, K3, sl 1, K1, PSSO, P8, K2tog, K3 *; YO, P2, K8, P2; rep from * to * once, YO, K1.

Row 2: P6, K8, P5, K2, P8, K2, P5, K8, P6.

Row 3: K2, *YO, K3, sl 1, K1, PSSO, P6, K2tog, K3*, YO, K1, P2, K8, P2, K1; rep from * to * once, YO, K2.

Row 4: P7, K6, P6, K2, P8, K2, P6, K6, P7.

Row 5: K3, *YO, K3, sl 1, Kl, PSSO, P4, K2tog, K3*, YO, K2, P2, K8, P2, K2; rep from * to * once, YO, K3.

Row 6: P8, K4, P7, K2, P8, K2, P7, K4, P8.

Row 7: K4, *YO, K3, sl 1, Kl, PSSO, P2, K2tog, K3*, YO, K3, P2, K8, P2, K3; rep from * to * once, YO, K4.

Row 8: P9, (K2, P8) 3 times, K2, P9.

Row 9: K5, *YO, K3, sl 1, Kl, PSSO, K2tog, K3*, YO, K4, P2, C8B, P2, K4; rep from * to * once, YO, K5.

Row 10: P19, K2, P8, K2, P19.

These 10 rows complete one patt.

Work in patt until strip measures about 54" long, ending by working a Row 10; BO.

Strip B (make 5)

With A, CO 12 sts.

Row 1 (right side): P2, K8, P2.

Row 2: K2, P8, K2.

Rows 3 through 8: Rep Rows 1 and 2 three times.

Row 9: P2, C8B, P2.

Row 10: Rep Row 2.

These 10 rows complete one patt.

Cont even in patt until strip measures same length as strip A, ending by working a Row 10; BO.

Finishing

Weave in ends, sew strips tog alternating strip A with strip B as shown in photo.

Fringe

Following Fringe instructions on page 221, cut 10" lengths of MC and A. Use 3 strands in each knot and knot fringe evenly along ends of throw, matching colors to strips.

#28 PRETTY PLAID

Designed by Joyce Nordstom for Coats and Clark

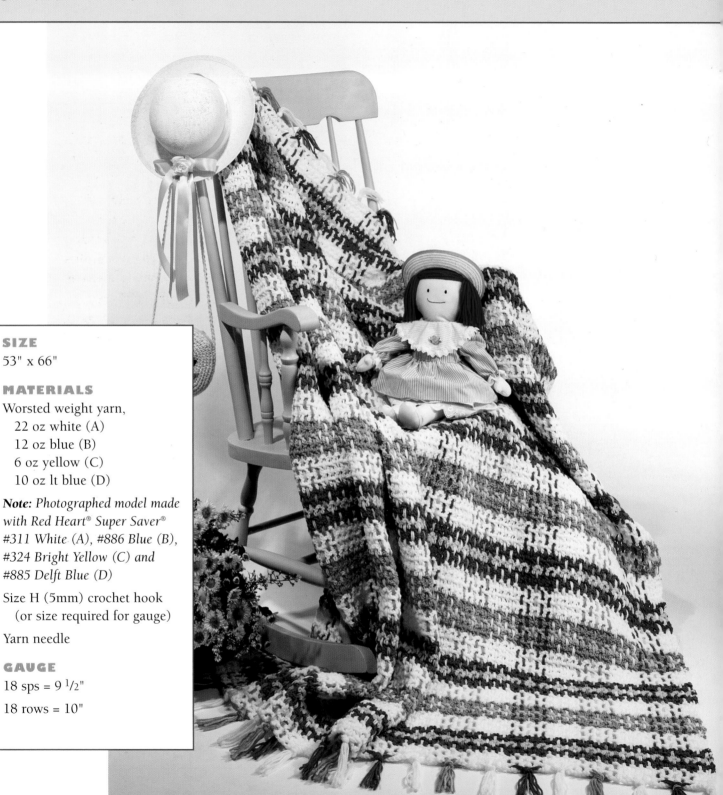

SIZE

53" x 66"

MATERIALS

Worsted weight yarn,
   22 oz white (A)
   12 oz blue (B)
   6 oz yellow (C)
   10 oz lt blue (D)

Note: Photographed model made with Red Heart® Super Saver® #311 White (A), #886 Blue (B), #324 Bright Yellow (C) and #885 Delft Blue (D)

Size H (5mm) crochet hook
   (or size required for gauge)

Yarn needle

GAUGE

18 sps = 9 $\frac{1}{2}$"

18 rows = 10"

INSTRUCTIONS

With A, ch 202.

Row 1 (right side): Dc in 6th ch from hook; *ch 1, skip next ch, dc in next ch; rep from * across: 99 sps; ch 4, turn.

Row 2: Skip first sp, dc in next dc, ch 1; *skip next sp, dc in next dc, ch 1; rep from * to last sp; skip next ch, dc in next ch; ch 4, turn.

Rep Row 2 for pattern in the following color sequence: 2 more rows A; *2 rows B, 1 row C, 2 rows B, 4 rows A**, 2 rows D, 1 row C, 2 rows D, 4 rows A; rep from * for color sequence 5 more times, then from * to ** once more. Finish off and weave in ends.

Weaving

Place afghan on a flat surface with right side facing. With yarn needle and 2 strands of yarn cut 12" longer than afghan, begin weaving first vertical row of sps by inserting needle down through first sp, then up through next sp; begin weaving next vertical row of sps by inserting needle up through first sp, then down through next sp. Continue weaving vertical rows in this alternating manner to other edge. Leave 6" strands of yarn at each end for fringe. Weave in the following sequence: (2 sps A, 2 sps B, 1 sp C, 2 sps B, 4 sps A, 2 sps D, 1 sp C, 2 sps D, 2 sps A) 5 times, 2 sps A, 2 sps B, 1 sp C, 2 sps B, 2 sps A.

Fringe

Following fringe instructions on page 221, group and knot yarn ends tog at top and bottom of afghan with consecutive white vertical rows knotted together and consecutive blue vertical rows knotted to with yellow center row as shown in photograph. Trim fringe ends as desired.

#29 SAILING ALONG

Designed by Janie Herrin

SIZE
56" x 63" before border

MATERIALS
Worsted weight yarn,
   28 oz blue
   24 oz white

Note: Photographed model made with Red Heart® Super Saver® #326 Soft White and Red Heart® Classic™ #848 Skipper Blue

Size H (5mm) crochet hook
   (or size required for gauge)

GAUGE
7 dc = 2"

Square = 7" x 7"

INSTRUCTIONS

Square (make 72)

With white, ch 5, join with sl st to form a ring.

Rnd 1: Ch 3 (equals first dc), in ring work 2 dc, (ch 1, 3 dc) 3 times, ch 1, join in 3rd ch of beg ch-3: 12 dc and 4 ch-1 corner spaces; ch 3, pull up a lp and drop yarn, do not cut.

Rnd 2: Join blue with sl st in center dc of any 3-dc group, work beg V-st, ch 2, V-st in same st; *ch 2, skip ch-1 sp, in center dc of next 3-dc group work (V-st, ch 2, V-st); rep from * around, ch 2, join in 3rd ch of beg ch-5, ch 3, pull up a lp and drop yarn, do not cut.

Rnd 3: Insert hook in dropped white lp on Rnd 1, sl st in sp of V-st, ch 3, dc in same sp; *(V-st, ch 2, V-st) in corner ch-2 sp, 2 dc in next V-st; working over ch-2, make

Beginning V-st: Ch 5 (equals first dc plus ch 2), dc in same st.

V-st: (dc, ch 2, dc) in st or sp indicated.

Long Dc (Ldc): YO, insert hook in st indicated, draw up a lp even with sts on hook, (YO, draw through 2 lps on hook) twice: Ldc made.

Note: Because each rnd starts with a new color, to avoid many ends to weave in, yarn is not finished off at end of each rnd but is picked up and worked in a later rnd.

Ldc in ch-1 sp 2 rows below, 2 dc in next V-st; rep from * around ending with sl st in 3rd ch of beg ch-3, ch 3, pull up lp and drop yarn, do not cut.

Rnd 4: Pick up blue from Rnd 2, sl st in Ldc, ch 3, 2 dc in same st; *3 dc in sp of V-st, in corner ch-2 sp work (3 dc, ch 2, 3 dc), 3 dc in next V-st, 3 dc in Ldc; rep from * around ending with sl st in 3rd ch of beg ch-3; ch 3, pull up a lp and drop yarn, do not cut.

Rnd 5: Pick up white from Rnd 3, sl st in center dc of 3-dc group at center of side, ch 3, dc in each of next 7 dc; *in corner ch-2 sp work (2 dc, ch 2, 2 dc), dc in each of next 15 dc; rep from * around ending with dc in last 7 dc, join, finish off.

Rnd 6: Pick up blue from Rnd 4, sl st in next dc, ch 2, hdc in same st, hdc in each dc around working (2 hdc, ch 2, 2 hdc) in each corner sp, end with sl st in beg hdc, finish off, weave in ends.

Joining

Hold two squares with right sides tog and with blue yarn, sew tog through back lps only along one side, carefully matching sts and corner sps. Join into 9 rows of 8 squares each.

Border

Rnd 1: Hold afghan with right side facing you and join blue with sc in sp at upper right corner; 2 sc in same st; sc in each st around, working 3 sc in each rem outer corner and adjusting sts to keep work flat, join in beg sc.

Rnd 2: Sl st in next sc, work (beg V-st, ch 2, V-st) in same st; * sk next 2 sc, V-st in next sc; rep from * to next corner, work (V-st, ch 2, V-st) in center sc of 3-sc corner group; rep from * twice, (sk next sc, V-st in next sc) across last side, join with sl st in 3rd ch of beg ch-3, finish off.

#3 COTTON CANDY

Designed by Jean Leinhauser

SIZE
40" x 40" before border

MATERIALS
Sport weight yarn,
 21 oz variegated,
 7 oz solid color

*Note: Photographed model made
with Patons® Astra #02948
Cotton Candy and #2936 Pale
Lavender*

Size F (5mm) crochet hook
 (or size required for gauge)

GAUGE
8 dc = 2"

INSTRUCTIONS

With variegated, ch 161.

Row 1: Sc in 2nd ch from hook and in each rem ch, ch 3 (counts as first dc of following row), turn: 160 sc.

Row 2: *Crdc over next 2 sc, dc in next sc; rep from * across, ch 3, turn.

Row 3: *Crdc over next 2 dc, dc in next dc; rep from * across, ending with dc in 3rd st of turning ch, ch 3, turn.

Rep Row 3 until piece measures about 40" or same as width, ch 1, turn.

Last Row: Sc in each dc to last dc, 3 sc in last dc for corner; continue working sc around rem 3 edges, working in sides of dc rows and working 3 sc in each rem corner sp. Adjust sts as needed to keep work flat. Finish off, weave in ends.

Border

Note: Adjust sts while working Rnd 1 so that at end you have a total uneven number of sts that can be divided by 3.

Rnd 1: Join solid color in center sc of any corner 3-sc group; ch 1, 3 sc in this st; work sc around entire afghan, working 3 sc in center sc of each corner group; join, do not turn.

Rnd 2: Sl st into center sc of first corner group; (ch 5, dc) in same st, ch 1; *dc in next sc, ch 1, sk next sc; rep from * around, working (dc, ch 2, dc) in each corner sc; join in 3rd ch of beg ch-5.

Rnd 3: Sl st into corner ch-2 sp; in same sp work (ch 6, dc, ch 2); *PC in next dc, ch 2; rep from * to next corner ch-2 sp, in sp work (dc, ch 3, dc, ch 2); rep from * around, ending last rep join in 3rd ch of beg ch-6.

Rnd 4: In beg ch-3 sp work (sc, ch 4, sc); *ch 4, sc in next ch-2 sp; rep from * around, working (sc, ch 4, sc) in each ch-3 corner sp, join in first sc.

Rnd 5: Sl st into ch-4 corner sp; in same sp work (sc, hdc, dc, ch 1, tr, ch 1, dc, hdc, sc), sc in next sc; * 6 dc in next ch-4 sp, sc in next sc; rep from * around, working (sc, hdc, dc, ch 1, tr, ch 1, dc, hdc, sc) in each ch-4 corner sp; join in first sc. Finish off, weave in ends.

#3 ARAN ISLE

Designed by Nazanin S. Fard

SIZE
61" x 61"

MATERIALS
Worsted weight yarn,
 75 oz off white

Note: Photographed model made with Bernat® Aran Style #5230 Natural

Size H (5mm) crochet hook,
 or size required for gauge

GAUGE
16 sc = 4"

INSTRUCTIONS

Strip 1 (make 7)

Ch 25.

Row 1 (wrong side): Sc in 2nd ch from hook, sc in each rem ch: 24 sc; ch 3 (counts as first dc of following row), turn.

Row 2: Dc in next sc; *skip next 3 sc, tr in next sc, working behind the tr just made, dc in the 3 skipped sts; rep from * across, ending with dc in last 2 sc, ch 3, turn.

Row 3: Dc in next dc; *skip next 3 dc, tr in next tr, then working in front of the tr just made, dc in the 3 skipped sts; rep from *across ending with dc in last 2 dc, ch 1, turn.

Row 4: Sc in each st, ch 1, turn.

Row 5: Sc in each st, ch 3, turn.

Row 6: Dc in each of next 2 sc; *BB, dc in each of next 3 sc; rep from * across, ending with dc in last 4 sc; ch 1, turn.

Row 7: Sc in first dc * sc in next 3 dc, sc in ch behind BB; rep from * across, ending with sc in last 2 dc, sc in 3rd ch of ch-3; ch 3, turn.

Rows 8 through 19: Rep Rows 6 through 7.

Rows 20 through 127: Rep Rows 2 through 19.

Rows 128 through 130: Rep Rows 2 through 4; at end of Row 130, finish off. Weave in ends.

Joining

Row 1: With wrong side of Strip 1 facing you, and with long edge at top, join yarn at upper right corner and sc in side of each sc row, 2 sc in side of each dc row, working only 1 sc in last dc row: 200 sc; ch 3, turn.

Row 2: Dc in next sc; *skip next 3 sc, tr in next sc; working behind the tr just made, dc into the 3 skipped sts; rep from * across, ending with dc in each of last 2 sc; ch 3, turn.

Row 3: Dc in next dc; *skip next 3 dc, tr in next tr, then working in front of the tr just made dc into the 3 skipped sts; rep from * across, ending with dc in each of last 2 dc; ch 1, turn.

Row 4: Sc in each st across: 200 sc; ch 1, turn.

Row 5: Hold another strip with wrong side facing; * insert hook into the next sc of first strip and the corresponding st on the 2nd strip, sl st; rep from * across, finish off.

Join rem strips in same manner. Then work Rows 1 through 4 on both outer side edges of afghan.

#32 DEEP PURPLE

Designed by Janie Herrin

SIZE
46" x 69" before border

MATERIALS
Worsted weight yarn,
  32 oz purple
  32 oz off white
  8 oz green
  5 oz shaded purple

Note: Photographed model made with Red Heart® Super Saver® #528 Medium Purple, #316 Soft White, #631 Lt Sage, and #985 Shaded Purples

Size H (5mm) crochet hook or
  size required for gauge

GAUGE
7 dc = 2"

One square = 11 $^1/_2$"

INSTRUCTIONS

Square (make 24)

With purple, ch 6, join with sl st to form a ring.

Rnd 1 (right side): Ch 1, in ring work *[sc, ch 1, (dc, ch 1) 5 times, sc]: petal made; ch 2, rep from * 3 times more, join with sl st in beg sc: 4 petals and 4 corner ch-2 sps.

Rnd 2: Ch 1, reaching back with hook sc in same ch-2 sp, ch 2, working behind petals, (sc in next ch-2 sp, ch 2) 3 times, join with sl st in beg sc.

Rnd 3: Sl st in next ch-2 sp, ch 1, in same sp work (sc, ch 3, sc), ch 3; *in next sp work (sc, ch 3, sc), ch 3; rep from * 2 times more, join in beg sc: 8 ch-3 sps.

Rnd 4: Sl st in next sp, ch 1, in same sp work (sc, ch 1, 5 dc, ch 1, sc): petal made; (in next ch-3 lp work petal) 7 times, do not join: 8 petals made.

Rnd 5: Sc around post of sc on Rnd 3 (2 rnds below); working ch-4 behind petals, ch 4, (sc around post of next sc on Rnd 3, ch 4) 7 times, ch 4, join in beg sc: 8 ch-4 sps.

Rnd 6: Sl st in next sp, ch 1, in same sp work (sc, ch 1, 7 dc, ch 1, sc): petal made; (in next ch-4 sp, work petal) 7 times, join.

Rnd 7: Working chains behind petals, sc around post of sc on Rnd 5, ch 5, (sc around post of next sc on Rnd 5, ch 5) 7 times, join.

Rnd 8: Sl st in next sp, ch 1, in same sp work (sc, ch 1, 9 dc, ch 1, sc) petal made; (in next sp work petal) 7 times, do not join.

Rnd 9: Working chains behind petals as before, sc around post of sc on Rnd 7, ch 7, (sc around post of next sc on Rnd 7, ch 7) 7 times, join, finish off.

Rnd 10: Join green with sl st in any ch-7 sp, in same sp work (beg CL, ch 3, CL) then (CL, ch 3, CL) 2 times, ch 1; * † in next ch-7 lp work 3 dc, ch 1 †; in next ch-7 lp work (CL, ch 3, CL) 3 times, ch 1; rep from * 2 times more; rep from † to † once, join in beg CL; finish off.

Rnd 11: Join white with sl st in any corner ch-3 sp between 3rd and 4th CL, ch 3, in same sp work (2 dc, ch 2, 3 dc): beg corner made; ch 1, (3 dc in next sp, ch 1) 4 times; * in next sp work (3 dc, ch 2, 3 dc): corner made; ch 1, (3 dc in next sp, ch 1) 4 times; rep from * around, join in beg ch-3.

Rnd 12: Sl st to next ch-2 corner sp, work beg corner, ch 1, (3 dc in next sp, ch 1) 5 times; *in next sp work corner, ch 1, (3 dc in next sp, ch 1) 5 times; rep from * around, join, finish off.

Rnd 13: Join shaded purple with sl st in any corner ch-2 sp, (ch 5, dc in same sp): beg

Continued on next page.

V-st made; ch 2, in same sp, work (dc, ch 2, dc): V-st made; ch 1, (V-st in next sp, ch 1) 6 times; * in next sp work (V-st, ch 2, V-st), ch 1, (V-st in next sp, ch 1) 6 times; rep from * around twice more, work last side as before, join in 3rd ch of beg ch-5, finish off.

Rnd 14: Join white with sl st in any corner ch-2 sp between V-sts, in same corner work (ch 5, dc, ch 2, V-st), ch 1; *(V-st in next ch-1 sp, ch 1) 7 times; in next corner ch-2 sp between V-sts work (V-st, ch 2, V-st), ch 1; rep from * around, join in 3rd ch of beg ch-5.

Rnd 15: Sl st to next ch-2 corner sp between V-sts, in same sp work (ch 5, dc, ch 2, V-st), ch 1; (V-st in next ch-1 sp, ch 1) 8 times; *in next corner sp between V-sts work (V-st, ch 2, V-st), ch 1; (V-st in next ch-1 sp, ch 1) 8 times; rep from * around, join in 3rd ch of beg ch-5.

Rnd 16: Ch 4, *in next ch-2 corner sp between V-sts, work (3 dc, ch 2, 3 dc): corner made, ch 1; (3 dc in next ch-1 sp, ch 1) 9 times; rep from * around ending with 2 dc in last sp, join in 3rd ch of beg ch-4, finish off.

Rnd 17: Join purple with sl st in any corner ch-2 sp, ch 3, in same sp work (2 dc, ch 2, 3 dc) ch 1; (3 dc in next sp, ch 1) 10 times; * in next ch-2 corner sp work (3 dc, ch 2, 3 dc), ch 1; (3 dc in next sp, ch 1) 10 times; rep from * around, join in 3rd ch of beg ch-3, finish off.

Joining

Hold 2 squares with right sides together and working through both thicknesses with purple, sew along one side with overcast st, carefully matching sts and corners. Join other squares in same manner, in 6 rows of 4 squares.

Border

Rnd 1: Hold piece with right side facing you and join purple with sc in outer corner sp at upper right, 2 sc in same sp, sc in each st and each joining across to next corner, 3 sc in corner; sc evenly around, adjusting sts as needed to keep work flat, and working 3 sc in each rem outer corner sp; join with sl st in beg sc.

Rnd 2: Ch 3, 2 dc in same st; *sk next dc, 3 dc in next st; rep from * around, join with sl st in 3rd ch of beg ch-3. Finish off purple.

Rnd 3: Join white with sc in same st, ch 2, 2 dc in same st, ch 1, skip next 2 dc of same 3-dc group; *sc in first dc of next 3-dc group, ch 2, 2 dc in same dc; ch 1, skip next 2 dc of same 3-dc group; rep from * around, ending join with sl st in beg sc, finish off.

#33 WAVES

Designed by Rita Weiss for Coats and Clark

SIZE
40" x 60".

MATERIALS
Worsted weight yarn,
  6 oz cream
  18 oz blue

Note: *Photographed model made with Red Heart® Plush™ #9103 Cream and #9823 French Blue*

29" Size 8 (5mm) circular knitting needle (or size required for gauge)

GAUGE
16 sts = 4" in patt

24 rows = 4"

PATTERN
Rows 1, 3, 5, 7, 9, 11: With blue, K5; *(K2tog) twice, (YO, K1) 3 times, YO; (sl 1, K1, PSSO) twice, K1; rep from * to last 4 sts, K4.

Rows 2, 4, 6, 8, 10, 12: K4, Purl to last 4 sts, K4.

Rows 13 through 16: With cream, knit.

INSTRUCTIONS

With cream, CO 165 sts; do not join, work back and forth in rows.

Rows 1 through 4: Knit.

Rep Rows 1 through 16 of pattern until piece measures 60" from beg, ending by working Row 16. BO loosely as to knit.

#34 POPCORN & LACE

Designed by Patons Design Staff

SIZE
54" x 60"

MATERIALS
Worsted weight yarn,
  42 oz off white

Note: *Photographed model made with
Patons® Canadiana #104 Aran*

Size J (6mm) crochet hook (or size
  required for gauge)

GAUGE
$12 \frac{1}{2}$ dc = 4"

4 rows = 4" in patt

Front post dc (FPdc): YO, insert hook from front to back to front around post of specified st, YO and draw up a lp, (YO and draw through 2 lps on hook) twice: FPdc made.

Back post dc (BPdc): YO, insert hook from back to front to back around post of specified st, YO and draw up a lp, (YO and draw through 2 lps on hook) twice: BPdc made.

Popcorn (PC): 4 dc in specified st, remove lp from hook, insert hook from the front into first of 4 dc and into dropped lp, draw dropped lp through first dc: PC made.

INSTRUCTIONS

Ch 185.

Foundation row (wrong side): Dc in 4th ch from hook, dc in next 4 chs; *skip next 2 chs, (2 dc, ch 2, 2 dc) in next ch, skip next 2 chs, dc in next 7 chs; skip next 2 chs, (2 dc, ch 2, 2 dc) in next ch, skip next 2 chs, dc in next 5 chs; rep from * to last ch; dc in last ch; ch 3, turn.

Row 1: Skip first st, FPdc around post of next st, dc in next st, PC in next st, dc in next st, FPdc around post of next st; *ch 2, (sc, ch 3, sc) in next ch-2 sp, ch 2, skip next 2 sts, FPdc around post of next st, dc in next 2 sts, PC in next st, dc in next 2 sts; FPdc around post of next st, ch 2, (sc, ch 3, sc) in next ch-2 sp, ch 2, skip next 2 sts; FPdc around post of next st, dc in next st, PC in next st, dc in next st, FPdc around post of next st; rep from * to last st; dc in next ch; ch 3, turn.

Row 2: Skip first st, BPdc around post of next FPdc, dc in next 3 sts, BPdc around post of next FPdc; *(2 dc, ch 2, 2 dc) in next ch-3 sp, BPdc around post of next FPdc, dc in next 5 dc, BPdc around post of next FPdc; (2 dc, ch 2, 2 dc) in next ch-3 sp, BPdc around post of next FPdc, dc in next 3 sts, BPdc around post of next FPdc; rep from * to last st; dc in 3rd ch of ch-3; ch 3, turn.

Row 3: Skip first st, FPdc around post of next BPdc, dc in next st, PC in next st, dc in next st, FPdc around post of next BPdc; *ch 2, (sc, ch 3, sc) in next ch-2 sp, ch 2, FPdc around post of next BPdc, (dc in next st, PC in next st) twice, dc in next st; FPdc around post of next BPdc, ch 2, (sc, ch 3, sc) in next ch-2 sp, ch 2; FPdc around post of next BPdc, dc in next st, PC in next st, dc in next st, FPdc around post of next BPdc; rep from * to last st; dc in 3rd ch of ch-3; ch 3, turn.

Row 4: Rep Row 2.

Rep Rows 1 through 4 until work measures 60", ending by working a Row 4. At end of last row, do not ch 3. Finish off and weave in ends.

Fringe

Following Single Knot Fringe instructions on page 221, cut strands 16" long and knot 4 strands in every ch-2 sp and in middle st of each dc section across top and bottom edges. Trim fringe.

#35 COMING UP ROSY

Designed by Bonnie Pierce

SIZE
28" x 35" before border

MATERIALS
Worsted weight yarn,
  8 oz white
  12 oz lt rose
  20 oz dk rose

Note: *Photographed model made with Red Heart® Classic™ #1 White, #755 Pale Rose, and #760 New Berry*

Size G (4mm) crochet hook
  (or size required for gauge)

GAUGE
7 sc = 2"

Square = 7" x 7"

INSTRUCTIONS

Square (make 20)

Note: Underlying center block is worked in lt rose for first 5 rnds; then dk rose section is worked over it.

With lt rose, ch 4, join with a sl st to form a ring.

Rnd 1: Ch 1, (sc in ring, ch 3) 4 times, join with sl st in first sc.

Rnd 2: Ch 1, sc in same sc; *† in next ch-3 sp work (sc, ch 3, sc) for corner; †*; sc in next sc; rep from * to * twice more, then repeat from † to † once; join in first sc.

Rnd 3: Ch 1, sc in same sc and in next sc; *† in next corner ch-3 sp work (sc, ch 3, sc) for corner †; sc in next 3 sc; rep from * twice more, then repeat from † to † once; sc in next sc; join in first sc.

Rnd 4: Ch 1, sc in same sc and in next 2 sc; † * corner in next corner; sc in next 5 sc †; rep from * twice more, then rep from † to † once; sc in next 2 sc; join in first sc.

Rnd 5: Ch 1, sc in same sc and in next 3 sc; * † corner in next corner †; sc in next 7 sc; rep from * twice more, then repeat from † to † once; sc in next 3 sc; join in first sc. Finish off.

Rnd 6: Join dk rose with Lsc in any corner ch-3 sp of Rnd 4; * † Lsc in ch-3 sp of same corner on Rnd 3, Lsc in ch-3 sp of same corner on Rnd 2, Lsc in ch-3 sp of same corner on Rnd 1, Lsc in center ring; Lsc in next corner ch-3 sp of Rnd 1, Lsc in same corner ch-3 sp of Rnd 2; Lsc in same corner ch-3 sp of Rnd 3; Lsc in same corner ch-3 sp of Rnd 4, ch 4 †; working over next side of square, Lsc in same ch-3 sp of Rnd 4; rep from * twice more, then rep from † to † once; join in first Lsc. Finish off.

Rnd 7: Join lt rose in any ch-4 sp; ch 1, in same sp work corner as for Rnd 2; * sc in next 9 sc, in next corner ch-4 sp work corner; rep from * twice more; sc in next 9 sc; join in first sc.

Rnd 8: Ch 1, sc in same sc as joining; * † corner in next corner †; sc in next 11 sc; rep from * twice more, then rep from † to † once; sc in next 10 sc; join in first sc.

Rnd 9: Ch 1, sc in same sc and in next sc; * † corner in next corner †; sc in next 13 sc; rep from * twice more, then rep from † to † once; sc in next 11 sc; join in first sc. Finish off.

Rnd 10: Join white in first sc to left of any corner ch-3 sp; ch 1, sc in same sc and in next 3 sc, sk next sc, 2 long sc in ch-4 sp of Rnd 6 below; * † sc in next 5 sc, sk next sc, 2 Lsc in next ch-4 sp on Round 6; sc in next 4 sc, working over next corner ch-3 sp, 2 Lsc in same ch-4 sp of Rnd 6: Lsc corner made †; sc in next 4 sc, sk next sc, 2 Lsc in same ch-4 sp of Rnd 6; rep from * twice more, then rep from † to † once to complete first corner; join in first sc. Finish off.

Continued on next page.

Rnd 11: Join lt rose in first corner Lsc; ch 1, 2 sc in same st; 2 sc in next Lsc: corner made; * sc in next 17 sc; 2 sc in each of next 2 Lsc ; rep from * twice more; sc in next 17 sc; join in first sc. Finish off.

Rnd 12: Join dk rose in 3rd sc in any corner; ch 1; 3 sc in same sc; * sc in next 20 sc, 3 sc in next sc; rep from * twice more; sc in next 20 sc; join in first sc.

Rnd 13: Ch 3, in 2nd sc of corner work (2 dc, ch 2, 2 dc) for corner; *† dc in next 22 sts †; (2 dc, ch 2, 2 dc) in next sc; rep from * twice more, dc in next 21 sts, join in 3rd ch of beg ch-3.

Rnd 14: Sc in each st around, working 3 sc in corner ch-2 sps, join in beg sc.

Rnd 15: Sc in each st around, working 3 sc in center sc of ech corner group; join in beg sc.

Finish off and weave in ends, leaving an 2 12" inch end for sewing.

Joining

Hold two squares with right sides tog and and sew along one side edge.

Join in this manner in 5 rows of 4 squares each.

Border

Rnd 1: With right side of afghan facing, join dk rose with sc in upper right-hand corner, 2 sc in same st; sc around entire outside edge, working 3 sc in each rem corner, and adjusting sts to keep work flat; join with sl st in beg sc.

Rnd 2: 3 sc in next sc, sc in each sc around, working 3 sc in center sc of each rem corner, join, finish off.

Rnd 3: Join lt rose with sc in center sc of any corner 3-sc group, 2 sc in same st; sc around, working 3 sc in each corner; finish off lt rose.

Rnd 4: Join white with sl st in center sc of any corner group; ch 1, 3 hdc in same st; hdc in each st around, working 3 hdc in each corner; join in beg hdc, finish off white.

Rnd 5: Join lt rose in center hdc of any corner group, 3 sc in same st; sc in each hdc around, working 3 sc in corners; join, finish off. Weave in all ends.

#36 JEWEL RIPPLE

SIZE
49" x 62".

MATERIALS
Worsted weight yarn,
   15 oz navy (A)
   29 oz variegated (B)

Note: Photographed model made with Red Heart® Super Saver® #387 Soft Navy (A) and #959 Gemstone(B)

36" Size 9 (5.5mm) circular knitting needle (or size required for gauge)

GAUGE
19 sts= 4" in patt
25 rows = 4" in patt

INSTRUCTIONS

With A, CO 234 sts; do not join, work back and forth in rows.

Lower Border
Rows 1 through 5: Knit; at end of Row 5, cut A.

Center Section
Row 1 (right side): With B, knit.

Row 2: Purl.

Row 3: (K2tog) 3 times; *(YO, K1) 6 times, (K2tog) 6 times; rep from * to last 12 sts; (YO, K1) 6 times, (K2tog) 3 times.

Row 4: Knit.

Rows 5 through 18: Rep Rows 1 through 4 three more times; then rep Rows 1 and 2 once more. At end of Row 18, cut B and attach A.

Row 19: With A, rep Row 3.

Rows 20 through 24: Knit. At end of Row 24, cut A.

Rep Rows 1-24 until afghan measures about 62" from CO row, ending by working a Row 23. BO with A.

Fringe
Following instructions for Single Knot Fringe on page 221, cut 12" strands of A and use 12 strands tog in each knot; tie a knot at each point along top and bottom of afghan.

#37 PINEAPPLE THROW

Designed by Janie Herrin

SIZE
41" x 58"

MATERIALS
Worsted weight yarn,
  36 oz cream

Size I (5.5mm) hook (or
  size required for gauge)

GAUGE
9 dc = 3"

INSTRUCTIONS

Ch 136.

Row 1 (right side): Sc in 2nd ch from hook and in each ch across; ch 3, turn: 135 sc. (**Note:** *turning ch equals first dc of next row now and throughout*)

Row 2: Dc in next 2 sc; *ch 2, skip 4 sc, 7 tr in next sc, ch 2, skip 4 sc, dc in next 6 sc; rep from * across, ending with dc in last 3 sc, ch 3, turn: base of 9 pineapples made.

Row 3: Dc in next dc; *ch 2, skip next dc and ch-2 sp, (dc in next tr, ch 1) 6 times; dc in next tr, ch 2, skip ch-2 sp and next dc, **dc in next 4 dc; rep from * across ending last rep at **, dc in last 2 dc, ch 3, turn.

Row 4: Dc in next dc; *ch 2, skip ch-2 sp, (sc in next ch-1 sp, ch 3) 5 times; sc in next ch-1 sp, ch 2, skip ch-2 sp and next dc, dc in next 2 dc; rep from * across ending with dc in last 2 dc, ch 3, turn.

Row 5: Dc in next dc; * ch 2, skip ch-2 sp, (sc in next ch-3 lp, ch 3) 4 times; sc in next ch-3 lp, ch 2, skip ch-2 sp, dc in next 2 dc; rep from * across ending with dc in last 2 dc, ch 3, turn.

Row 6: 2 dc in next dc; *ch 2, skip ch-2 sp, (sc in next ch-3 lp, ch 3) 3 times; sc in next ch-3 lp, ch 2, skip ch-2 sp, 2 dc in each of next 2 dc; rep from * across ending with 2 dc in next dc, dc in last dc, ch 3, turn.

Row 7: Dc in next dc, 2 dc in next dc; *ch 2, skip ch-2 sp, (sc in next ch-3 lp, ch 3) twice; sc in next ch-3 lp, ch 2, skip ch-2 sp, 2 dc in next dc; dc in next 2 dc, 2 dc in next dc; rep from * across ending with 2 dc in next dc, dc in last 2 dc, ch 3, turn.

Row 8: Dc in next 2 dc, 2 dc in next dc; *ch 2, skip ch-2 sp, sc in next ch-3 lp, ch 3, sc in next ch-3 lp; ch 2, skip ch-2 sp, 2 dc in next dc, dc in next 4 dc, 2 dc in next dc; rep from * across ending with 2 dc in next dc, dc in last 3 dc, ch 3, turn.

Row 9: Dc in next 3 dc, 2 dc in next dc; *ch 2, skip ch-2 sp, sc in next ch-3 lp; ch 2, skip ch-2 sp, 2 dc in next dc, dc in next 6 dc, 2 dc in next dc; rep from * across ending with 2 dc in next dc, dc in last 4 dc, ch 3, turn.

Row 10: Dc in next 4 dc, 2 dc in next dc; *ch 2, skip both ch-2 sps, 2 dc in next dc, dc in next 8 dc, 2 dc in next dc; rep from * across ending with 2 dc in next dc, dc in last 5 dc, ch 3, turn.

Row 11: Dc in next 2 dc; *ch 2, skip 4 dc, 7 tr in next ch-2 sp, ch 2; skip 4 dc, 2 dc in next dc, dc in next 2 dc, 2 dc in next dc; rep from * across ending with skip 4 dc, dc in last 3 dc, ch 3, turn.

Rep Rows 3 through 11 nine times more, then Rep Rows 3 thru 10 once; do not ch 3 at end of last row.

Ch 1, turn, sc in first dc and in next 5 dc, 2 sc in next dc; *2 sc in ch-2 sp, sc in next 12 dc; rep from * across ending with 2 sc in next dc, sc in last 6 dc; finish off. Weave in ends.

Fringe
Following Single Knot Fringe instructions on page 221, cut strands 16" long and knot 2 strands in each st across on each short end.

Trim fringe.

#38 AMERICANA

Designed by Janie Herrin

SIZE
48" x 64" before border

MATERIALS
Worsted weight yarn,
   11 oz red (A)
   21 oz white (B)
   21 oz blue (C)

Note: *Photographed model made with Red Heart® Classic™ #902 Jockey Red(A), #1 White (B), and #848 Skipper Blue (C)*

Size H (5mm) crochet hook
   (or size required for gauge)

GAUGE
3 dc = 1"

Square = 8" x 8"

INSTRUCTIONS

Square (make 48)

With Color A, ch 5, join with sl st to form a ring.

Rnd 1: Ch 3 (counts as a dc), 2 dc in ring; (ch 2, 3 dc in ring) 3 times; ch 2, join with a sl st in 3rd ch of beg ch-3; sl st in next 2 dc and into ch-2 sp.

Rnd 2: Ch 5 (counts as a dc and ch-2 sp), (dc, ch 2, V-St) in same ch-2 sp (first corner made); * in next ch-2 sp work (V-st, ch 2, V-st) (next corner made); rep from * once more, (V-st, ch 2, V-st) in next sp (last corner made), sl st in 3rd ch of beg ch-5; sl st into next ch-2 sp.

Rnd 3: Ch 3, 2 dc in same sp; *ch 1, skip V-st, 3 dc in next sp (betweenV-sts), ch 1, (3 dc, ch 2, 3 dc) in next corner ch-2 sp; rep from * around, ending with 3 dc, ch 2, join with sl st to beg ch-3: 12, 3-dc groups made; finish off Color A.

Rnd 4: Join Color B with sl st in any corner sp; (ch 3, dc, ch 2, 2 dc) all in same sp; *dc in next 3 dc; (tr in ch-2 sp of V-st one row below, dc in each of next 3 dc) twice; (2 dc, ch 2, 2 dc) in next corner sp; rep from * twice; dc in next 3 dc, (tr in ch-2 sp of V-st one row below, dc in each of next 3 dc) twice, join in top of beg ch-3.

Rnd 5: Sl st to corner sp, (ch 5, dc, ch 2, V-st) in same corner sp;*(sk 3 sts, V-st in next dc) 3 times, sk 3 dc; in next corner sp work (V-st, ch 2, V-st), rep from * twice; (sk 3 sts, V-st in next dc) 3 times, sk 3 dc, join with sl st in 3rd ch of beg-5; sl st to next sp.

Rnd 6: Ch 4 (counts as dc plus ch-1), skip next V-st; *in next corner sp work (3 dc, ch 2, 3 dc); ch 1, (skip next V-st, 3 dc in next sp between V-sts, ch 1) 4 times, rep from * twice, ending with 2 dc in last sp, join with sl st to 3rd ch of beg ch-4; finish off Color B.

Rnd 7: Join Color C in any ch-2 corner sp; (ch 3, dc, ch 2, 2 dc) all in same sp; *dc in next 3 dc; (tr in ch-2 sp of V-st one row below, dc in each of next 3 dc) 5 times; (2 dc, ch 2, 2 dc; in next corner sp; rep from * twice, dc in next 3 dc; (tr in next ch-2 sp of V-st one row below, dc in each of next 3 dc) 5 times, join in top of beg ch-3.

Rnd 8: Sl st in next dc, 3 sc in ch-2 sp; sc in each st around, working 3 sc in each rem corner sp; finish off, weave in ends.

Joining

To join, hold two squares with right sides tog and with Color C, sew with overcast st along one side, carefully matching sts and corners. Continue joining into 8 rows of 6 squares each.

Border

Rnd 1: With right side facing, join Color A with a sl st in upper right corner; ch 1, 3 sc in same st; work one rnd sc around entire outer edge, adjusting sts as needed to keep work flat, and working 3 sc in each outer corner st; join, finish off Color A.

Rnd 2: With right side facing, join color B in center sc of any 3-sc corner group; (ch 3, 2 dc, ch 3, 3 dc) all in same sc; *dc in each sc to next 3-sc corner group, work (3 dc, ch 3, 3 dc) in same sc; rep from * twice, dc in each rem sc, join to 3rd ch of beg ch-3; finish off Color B.

Rnd 3: With right side facing, join Color C in ch-3 sp of any corner group; ch 1, 3 sc in same sp; *sc in each dc to next corner sp, 3 sc in ch-3 sp; rep from * twice, sc in each rem dc; join, finish off. Weave in ends.

#39 LEMONADE SKIES

Designed by Trish Kristoffersen for Coats & Clark

SIZE
48" x 68"

MATERIALS
Worsted weight yarn,
24 oz white (A)
28 oz yellow (B)
12 oz blue (C)

Note: Photographed model made with Red Heart Super Saver #311 White (A), #322 Pale Yellow (B) and #347 Light Periwinkle (C)

Size H (5mm) crochet hook (or size required for gauge)

25 yards of 1/4" wide ribbon

Sewing thread to match ribbon

Sewing needle

Yarn needle

GAUGE
In patt: 5 rows = 4"

Strip measures 4 1/4" wide x 67" long

INSTRUCTIONS

Strip (make 11)

With A, ch 6, join with sl st to form a ring.

Row 1 (right side): Ch 3; (fPc, ch 3, fPc, dc) in ring; ch 3, turn.

Row 2: In ch-3 sp between popcorns work (bPc, ch 3, bPc); dc in 3rd ch of beg ch-3; ch 3, turn.

Row 3: In ch-3 sp between popcorns work (fPc, ch 3, fPc); dc in 3rd ch of beg ch-3; ch 3, turn.

Rows 4 through 69: Rep Rows 2 and 3 alternately 33 times more. Finish off and weave in ends.

Border

Rnd 1: With right side facing, join B with sl st in ch-3 sp between popcorns on Row 69; ch 3, 10 dc in same sp; *3 dc around row edge (a ch-3 sp or a dc post)**; rep from * to ** 68 times more along side; 11 dc in ring; rep from * to ** 69 times along opposite side; join with sl st in 3rd ch of beg ch-3.

Rnd 2: Ch 1, sc in same ch as joining; **(sc in back 1p of next dc, 2 sc in both 1ps of next dc) 4 times; *sc in back lp of next dc, sc in both 1ps of next 2 dc; rep from * along side, end 2 dc before next 11-dc group; sc in back 1p of next dc, sc in both

1ps of next dc***; sc in both 1ps of first dc of next 11-dc group; rep from ** around, end at ***; join with sl st in first sc.

Rnd 3: Ch 1, sc in each sc around; join with sl st in first sc. Finish off and weave in ends.

Rnd 4: With right side facing, join C with sl st in same sc as joining; ch 1, sc in same sc; *dc in front lp of dc on Rnd 1 below next st, skip sc behind dc just worked**; sc in next 2 sc, rep from * to last sc, end at **; sc in last sc, join with sl st in first sc. Finish off and weave in ends.

Arrange strips so that top of strip is alternately at top or bottom of afghan. Sew strips tog through both 1ps omitting 17 sts at each end.

Edging

Hold piece with right side facing; join C with sl st in any dc along side edge; ch 1, sc in same dc; *ch 2, 2 dc in side of sc just made, skip next 2 sc**, sc in next dc; rep from * around entire afghan, end at **, working a sc only in the dc where strips are sewn together; join with sl st in same dc as joining. Finish off and weave in ends.

Finishing

Thread yarn needle with ribbon and weave in and out between center of popcorn rows as shown in photograph. Fold back and with sewing needle and thread, tack ends down on wrong side.

#40 EVENING SHADOWS

Designed by Janie Herrin

SIZE
30" x 42" before border

MATERIALS
Worsted weight yarn,
 21 oz light mauve
 17 1/2 oz medium mauve

Note: *Photographed model made with Bernat® Berella® 4, #01305 Soft Mauve and #01306 True Mauve*

Size H (5mm) crochet hook or
 size required for gauge

GAUGE
7 dc = 2"

Square = 6" x 6"

INSTRUCTIONS

Square (make 35)

With med mauve, ch 6, join with sl st to form a ring.

Rnd 1: Ch 3 (equals first dc), 15 dc in ring, join with sl st in 3rd ch of beg ch-3: 16 dc.

Rnd 2: Ch 3, 4 dc in same st; *ch 1, skip next dc, sc in next dc, ch 1, skip next dc, 5 dc in next dc; rep from * around ending with sl st in 3rd ch of beg ch-3.

Rnd 3: Ch 1, sc in same st; *ch 2, skip next dc, in next dc work (sc, ch 2, sc), ch 2, skip next dc, sc in next dc; ch 2, sc in sc, ch 2, sc in next dc; rep from * around ending with sl st in beg sc; finish off.

Rnd 4: Join lt mauve with sl st in next sp, ch 1, sc in same sp; *ch 2, (sc, ch 2, sc) in corner sp; (ch 2, sc in next sp) 4 times; rep from * around ending with sl st in beg sc.

Rnd 5: Ch 5 (equals first dc plus ch 2), *skip next sp, in corner sp work (dc, ch 5, dc), (ch 2, skip next sp, dc in next sc) 4 times, ch 2; rep from * around ending with ch 2, sl st in 3rd ch of beg ch 5.

Rnd 6: Work beg V-st; *in corner sp work (V-st, ch 3, V-st), skip next dc, (V-st in next dc) 4 times; rep from * around, end with V-st in last 3 dc, sl st in 3rd ch of beg ch 5.

Rnd 7: Sl st in ch-2 sp of next V-st, ch 1, 3 sc in same sp; 3 sc in ch-2 sp of each V-st around, working 5 sc in each corner ch-3

sp, join in beg sc; finish off. Weave in ends.

Joining

To join, hold two squares with right sides tog and with lt mauve sew with overcast st through outer lps only along one side, carefully matching sts and corners. In same manner, continue joining in 7 rows of 5 squares each.

Border

Rnd 1: Hold afghan with right side facing you; join lt mauve in upper right corner sp, 3 sc in same sp; sc in each st and joining around, adjusting sts to keep work flat and working 3 sc in each outer corner sp; join in beg sc.

Rnd 2: Ch 3, 2 dc in same sc; *sk next sc, 3 dc in next sc; rep from * around, join in 3rd ch of beg ch-3, finish off.

Rnd 3: Join med mauve in any dc, ch 3, 2 dc in same dc; 3 dc in each dc around, join with sc in 3rd ch of beg ch-3

Rnd 4: *Ch 4, sk next dc, sc in next dc; rep from * around; join, finish off. Weave in ends.

#41 TIFFANY ROSE

Designed by Joyce Vanderslice for Coats and Clark

SIZE
52" x 67"

MATERIALS
Worsted weight yarn,
 11 oz rose (A)
 12 oz off-white (B)
 10 oz lt green (C)
 18 oz dk green (D)

Note: Photographed model made with Red Heart® Super Saver® #374 Country Rose (A), #313 Aran (B), #631 Light Sage (C), and #633 Dark Sage (D)

Size J (6mm) crochet hook (or
 size required for gauge)

GAUGE
Square = 6 ³/₄" x 6 ³/₄"
Stripe patt = 2 ¹/₂" wide

INSTRUCTIONS

Note: Always join new color with right side facing.

Square (make 49)

With A, ch 4; join with sl st to form a ring.

Rnd 1 (right side): Ch 1, 8 sc in ring: 8 sc; join with sl st in first sc.

Rnd 2: Beg PC, ch 3; (PC, ch 3) 7 times; join with sl st in top of beg PC. Finish off and weave in ends.

Rnd 3: Join B with sl st in any ch-3 sp; ch 3 (counts as dc), dc in same sp, *9 dc in next (corner) sp**, 2 dc in next sp; rep from * around, end at **: 44 dc; join with sl st in 3rd ch of beg ch-3.

Rnd 4: Ch 3 (counts as dc), dc in next dc; *ch 3, skip next 3 dc, dc in next dc, (dc, ch 2, dc) in next dc, dc in next dc, ch 3, skip next 3 dc**, dc in next 2 dc; rep from * around, end at **: 24 dc, 8 ch-3 sps and 4 corner ch-2 sps; join as before. Finish off and weave in ends.

Rnd 5: Join C with sl st in any corner ch-2 sp, ch 6, 2 dc in same sp; *(dc in next 2 dc, 3 dc in next ch-3 sp) twice, dc in next 2 dc**, (2 dc, ch 3, 2 dc) in corner ch-2 sp; rep from * around, end at **; dc in first corner ch-2 sp: 64 dc and 4 corner ch-3 sps; join with sl st in 3rd ch of ch-6. Finish off and weave in ends.

Rnd 6: Join D with sl st in any corner ch-3 sp; ch 1, *3 sc in corner sp, sc in next 16 dc; rep from * around: 76 sc; join with sl st in first sc. Finish off and weave in ends.

Joining

***With D, sew 7 squares tog in a strip through the back 1ps. Now work stripe pat on one side only of strip as follows:

Stripe pattern

Row 1: Join D with sl st in back 1p of center sc of 3 sc at corner of first square; ch 1, working in back 1p of each sc across, sc in same sc as joining, sc in next 19 sc on same square, (sc in next 20 sc on next square) 6 times: 140 sc; ch 3 (counts as dc on next row), turn.

Row 2: Skip first sc, dc in each sc across, changing to A in last st: 140 dc; ch 3 (counts as dc on next row), turn.

Row 3: With A, skip first dc, *Crdc in next 2 dc; rep from * to last st; dc in 3rd ch of ch-3 changing to D: 69 Crdc and 2 dc; ch 3 (counts as dc on next row), turn.

Row 4: With D, skip first dc, dc in each dc across and in 3rd ch of ch-3: 140 dc; ch 1, turn.

Continued on next page.

Row 5: Sc in each dc across and in 3rd ch of ch-3. Finish off and weave in ends.

Rep from *** (under Joining) 5 times more: 6 strips of 7 squares completed. Join strips, side by side, sewing strip edges with stripe patt adjacent to edge of strip without stripe patt and working through back lps. Sew rem 7 squares together for 7th strip and sew to stripe patt edge of a completed strip through back lps (top and bottom edges of afghan do not have stripe patt).

Border

Rnd 1: Join D with sl st in back lp of center sc of 3 sc at top right corner of afghan; working in back lps around, ch 1, *3 sc in corner sc, sc in next 19 sc on same square, (sc in next 20 sc on next square) 5 times, sc in next 19 sc on next square, 3 sc in corner sc, sc in next 19 sc on same square, 8 sc across stripe pat (work 1 sc in edge of each sc row and 2 sc around post [vertical bar] of each dc row), (sc in next 20 sc on next square, 8 sc across stripe pat as before) 5 times, sc in next 19 sc on next square; rep from * around; join with sl st in first sc.

Rnd 2: Ch 3, skip first sc, *2 dc in corner sc, dc in each sc to next corner; rep from * around; join with sl st in 3rd ch of ch-3. Finish off and weave in ends.

Rnd 3: Join A with sl st in 2nd dc of any 2 corner dc; ch 3 (counts as dc), dc in dc before joining to make first Crdc, *Crdc in next 2 dc; rep from * around; join as before. Finish off and weave in ends.

Rnd 4: Join D with sl st in any dc; ch 3 (counts as dc), dc in next dc and in each dc around, working 2 dc in each of 2 dc in corner Crdc; join.

Rnd 5: Ch 1, sc in each dc around, working 2 sc in 2nd and 3rd dc of corner dc; join with sl st in first sc. Finish off and weave in ends.

Rnd 3: Ch 4, (dc in next dc, ch 1) 3 times; *in corner ch-3 sp work (dc, ch 3, dc); (ch 1, dc in next dc) 5 times, ch 1; rep from * around, ending (dc, ch 3, dc) in last corner sp, ch 1, dc in next dc, ch 1, join in 3rd ch of beg ch-4.

Rnd 4: Ch 4, (dc in next dc, ch 1) 4 times; * in corner ch-3 sp work (dc, ch 3, dc); (ch 1, dc in next dc) 7 times, ch 1; rep from * around, ending (dc, ch 3, dc) in last corner sp, (ch 1, dc in next dc) twice, ch 1, join to 3rd ch of beg ch-4.

Rnd 5: Ch 4, (dc in next dc, ch 1) 5 times; * in corner ch-3 sp work (dc, ch 3, dc); (ch 1, dc in next dc) 9 times, ch 1; rep from * around, ending (dc, ch 3, dc) in last corner sp, (ch 1, dc in next dc) 3 times, ch 1, join in 3rd ch of beg ch-4.

Rnd 6: Ch 1, sc in same st and in each ch-1 sp and dc around, working 3 sc in each corner sp, join to beg sc; finish off.

Ruffles

First Ruffle

With right side facing, join ombre yarn with sc around post (vertical bar) of first dc on Rnd 2, (ch 2, sc around same st) twice, *ch 3, working from right to left, sc around post of next dc on same rnd, (ch 2, sc around same st) twice; rep from * around ending with ch 3, join to beg sc; finish off.

Second Ruffle

With right side facing, join ombre yarn with sc around post of first dc on Rnd 4, and work as for First Ruffle. Finish off, weave in ends.

Joining

To join, hold two squares with right sides tog, and sew with overcast st along one edge, carefully matching sts and corners. Join squares in 4 rows of 5 squares each.

Border

Rnd 1: Hold piece with right side facing you and one short end at top. Join lt blue yarn with sc in first st at upper right; 2 sc in same st for corner; sc around entire afghan, working 3 sc in each rem outer corner st and adjusting sts as needed to keep work flat and edges straight; finish off.

Rnd 2: Join ombre with sc in center sc of 3-sc group at right top; work as for Rnd 1; finish off.

#44 TWO SIDES TO THE STORY

Designed by Kathleen Stuart

SIZE
41" x 41" before border

MATERIALS
Worsted weight yarn,
 24 oz ombre
 12 oz white

Note: Photographed model made with Red Heart® Super Saver® #996 Ocean and #322 White

Size J (6mm) crochet hook (or size required for gauge)

GAUGE
16 sts (5 blocks) = 5"

8 rows (4 blocks) = 3"

Dc cluster (dcCL): (YO, insert hook in specified st, YO and pull up a lp, YO and draw through 2 lps on hook) twice; YO and draw through all 3 loops on hook: dcCL made.

To change colors: Work last st in first color until one step remains; work last step with new color, and continue with it.

INSTRUCTIONS

With white, ch 132.

Row 1: Sc in 2nd ch from hook and in each rem ch: 131 sc.

Row 2: Ch 5 (counts as dc and ch-2 sp), turn; skip next 2 sc, dc in next sc; *ch 2, skip next 2 sc, dc in next sc; rep from * across, changing to ombre in last dc: 43 ch-2 spaces; cut white.

Note: You will now cut working color at end of each row; leave at least a 4" end before cutting for weaving in later. You may wish to weave in ends every few rows as you work, rather than leaving them all for later.

Row 3: Ch 1, turn; sc in first dc; *working behind next ch-2 sp, work dcCL in each of next 2 skipped sc on row below, sc in next dc; rep from * across, changing to white in last sc: 86 dcCL; cut ombre.

Row 4: Ch 5 (counts as dc and ch-2), turn; skip next 2 sts, dc in next sc; *ch 2, skip next 2 sts, dc in next sc; rep from * across changing to ombre in last dc: 43 ch-2 spaces; cut white.

Row 5: Ch 1, turn; sc in first dc; *working behind next ch-2 sp, work dcCL in each of next 2 dcCL two rows below, sc in next dc; rep from * across changing to white in last sc; cut ombre.

Rep Rows 4 and 5 until piece measures about 41", ending by working a Row 5. Finish off, weave in all ends.

Border

Hold afghan with Row 5 side facing you, and last row at top.

Rnd 1: Join white with a sl st in first st at upper right corner; ch 1, 3 sc in same st; sc in first st of last row, 2 sc in same space for corner; work sc evenly around all four sides of afghan, adjusting sts to keep work flat, and working 3 sc in each outer corner.

Count sts as you go: you will need a multiple of 10 sts (any number that can be divided by 10 evenly) for next rnd. Join with a sl st in beg sc.

Rnd 2: Sl st into next sc, (ch 3, dc, ch 2, 2 dc) all in same sc; *ch 2, skip next 2 sc, sc in next 5 sc, ch 2, skip 2 sc, work shell of (2 dc, ch 2, 2 dc) all in next sc; rep from * around ending last rep ch 2, skip next 2 sc, sc in next 5 sc, ch 2, skip 2 sc, join with a sl st in 3rd ch of beg ch-3.

Rnd 3: Sl st in next dc and into ch-2 sp; in ch-2 sp work (ch 3, 2 dc, ch 2, 3 dc); *ch 3, skip ch-2 sp and next sc, sc in next 3 sc, ch 3, skip next sc and ch-2 sp, in ch-2 sp of next shell work (3 dc, ch 2, 3 dc); rep from * around, ending last rep ch 3, skip next ch-2 sp and next sc, sc in next 3 sc, ch 3, skip next sc and ch-2 sp, join with a sl st in 3rd ch of beg ch-3. Finish off, weave in all ends.

#45 SUMMER SUNSHINE

Designed by Jane Herrin

SIZE
49" x 54"

MATERIALS
Worsted weight yarn,
  16 oz light yellow
  24 oz light blue
  24 oz medium blue

Note: *Photographed model made with Caron® Simply Soft® #9726 Soft Yellow, #9709 Light Country Blue, and #9710 Country Blue*

Size H (5mm) crochet hook or
  size required for gauge

GAUGE
7 dc = 2"

STITCH GUIDE

DC Decrease (DCdec): Keeping last lp of each dc on hook, dc in each of next 2 chs or sts, YO and draw through all 3 lps on hook: DCdec made.

Cluster (CL): YO, draw up a lp in next ch or st, (YO, draw up a lp in same ch or st) twice, YO, draw through all 7 lps on hook: CL made.

Color Change: Work last st with old color until 2 lps rem on hook, YO with new color and draw through both lps on hook; cut old color.

INSTRUCTIONS

With med blue, ch 173.

Row 1 (right side): Dc in 5th ch from hook, (DCdec over next 2 chs) twice; ch 1, (CL in next ch, ch 1) 5 times; *(DCdec over next 2 chs) 6 times; ch 1, (CL in next ch, ch 1) 5 times; rep from * to last 6 chs, (dec over next 2 chs) 3 times; ch 1, turn.

Row 2: Sc in each st and in each ch across to last dc, sc in last dc (do not sc in ch-3); ch 3 (counts as first dc of following row), turn.

Row 3: Dc in next sc, DCdec twice; *ch 1, (CL in next sc, ch 1) 5 times, DCdec 6 times; rep from * across to last 6 sc, DCdec 3 times; ch 1, turn.

Row 4: Rep Row 2, changing to lt blue in last st .

Rows 5 through 8: With lt blue, rep Row 3, then Rows 2 and 3 in sequence, changing to yellow at end of Row 8.

Rows 9 and 10: With yellow, Rep Rows 2 and 3, changing to med blue at end of Row 10.

Rows 11 through 14: Rep Rows 2 and 3, changing to lt blue at end of Row 14.

Continue to rep Rows 2 and 3, in this color sequence:

*4 rows lt blue

4 rows med blue

2 rows yellow

Rep colors from * until piece measures about 54" long, end last sequence by working 4 rows lt blue, then 4 rows med blue.

Finish off, weave in ends.

Fringe

Following instructions on page 221 for Single Knot Fringe, cut strands 18" long from all three colors. Use one strand of each color in each knot, and tie knots across each short end, spaced in every other st. Trim fringe evenly.

#46 STARRY NIGHT

SIZE
47 1/2" x 66 1/2" before border

MATERIALS
Worsted weight yarn,
   17 oz navy (A)
   4 oz white (B)
   4 oz lt blue (C)
   6 oz med blue (D)
   7 oz dk blue (E)
   6 oz royal blue (F)

Note: Photographed model made with Red Heart® Super Saver® #387 Soft Navy (A), #316 Soft White (B), #381 Light Blue (C), #885 Delft Blue (D), #886 Blue (E), and #385 Royal (F)

Size J (6mm) crochet hook (or
   size required for gauge)

GAUGE
Square = 9 1/2" x 9 1/2"

INSTRUCTIONS

Note: Always join new color with right side facing.

Square (make 35)
With A, ch 4; join with sl st to form a ring.

Rnd 1 (right side): Ch 1, 8 sc in ring: 8 sc; join with sl st in first sc. Finish off and weave in ends.

Rnd 2: Join B with sl st in any sc; ch 2 (counts as hdc), hdc in same sc as joining, 2 hdc in each sc around: 16 hdc; join with sl st in 2nd ch of beg ch-2.

Rnd 3: Beg Cl, ch 2; *Cl in next hdc, ch 2; rep from * around: 16 Cl; join with sl st in top of beg Cl (first dc). Finish off and weave in ends.

Rnd 4: Join C with sl st in any ch-2 sp; ch 3, (2 dc, ch 2, 3 dc) in same sp for corner, *(2 dc in next ch-2 sp) 3 times**, (3 dc, ch 2, 3 dc) in next ch-2 sp for corner; rep from * around, end at **; join with sl st in 3rd ch of beg ch-3. Finish off and weave in ends.

Rnd 5: Join D with sl st in any corner ch-2 sp; ch 2, (hdc, ch 2, 2 hdc) in same sp; *hdc in next 12 dc**, (2 hdc, ch 2, 2 hdc) in next corner ch-2 sp; rep from * around, end at **; join with sl st in 2nd ch of beg ch-2. Finish off and weave in ends.

Rnd 6: Join E with sl st in any corner ch-2 sp; ch 3, (dc, ch 3, 2 dc) in same sp; *ch 1, (skip next hdc, dc in next 4 hdc, ch 1) 3 times, skip next hdc**, (2 dc, ch 3, 2 dc) in next ch-2 sp; rep from * around, end at **; join with sl st in 3rd ch of beg ch-3. Finish off and weave in ends.

Rnd 7: Join F with sl st in any corner ch-3 sp; ch 1, (sc, ch 3, sc) in same sp; *sc in next 2 dc, [ch 1, skip next st (ch or dc), sc in next 2 sts (ch or dc)] 6 times**; (sc, ch 3, sc) in next corner ch-3 sp; rep from * around, end at **; join with sl st in first sc. Finish off and weave in ends.

Rnd 8: Join A with sl st in any corner ch-3 sp; (beg Cl, ch 2, Cl, ch 3, Cl, ch 2, Cl) in same sp; *skip next 3 sc, [(Cl, ch 2, Cl) in next ch-1 sp, skip next 2 sc] 6 times, skip next sc**, (Cl, ch 2, Cl, ch 3, Cl, ch 2, Cl) in next corner ch-3 sp; rep from * around, end at **; join with sl st in top of beg Cl (first dc).

Rnd 9: Sl st in next ch-2 sp; ch 1, 3 sc in same sp; *(2 sc, ch 2, 2 sc) in corner ch-3 sp, 3 sc in each ch-2 sp to next corner; rep from * around; join with sl st in first sc. Finish off and weave in ends.

Sew squares together with whip stitch through back 1ps into 5 rows of 7 squares each.

Border

Rnd 1: Join F with sl st in any corner ch-2 sp, ch 1, (sc, ch 2, sc) in same sp; *sc in each sc to next corner**, (sc, ch 2, sc) in next corner ch-2 sp; rep from * around, end at **; join with sl st in first sc.

Rnd 2: Sl st in next corner ch-2 sp, ch 1, (sc, ch 2, sc) in same sp; *sc in each sc to next corner**, (sc, ch 2, sc) in next corner ch-2 sp; rep from * around, end at **; join with sl st in first sc. Finish off and weave in ends.

#47 SAGE WHEEL

Designed by Janie Herrin

SIZE
37 ¹/₂" x 52 ¹/₂" before border

MATERIALS
Worsted weight yarn,
  24 oz rose
  12 oz cream
  6 oz pale green

Note: Photographed model made with TLC® Amoré™ #3710 Rose, #3103 Vanilla, and #3625 Celery

Size H (5mm) crochet hook
  (or size required for gauge)

GAUGE
7 dc = 2"

Square = 7 ¹/₂" x 7 ¹/₂"

INSTRUCTIONS

Square (make 35)
Beginning with green, ch 5, join with sl st to form a ring.

Rnd 1: Ch 3 (counts as first dc of rnd), 11 dc in ring, join with sl st in 3rd ch of beg ch-3: 12 dc.

Rnd 2: Ch 5 (counts as first dc plus ch 2), dc in next dc; *ch 2, dc in next dc, rep from * around, ch 2, join with sl st in 3rd ch of beg ch-5, finish off green.

Rnd 3: Join cream with sc in any ch-2 sp; *ch 3, sc in next ch-2 sp, rep from * around, ending ch 3, join with sl st in beg sc: 12 ch-3 lps.

Rnd 4: Sl st in next lp, (ch 3, 2 dc, ch 2, 3 dc in same lp): beg corner made; * † ch 3, (sc in next lp, ch 3) twice; † in next lp work (3 dc, ch 2, 3 dc): corner made; rep from * 2 times more, then rep from † to † once, join with sl st in beg ch-3; finish off cream.

Rnd 5: Join rose with sl st in any corner sp, work beg corner as before; *ch 3, sc in next lp, 3 dc in next lp, sc in next lp, ch 3, work corner in next lp; rep from * around, end with sl st beg ch-3.

Rnd 6: Ch 3, dc in next 2 dc; *(2 dc, ch 2, 2 dc) in next lp for corner; dc in next 3 dc, 2 dc in next lp, ch 3, sc in center dc of next 3-dc group, ch 3, 2 dc in next lp, dc in next 3 dc; rep from * around, ending Ch3, 2 dc in last lp, join.

Rnd 7: Ch 3, dc in next 4 dc; * † (2 dc, ch 2, 2 dc) in next sp, dc in next 6 dc, skip next dc, 2 dc in next lp, ch 2, 2 dc in next lp, skip next dc, † dc in next 6 dc; rep from * around, 2 times more then rep from † to † once; end dc in next dc, join, finish off.

Rnd 8: Join cream with sc in any corner sp, 2 sc in same sp; *skip first dc, sc in next 9 dc, 2 sc in next sp, sc in next 10 dc, 3 sc in next sp; rep from * around, omit last 3 sc, join with sl st in beg sc; finish off. Weave in ends.

Joining

To join, hold 2 squares with right sides tog and sew with cream with overcast st along one side, carefully matching sts and corners. Continue joining in this manner for 7 rows of 5 squares each.

Border

Hold afghan with right side facing; join green in first outer corner sp at upper right.

Rnd 1: Ch 1, (hdc, ch 2, hdc) in same sp; hdc in each st around outer edge of afghan, adjusting sts to keep work flat, and working (hdc, ch 2, hdc) in each rem outer corner sp; join in beg hdc, finish off green.

Rnd 2: Join rose in any ch-2 corner sp; (ch 3, 2 dc, ch 3, 3 dc) in same sp; *3 dc in each hdc to next corner, (3 dc, ch 3, 3 dc) in corner ch-2 sp; rep from * twice more, 3 dc in each rem hdc, join; finish off rose.

Rnd 3: Join cream in ch-3 sp of any corner, 3 sc in same sp; *sc in each dc to next corner, 3 sc in ch-3 sp; rep from * twice, sc in each rem dc, join, finish off.

#48 ROSE RIPPLE

SIZE
46"x 60"

MATERIALS
Worsted weight yarn,
48 oz rose

Note: *Photographed model made with TLC® Amoré™ #3710 Rose*

Size J (6mm) crochet hook (or size required for gauge)

GAUGE
6 sc and 7 sc rows = 4"

INSTRUCTIONS

Ch 210 loosely.

Foundation Row (wrong side): Sc in 2nd ch from hook and in next 4 chs, 3 sc in next ch; *sc in next 3 chs, sk 2 chs; sc in next 3 chs, 3 sc in next ch; rep from * to last 5 chs, sc in each of rem 5 chs; ch 1, turn.

Row 1: Working in back lp only (lp away from you) of each st, sc dec over next 2 sts, sc next 4 sts, 3 sc in next st; * sc in next 3 sts, skip 2 sts; sc in next 3 sts, 3 sc in next st; rep from * to last 6 sts, sc in next 4 sts, sc dec over last 2 sts; ch 1, turn.

Rows 2 through 6: Rep Row 1.

Row 7: Working in both lps of each sc, sc dec over first 2 sc, sc in next 4 sc; work (scPC, sc, scPC) in next sc; *sc in next 3 sc, skip 2 sc, sc in next 3 sc; work (scPC, sc, scPC) in next sc; rep from * to last 6 sc, sc in each of next 4 sc, sc dec over last 2 sc; ch 1, turn.

Row 8: Working in both lps of each st, rep Row 1.

Row 9: Working in both lps of each sc, sc dec over first 2 sc, sc in each of next 2 sc; scPC in next sc, sc in next sc; work (scPC, sc, scPC) in next sc; *sc in next sc, scPC in next sc, sc in next sc; skip 2 sc, sc in next sc; sc PC in next sc, sc in next sc; work (scPC, sc, scPC) in next sc; rep from * to last 6 sc, sc in next sc, scPC in next sc; sc in each of next 2 sc, sc dec over last 2 sc; ch 1, turn.

Row 10: Rep Row 8.

Rep Rows 1 through 10 nine times more, then rep Rows 1 through 4 once. Finish off. Weave in all ends.

#49 DREAM PANELS

Designed by Trish Kristoffersen for Coats and Clark

SIZE
45" x 63"

MATERIALS
Worsted weight yarn,
   17 oz off-white (A)
   9 oz lt green (B)
   6 oz dk green (C)

Note: *Photographed model made with Red Heart® Super Saver® #313 Aran (A), #631 Light Sage (B) and #633 Dark Sage (C)*

Size I (5.5mm) crochet hook
   (or size required for gauge)

GAUGE
14 sts = 4 1/2" in patt
Panel = 9" wide

INSTRUCTIONS

Panel (make 5)
With A ch 172.

Note: *Panel begins at center and is worked in rounds, working around both sides of beg chain.*

Rnd 1 (right side): 2 dc in 4th ch from hook; *ch 3, skip next 3 chs, sc in next 7 chs, ch 3, skip next 3 chs**, 5 dc in next ch; rep from * to last ch, end at **; (3 dc, ch 5, 3 dc) in last ch; rotate work and now working in unused lps on opposite side of beg ch, rep from * across, end at **; 3 dc in same ch as first 2 dc, ch 5; join with sl st in last ch of starting ch back on first side of beg ch.

Rnd 2: Sl st in next dc, beg shell in same dc; *ch 3, skip next sc, sc in next 5 sc, ch 3, skip next dc; shell in next dc**; ch 3, skip next dc, shell in next dc; rep from * across, end at **; ***ch 5, 3 sc in ch-5 sp, ch 5***, skip next dc, shell in next dc; rep

Beg shell: Ch 3, 4 dc in same st.

Shell: 5 dc in same st.

Shell over shell: 5 dc in 3rd dc of next shell.

Beg cluster (beg CL): Ch 2, (YO, insert hook in specified st, YO and draw up a lp, YO and draw through 2 lps on hook) twice, YO and draw through all 3 lps on hook: beg cl made.

3 dc cluster (3dcCL): (YO, insert hook in 3rd dc of next shell, YO and draw up a lp, YO and draw through 2 lps on hook) 3 times, YO and draw through all 4 lps on hook: 3-dc-cl made.

Double tr (dtr): YO hook 3 times, (YO and draw through 2 lps) 4 times, YO and draw through all 4 lps: dtr made.

from * across, end at **; rep from *** to ***; join with sl st in 3rd ch of beg shell.

Rnd 3: Sl st in next 2 dc, beg shell in same dc; *ch 3, skip next sc, sc in next 3 sc, ch 3; shell over shell**; ch 3, sc in ch-3 sp, ch 3, shell over shell; rep from * across, end at **; ***ch 5, sc in ch-5 sp, ch 5, sc in next sc, ch 5, skip next sc, sc in next sc, ch 5, sc in next ch-5 sp, ch 5***, shell over shell; rep from * across, end at **; rep from *** to ***; join as before.

Rnd 4: Sl st in next 2 dc, beg shell in same dc; *ch 3, skip next sc, sc in next sc, ch 3, shell over shell **, (ch 3, sc in next ch-3 sp) twice, ch 3, shell over shell; rep from * across, end at **; ***ch 3, sc in next ch-5 sp, (ch 5, sc in next ch-5 sp) 4 times, ch 3***, shell over shell; rep from * across, end at **; rep from *** to ***; join.

Rnd 5: Sl st in next 2 dc; beg CL in same dc; *ch 1; 3dcCL in next shell**; ch 4, (sc in next ch sp, ch 3) twice, sc in next ch sp, ch 4, 3dcCL in next shell; rep from * across, end at **; ***ch 5, sc in next ch sp, (ch 6, sc in next ch sp) 5 times, ch 5***, 3dcCL in next shell; rep from * across, end at **; rep from *** to ***; join with sl st in top of beg CL. Finish off and weave in ends.

Rnd 6: Join B with sl st in ch-1 sp after joining, ch 1, sc in same ch-1 sp; *4 sc in next ch sp, (3 sc in next ch sp) twice, 4 sc in next ch sp, sc in ch-1 sp; rep from * across; (3 sc, 2 hdc) in next ch-5 sp, 6 hdc in next ch sp, 6 dc in next ch sp, (dc, 2 tr, dtr, 2 tr, dc) in next ch sp, 6 dc in next ch sp, 6 hdc in next ch sp, (2 hdc, 3 sc) in next ch sp **, sc in ch-1 sp; rep from * across, end at **; join with sl st in first sc. Finish off and weave in ends.

Rnd 7 (work all sts in BLO): Join C with sl st in back lp of any sc along long edge, ch 3, *dc in next sc and in each sc across, 3 dc in first hdc along side, dc in next 16 sts, (2 dc, ch 2, 2 dc) in dtr, dc in next 16 sts, 3 dc in next hdc; rep from * around; dc in each sc to beg of rnd; join with sl st in 3rd ch of beg ch-3. Finish off and weave in ends.

Rnd 8: Join B with sl st in center dc of 3-dc group after an end, ch 1; **3 sc in center dc, *sc in next dc, tr in front lp of st below next dc (skip dc behind tr)***, sc in next dc; rep from * across to next 3-dc group, end at ***; sc in next dc, 3 sc in next (center) dc, (sc in next dc, tr in front lp of st below next dc skip dc behind tr, sc in next dc) 6 times, sc in next dc, sc in ch-2 sp, tr in front lp of dtr, sc in same ch-2 sp, sc in next dc, (sc in next dc, tr in front lp of st below next dc skip dc behind tr, sc in next dc) 6 times; rep from ** across; join with sl st in first sc. Finish off and weave in ends.

Finishing

With right sides together sl st panels tog through back lps from center sc of a 3-sc group along side edge to center sc of next 3-sc group of same long edge.

#50 ROSY RUFFLES

Designed by Janie Herrin

SIZE
49" x 49" before border

MATERIALS
Worsted weight yarn,
   12 oz rose
   36 oz oz raspberry

Note: *Photographed model made with Caron Simply Soft #9221 Victorian Rose and #9723 Raspberry*

Size H (5mm) crochet hook
   (or size required for gauge)

GAUGE
7 dc = 2"

Square = 7" x 7"

INSTRUCTIONS

Square (make 49)
With rose, ch 4, join with a sl st to form a ring.

Rnd 1: Ch 3 (counts as a dc), 15 dc in ring, join with sl st in 3rd ch of beg ch-3: 16 dc.

Rnd 2: Ch 3, 2 dc in same st, ch 2, skip next st; * 3 dc in next st, ch 2, skip next st; rep from * 6 times more; join in 3rd ch of beg ch-3, finish off.

Rnd 3: Join raspberry with sc in any ch-2 sp; working in front of same ch-2, FPtr in skipped dc 2 rows below, sc in same ch-2 sp as first sc made, ch 3, skip next 3 dc;

Front Post Triple Crochet (FPtr): YO twice, insert hook from front to back to front around post (vertical bar) of indicated st, and pull up a lp; (YO and draw through 2 lps on hook) 3 times: FPtr made.

*in next ch-2 sp work (sc, FPtr in skipped dc 2 rows below as before, sc) ch 3, skip next 3 dc; rep from * 6 times more; join with sl st in beg sc.

Rnd 4: Ch 2, (equals first hdc), hdc in each of next 2 sts; * † in next ch-3 sp work (2 dc, ch 3, 2 dc): corner made, hdc in each of next 3 sts, 3 sc in next ch-3 sp, † hdc in each of next 3 sts; rep from * 2 times more then rep from † to † once; join in beg ch-2, finish off.

Rnd 5: Join rose with sc in any corner ch-3 sp, 2 sc in same sp; * † sc in next 3 sts, FPtr around post of tr 2 rows below, (skip st behind FPtr), sc in next 6 sts, work FPtr around post on next tr 2 rows below, (skip st behind FPtr), sc in next 2 sts, † 3 sc in next corner ch-3 sp; rep from * 2 times more, then rep from † to † once; join in beg sc, finish off.

Rnd 6: Join raspberry with sl st in center sc of any corner 3-sc group, ch 3, in same st work (dc, ch 2, 2 dc), dc in each st around, working (2 dc, ch 2, 2 dc) in each corner sc; join in beg ch-3, finish off. Weave in all ends.

Joining

To join, hold two squares with right sides tog and with lavender, sew together with overcast st through outer lps, along one side edge, carefully matching sts and corners. Join squares in 7 rows of 7 squares each.

Border

Rnd 1: Hold piece with right side facing you and join raspberry with sc in upper right corner sp, 2 sc in same sp; sc around outer edges, adjusting sts as needed to keep work flat, and working 3 sc in each rem outer corner sp; join with sl st in beg sc.

Rnd 2: Sl st in next sc, ch 3 (counts as a dc), 4 dc in same sc; *sk 2 sc, ch 1, 5 dc in next sc; rep from * around, ending ch 1, join with sl st in 3rd ch of beg sc. Note: to come out even with the repeat, if necessary sk 1 or 3 sc instead of 2 in a few places on last side.

Rnd 3: Ch 5 (counts as a dc and ch-2 sp); *in next dc work (dc, ch 2, dc); rep from * around, join in 3rd ch of beg ch-5.

Rnd 4: Sc in ch-2 sp, (ch 8, sc in same sp); *ch 4, in next ch-2 sp work (sc, ch 8, sc); rep from * around, join in beg sc, finish off.

#51 RICH CABLES

Designed by Patons Design Department

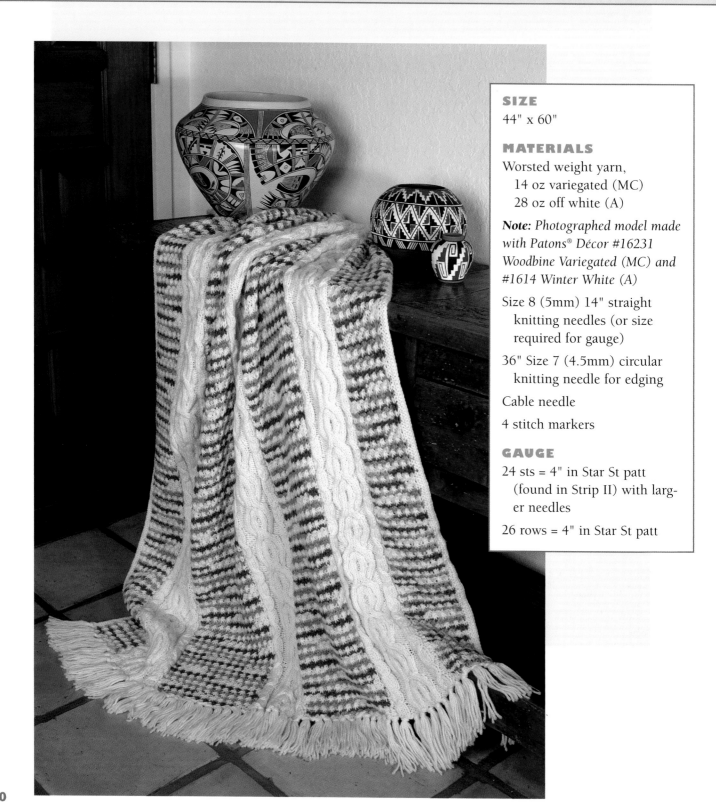

SIZE
44" x 60"

MATERIALS
Worsted weight yarn,
   14 oz variegated (MC)
   28 oz off white (A)

Note: Photographed model made with Patons® Décor #16231 Woodbine Variegated (MC) and #1614 Winter White (A)

Size 8 (5mm) 14" straight
   knitting needles (or size
   required for gauge)

36" Size 7 (4.5mm) circular
   knitting needle for edging

Cable needle

4 stitch markers

GAUGE
24 sts = 4" in Star St patt
   (found in Strip II) with larger needles

26 rows = 4" in Star St patt

STITCH GUIDE

C4F = Sl next 2 sts onto a cable needle and leave at front of work, K2, then K2 from cable needle.

C4B = Sl next 2 sts onto a cable needle and leave at back of work, K2, then K2 from cable needle.

C5F = Sl next 3 sts onto a cable needle and leave at front of work, P2, then K3 from cable needle.

C5B = Sl next 2 sts onto a cable needle and leave at back of work, K3, then P2 from cable needle.

C6F = Sl next 3 sts onto a cable needle and leave at front of work, K3, then K3 from cable needle.

C6B = Slip next 3 sts onto a cable needle and leave at back of work, K3, then K3 from cable needle.

PATTERNS

Panel Pattern A (worked over 24 sts)

Row 1 (right side): P6, K12, P6.

Row 2 and all even-numbered rows: Knit all knit sts and purl all purl sts.

Row 3: P6, C6B, C6F, P6.

Row 5: P4, C5B, K6, C5F, P4.

Row 7: P4, K3, P2, K6, P2, K3, P4.

Row 9: P2, (C5B) twice, (C5F) twice, P2.

Row 11: (P2, K3) twice, P4, (K3, P2) twice.

Row 13: P2, (C5F) twice, (C5B) twice, P2.

Row 15: P4, C5F, K6, C5B, P4.

Row 16: Rep Row 2.

These 16 rows form Panel Patt A.

Panel Pattern B (worked over 4 sts)

Row 1: (RS), Knit.

Row 2 and all even-numbered rows: Purl.

Row 3: Knit.

Row 5: C4F.

Rows 7 and 9: Knit,

Row 11: C4B,

Row 13: Knit.

Row 14: Purl.

These 14 rows form Panel Patt B.

INSTRUCTIONS

Strip I (make 3)

With A and straight needles, CO 36 sts.

Row 1 (right side): P2, place a marker on needle; work Row 1 of Panel Patt B, place marker; work Row 1 of Panel Patt A, place marker; work Row 1 of Panel Patt B, place marker; P2.

Note: *Sl markers up each row as you work.*

Row 2: Work Row 2 of each panel: patterns are now established.

Continue working panels in patterns (note that Panel A has two more rows than Panel B) until piece measures about 60" long, ending by working a 16th row of Panel A; BO, weave in ends.

Strip II (make 2):
Star Stitch Pattern

With MC and straight needles, cast on 49 sts.

Row 1: With MC, knit.

Row 2: P 1; * P3tog, leaving sts on needle, yrn, P3tog the same 3 sts again: Star Stitch made; P 1; rep from * across.

Continued on next page.

Row 3: With A, knit.

Row 4: P3, work Star St, *Pl, Star St; rep from * to last 3 sts, P3.

These 4 rows form Star St Patt.

Rep Rows 1 through 4 until piece measures same length as Strip I; BO.

Strip III (make 2)

With MC and straight needles, cast on 25 sts,

Rep Rows 1 through 4 of Strip II until piece measures same length as Strip I; BO.

Joining

Sew strips tog in following sequence from left to right: Panel III, Panel I, Panel II, Panel I, Panel II, Panel I. Panel III.

Side Edgings

With A and circular needle, pick up and knit 285 sts along one side edge of afghan.

Knit 3 rows, then BO as to knit.

Work other side edge the same.

Fringe

Following Single Knot Fringe instruction on page 221, cut A into 14" lengths. Using 3 lengths in each knot, tie fringe evenly across each short end of piece; trim fringe.

#52 CHEVRONS & DIAMONDS

SIZE
49" x 60"

MATERIALS
Worsted weight yarn,
  50 oz purple

Note: *Photographed model
made with TLC® Heathers™
#2455 Purple Haze*

Size I (5.5mm) crochet hook
  (or size required for gauge)

GAUGE
17 sts = 6" in patt

20 rows = 6" in patt

PATTERN GUIDE

CHEVRON PATTERN A
(worked over 22 sts)

Row 1 (right side): Sc in next 22 sts.

Row 2 (and all even-numbered rows): Sc in next 22 sts.

Row 3: (Sc in next sc, FPdc) twice, sc in next 5 sc, FPdc 4 times, sc in next 5 sc, (FPdc, sc in next sc) twice.

Row 5: (Sc in next sc, FPdc) twice, sc in next 4 sc, FPdc twice, sc in next 2 sc, FPdc twice; sc in next 4 sc, (FPdc, sc in next sc) twice.

Row 7: (Sc in next sc, FPdc) twice, sc in next 3 sc, FPdc twice, sc in next 4 sc, FPdc twice; sc in next 3 sc, (FPdc, sc in next sc) twice.

Row 9: (Sc in next sc, FPdc) twice, sc in next 2 sc, FPdc twice, sc in next 6 sc, FPdc twice; sc in next 2 sc, (FPdc, sc in next sc) twice.

Row 11: (Sc in next sc, FPdc) twice, sc in next sc, FPdc twice, sc in next 2 sc, FPdc 4 times, sc in next 2 sc, FPdc twice, sc in next sc, (FPdc, sc in next sc) twice.

Row 13: (Sc in next sc, FPdc) twice, (FPdc twice, sc in next 2 sc) 3 times, FPdc twice, (FPdc, sc in next sc) twice.

Row 14: Rep Row 2.

Rep Rows 7 through 14 for Chevron Pattern A.

DIAMOND PATTERN B
(worked over 35 sts)

Row 1 (right side): Sc in next 35 sts.

Row 2: (Sc in next sc, tr in next sc) 5 times, sc in next 7 sc, tr in next sc, sc in next 7 sc, (tr in next sc, sc in next sc) 5 times.

Row 3 (and every odd-numbered row): Sc in next 35 sts.

Row 4: (Tr in next sc, sc in next sc) 5 times, sc in next 6 sc, tr in next sc, sc in next sc, tr in next sc, sc in next 6 sc, (sc in next sc, tr in next sc) 5 times.

Row 6: (Sc in next sc, tr in next sc) 4 times, sc in next 7 sc, tr in next sc, (sc in next sc, tr in next sc) twice, sc in next 7 sc, (tr in next sc, sc in next sc) 4 times.

Row 8: (Tr in next sc, sc in next sc) 4 times, sc in next 6 sc, tr in next sc, (sc in next sc, tr in next sc) 3 times, sc in next 6 sc, (sc in next sc, tr in next sc) 4 times.

Row 10: (Sc in next sc, tr in next sc) 3 times, sc in next 7 sc, tr in next sc, (sc in next sc, tr in next sc) 4 times, sc in next 7 sc, (tr in next sc, sc in next sc) 3 times.

Row 12: (Tr in next sc, sc in next sc) 3 times, sc in next 6 sc, tr in next sc, (sc in next sc, tr in next sc) 5 times, sc in next 6 sc, (sc in next sc, tr in next sc) 3 times.

Row 14: (Sc in next sc, tr in next sc) twice, sc in next 7 sc, tr in next sc, (sc in next sc, tr in next sc) 6 times, sc in next 7 sc, (tr in next sc, sc in next sc) twice.

Row 16: Tr in next sc, sc in next sc, tr in next sc, sc in next 7 sc, tr in next sc, (sc in next sc, tr in next sc) 7 times, sc in next 7 sc, tr in next sc, sc in next sc, tr in next sc.

Row 18: Sc in next sc, tr in next sc, sc in next 7 sc, tr in next sc, (sc in next sc, tr in next sc) 8 times, sc in next 7 sc, tr in next sc, sc in next sc.

Row 20: Tr in next sc, sc in next 7 sc, tr in next sc, (sc in next sc, tr in next sc) 9 times, sc in next 7 sc, tr in next sc.

Row 22: Rep Row 18.

Row 24: Rep Row 16.

Row 26: Rep Row 14.

Row 28: Rep Row 12.

Row 30: Rep Row 10.

Row 32: Rep Row 8.

Row 34: Rep Row 6.

Row 36: Rep Row 4.

Row 38: Rep Row 2.

Row 40: (Tr in next sc, sc in next sc) 6 times, sc in next 11 sc, (sc in next sc, tr in next sc) 6 times.

Rep Rows 1 through 40 for Diamond Pattern B.

INSTRUCTIONS

Ch 139.

Row 1 (right side): Sc in 2nd ch from hook and in each ch across: 138 sc; ch 1, turn.

Row 2: Sc in first sc, work Pat A Row 2 across next 22 sts, (work Pat B Row 2 across next 35 sts, work Pat A Row 2 across next 22 sts) twice, sc in last sc; ch 1, turn.

Row 2 establishes pattern placement. Continue in this manner, working appropriate rows of each pattern until Diamond Pat B Rows 1 through 40 have been worked 4 times and Rows 1 through 38 have been worked once more (5 diamonds), end Chevron Pat A Row 14, wrong-side row; ch 1, turn to work Edging on right side.

Edging

Rnd 1: 3 sc in first st for corner; sc in each st across top, 3 sc in last st for corner, sc evenly down side (work about 4 sc per every 5 rows), 3 sc in first st of lower edge for corner, sc across lower edge, 3 sc in last st for corner, sc evenly up next side as before; join with sl st in first sc; ch 1, do not turn.

Rnd 2: Work one rnd Reverse Sc around entire piece; join with sl st in first st. Finish off and weave in ends.

#53 MARVELOUS MAUVE

Designed by Janie Herrin

SIZE
48" x 60" before border

MATERIALS
Worsted weight yarn,
 21 oz mauve
 14 oz lt mauve
 11 oz green

Note: Photographed model made with Bernat® Berella® "4" #01306 True Mauve, #01305 Soft Mauve, and #08876 Deep Sea Green

Size H (5mm) crochet hook
 (or size required for gauge)

GAUGE
7 dc = 2"

Square = 12" x 12"

INSTRUCTIONS

Square (make 20)

With mauve, ch 5, join with a sl st to form a ring.

Rnd 1: Ch 5 (equals first dc plus ch 2), (dc in ring, ch 2) 7 times, join in 3rd ch of beg ch 5: 8 ch-2 sps.

Rnd 2: Sl st in next ch-2 sp, ch 2, in same sp work (3 hdc, ch 1); in each rem sp work (3 hdc, ch 1); join with sl st to beg hdc: 8 ch-1 sps.

Rnd 3: Ch 1, working in front of joining and reaching back with hook, sc in last ch-1 sp made, ch 5, (sc in next ch-1 sp, ch 5) around, join in beg sc.

Rnd 4: Sl st in next ch-5 lp, ch 1, in same lp and in each lp around work (sc, hdc, dc, tr, dc, hdc, sc), join in beg sc: 8 petals made; ch 3, pull up lp and drop yarn (to be picked up later), do not cut yarn

Rnd 5: Join lt mauve with sl st between any 2 sc between petals, ch 7, sc in next tr, ch 4; *dc between next 2 sc, ch 4, sc in next tr, ch 4; rep from * around, join in 3rd ch of beg ch- 7: 16 ch-4 lps.

Rnd 6: Sl st in next lp, ch 1, in same lp and in each lp around work (sc, ch 1, dc, tr, dc, ch 1, sc), join; ch 3, pull up lp and drop yarn (to be picked up later), do not cut.

V-st: (dc, ch 2, dc) in st or sp indicated.

Back Post Double Crochet (BPdc): YO, insert hook from back to front to back around post (vertical bar) of specified st, YO and up a lp; (YO and draw through 2 lps on hook) twice: BPdc made.

Front Post Double Crochet (FPdc): YO, insert hook from front to back to front around post (vertical bar) of specified st, YO and draw up a lp; (YO and draw through 2 lps on hook) twice: FPdc made.

Rnd 7: Place dropped mauve lp from Rnd 4 on hook, sc in first sc of nearest petal; *ch 5, sc in each of next 2 sc; rep from * around, end with last sc, join in beg sc: 16 lps; finish off.

Rnd 8: Join green with sc in any ch-5 lp, 4 sc in same lp, ch 2, (5 sc in next lp, ch 2) around, join; ch 3, pull up lp and drop yarn as before, do not cut.

Rnd 9: Place dropped lt mauve lp from Rnd 6 on hook, sc in first sc of nearest 5-sc group, *ch 3, skip 3 sc, sc in next sc, ch 3, skip ch-2 sp, sc in next sc; rep from * around, end with ch 3, join in beg sc: 32 ch-3 sps.

Rnd 10: Sl st in next sp, ch 4, 6 tr in same sp; *ch 1, 2 dc in next sp, ch 1, 2 hdc in next sp; ch 1, (2 sc, ch 1) in each of next 3 sps, 2 hdc in next sp, ch 1, 2 dc in next sp, ch 1, 7 tr in next sp; rep from * around, end with ch-1, join in beg tr: four 7-tr groups, 32 ch-1 sps.

Rnd 11: Place dropped green lp from Rnd 8 on hook, sl st in ch-1 sp before 7-tr group, ch 5, dc in same sp (beg V-st made); *BPdc in next 3 tr, in next tr work (V-st, ch 2, V-st); BPdc in next 3 tr, (V-st in next ch-1 sp) 8 times; rep from * around, end with last 7 V-sts, join in 3rd ch of beg ch 5; finish off.

Rnd 12: Join mauve with sl st in any corner ch-2 sp, ch 3 (equals first dc), in same sp work (dc, ch 2, 2 dc): beg corner made; *FPdc in first dc of V-st, ch 1, FPdc in 2nd dc of same V-st, BPdc in next 3 dc, (FPdc in first dc of next V-st, ch 1, FPdc in 2nd dc of same V-st) 8 times, BPdc in next 3 dc, FPdc in first dc of next V-st, ch 1, FPdc in 2nd dc of same V-st; (2 dc, ch 2, 2 dc) in ch-2 sp: corner made; rep from * around, end with last FPdc, join in beg dc.

Rnd 13: Sl st in next dc and into ch-2 sp, work beg corner; *ch 1, skip 3 sts, 2 dc in next ch-1 sp, ch 1, 2 dc in center st of 3-BPdc, ch 1; (2 dc in next ch-1 sp, ch 1) 8 times, 2 dc in center st of next 3-BPdc, ch 1, 2 dc in next ch-1 sp, ch 1, work corner in corner sp; rep from * around, ch 1, join to beg dc; finish off, weave in ends.

Joining

Hold two squares with right sides tog and with mauve, sew with overcast st along one side, carefully matching sts and chs.

Join squares in 5 rows of 4 squares each.

Border

Rnd 1: Hold afghan with right side facing you and join mauve in upper right corner with sc; 3 sc in same st, sc evenly around, adjusting sts as needed to keep work flat, and working 3 sc in each rem outer corner sp; join with sl st to beg sc; sl st in next sc. Finish off.

#54 JUST PEACHY

Designed by Jean Leinhauser

SIZE
33" x 45" before border

MATERIALS
Sport weight yarn,
   28 oz peach

Note: *Photographed model made with Patons Astra #0714 Mango*

Size E (3.5mm) crochet hook
   or size required for gauge

GAUGE
5 dc = 1"

3 dc rows = 1"

INSTRUCTIONS

Ch 166.

Row 1: Sc in 2nd ch from hook and in each rem ch: 165 sc; ch 3 (counts as first dc of all following rows), turn.

Row 2 (right side): Dc in next 4 sc; * ch 4, sk next 4 sc, sc in next sc; ch 3, sk next sc, sc in next sc; ch 4, sk next 4 sc, dc in next 5 sc; rep from * across, ch 3, turn.

Row 3: Dc in next 4 dc; *ch 2, sc in next ch-4 sp; ch 1, 7 dc in next ch-3 sp; ch 1, sc in next ch-4 sp; ch 2, dc in next 5 dc; rep from * across; ch 3, turn.

Row 4: Dc in next 4 dc; *ch 1, sk next sc, CL (see Special Stitch) in next dc; (ch 3, sk next dc, CL in next dc) 3 times; ch 1, sk next sc, dc in next 5 dc; rep from * across; ch 3, turn.

Row 5: Dc in next 4 dc; *ch 2, sk next ch-1 sp, sc in next ch-3 sp; (ch 3, sc in next ch-3 sp) twice; ch 2, sk next CL, dc in next 5 dc; rep from * across; ch 3, turn.

Row 6: Dc in next 4 dc; *ch 4, sk next ch-2 sp, sc in next ch-3 sp, ch 3, sc in next ch-3 sp, ch 4, dc in next 5 dc; rep from * across; ch 3, turn.

Rep Rows 3 through 6 until piece measures about 45" from beg ch; at end of last Row 6, ch 1 instead of 3, turn.

Last Row: Sc in each sc and each dc, work 4 sc in each ch-4 sp and 3 sc in each ch-3 sp; ch 1, turn.

Border

Rnd 1: (Sc, ch 1, sc) in first st; work in sc around all four sides, working (sc, ch 1, sc) in rem 3 corners; adjust sts as you work to keep work flat; join with a sl st in beg sc.

Rnd 2: Ch 3, dc in same sp; *2 dc in each sc to next corner, 7 dc in corner ch-1 sp; rep from * 3 times more, 2 dc in each rem sc, join with a sl st in 3rd ch of beg ch-3.

Rnd 3: Ch 4 (counts as a dc and ch-1); *dc in next dc, ch 1; rep from * around, join with sc in 3rd ch of beg ch-4.

Rnd 4: Ch 1, sc in joining; *ch 2, sc in next dc; rep from * around, end ch 2, join in beg sc. Finish off, weave in ends.

#55 VINEYARD VIEW

SIZE
52" x 58"

MATERIALS
Bulky weight yarn,
  24 oz violet (MC)
  15 oz green (A)
  15 off white (B)

Note: Photographed model made with Lion Brand® Jiffy® #191 Violet, #181 Country Green and #099 Fisherman

Size N (9 mm) crochet hook (or size required for gauge)

6" piece of cardboard

GAUGE
Block = 5 ³/₄" x 6 ¹/₂".

INSTRUCTIONS

Block (make 40 with MC and A; and 40 with MC and B: 80 blocks total)

With A or B, ch 4, join with a sl st to form a ring.

Rnd 1: Ch 4 {counts as a dc and ch-1 sp}, (dc in ring, ch 1) 11 times, join with sl st in 3rd ch of beg ch-4; finish off.

Rnd 2: Join MC in last sl st, ch 2, beg CL in next ch-1 sp, ch 2; CL in next ch-1 sp, ch 2; rep from * around, join in top of beg CL, finish off.

Rnd 3: Join A or B with sl st in any ch-2 sp; ch 1, sc in same sp; * YO, working around and over Rnd 2 ch-2, insert hook in Rnd 1 dc below, pull up a long lp, (YO and pull through 2 lps on hook) twice (long dc made); sc in top of next cluster, sc in next ch-2 sp; rep from * around, end with long dc in last Rnd 1 dc, sc in last cluster, join in first sc: 36 sts.

Rnd 4: Ch 3 [counts as first dc], work (dc, ch 1, 2 dc) in same place for first corner; * dc in next 7 sts, (2 dc, ch 1, 2 dc) in next st for corner, dc in next st, hdc in next st, sc in next 5 sts, hdc in next st, dc in next st, (2 dc, ch 1, 2 dc) in next st for corner; rep from * once more to first corner, join in top of beg ch-3; finish off.

Rnd 5: Join MC with sl st in any ch-1 corner sp, ch 1, 2 dc in same sp; * sc in each st to next corner sp, 3 sc in ch-1 corner sp; rep from * around, join in first sc; finish off, weave in ends.

Finishing

Afghan is 8 blocks wide and 10 blocks long. With MC, whipstitch blocks tog through both lps in corresponding sts on adjoining blocks, alternating colors in checkerboard pattern. Note: Blocks are rectangular, not square. Make sure all blocks are oriented with (dc, hdc, 5 sc, hdc, dc) edge of Rnd 4 at top and bottom.

Border

Rnd 1: With right side facing, join MC with sl st in any corner, ch 1; * sc in each st across to next corner, 3 sc in corner; rep from * around, join in first sc, turn.

Rnd 2: Ch 1; * sc in each st to center corner st, 3 sc in corner st: rep from * around, join in first sc; finish off.

Tassel (make 4)

Wrap MC 30 times around 6" piece of cardboard. Bring a separate double strand of MC under strands along one edge of cardboard and tie strands tightly tog. Cut strands along opposite edge and remove cardboard. Cut another strand of MC 36" long, double it, and wrap tightly around tassel, 1 1/4" from top. Tie tightly, secure ends, and tuck into tassel. Trim tassel ends even. Sew a tassel securely to each corner of afghan.

#56 POLKA DOT COUNTRY

Designed by Janie Herrin

SIZE
47" x 66" before border

MATERIALS
Worsted weight yarn,
  24 oz white (MC)
  4 oz deep rose (A)
  8 oz medium rose (B)
  9 oz medium blue (C)

Note: Photographed model made with Red Heart® Super Saver® #316 Soft White (MC), #374 Country Rose (A), #372 Rose Pink (B), and #382 Country Blue (C).

Size H (5mm) crochet hook
  (or size required for gauge)

GAUGE
7 dc = 2"

First 2 rnds of square = 2 $\frac{1}{2}$"

 8-rnd Square = 9"

INSTRUCTIONS

Square (make 35)
With A, ch 6, join to form a ring

Rnd 1: Ch 4 (counts as first tr), in ring work 19 tr, join to beg ch-4: 20 tr.

Rnd 2: Ch 1, in same st work (sc, ch 1); (sc, ch 1) in next st and in each st around, join with sl st in beg sc: 20 ch-1 sps. Finish off.

Rnd 3: Join MC with sl st in any ch-1 sp, ch 1, work (PS, ch 1) in same sp and in each ch-1 sp around, join in top of beg PS: 20 PS and 20 ch-1 sps. Finish off.

Rnd 4: Join B with sc in any ch-1 sp, ch 3; *sc in next sp, ch 3; rep from * around, join in beg sc: 20 ch-3 lps.

Rnd 5: Sl st into next lp, ch 3, in same lp work 2 dc; *ch 5 for corner, in next lp work 3 dc, in next lp work 3 hdc, 3 sc in next lp, 3 hdc in next lp, 3 dc in next lp; rep from * around, ending with sl st in 3rd ch of beg ch-3; finish off.

Rnd 6: Join MC with sl st in any corner ch-5 sp, ch 3, in same sp work 8 dc; *(ch 3, skip next 3 sts, sc in sp) 4 times, ch 3, 9 dc in corner lp; rep from * around, ending ch 3, join.

Rnd 7: Sl st in next dc, ch 1, sc in same st; *ch 3, skip next dc, sc in next dc, ch 5, (skip next dc, sc in next dc, ch 3) twice, skip next dc, in ch-3 lp work sc, ch 1; (dc, ch 2, dc in next lp) 3 times: 3 V-sts made; ch 1, sc in next lp, ch 3, skip next dc, sc in next dc; rep from * around ending with sl st in beg sc; finish off.

Rnd 8: Join C with sl st in any corner ch-5 lp, ch 3, in same lp work (2 dc, ch 3, 3 dc); *(3 dc in next ch-3 lp) twice, 3 dc in each of next 3 V-sts, (3 dc in next ch-3 lp) twice, in corner lp work (3 dc, ch 3, 3 dc); rep from * around, join, finish off.

Joining

Join 5 squares across by 7 squares down as follows:

First Square

With right side of square facing, join MC with sc in any corner ch-3 sp; *ch 5, sc in same sp, ch 3, (skip next 3 dc, sc in sp before next dc, ch 3) 8 times, sc in next corner ch-3 sp; rep from * around ending with sl st in beg sc; finish off.

Work rem squares same as First Square, joining 5 squares across by 7 squares down as follows: remove hook from the center ch of each ch-lp where joining ch-lps meet, insert hook into corresponding ch lp of previous square and pick up dropped lp, pull through and join with sl st, (sl st counts as center ch of joining chlp). ***Note:*** *When joining corners, always join into the same st as previous joining.*

Border

Rnd 1: With right side facing, join MC with sc in any corner ch-5 lp, ch 3, sc in same sp; *ch 3, (sc in next ch-3 lp, ch 3) 9 times, sc in joining between two squares; rep from * across to next corner ch-5 lp; in corner lp work (sc, ch 3, sc), work in same manner around entire afghan ending with sl st in beg sc.

Rnd 2: Sl st in corner ch-3 lp, ch 3, (2 dc, ch 2, 3 dc) in same lp; * † (3 dc in next ch-3 lp) across to next corner, † in corner lp work (3 dc, ch 2, 3 dc); rep from * 2 times more then rep from † to † once, join.

Rnd 3: Sl st in next 2 dc; * in corner ch-2 sp work (sc, ch 2, dc, ch 1) twice, (skip 3 dc in sp before next dc, work (sc, ch 2, dc, ch 1) across to next corner; rep from * around entire afghan, ending with sl st in beg sc, finish off.

#57 COZY MILE-A-MINUTE

Designed by Kelly Robinson for Coats and Clark

SIZE
48" x 65"

MATERIALS
Worsted weight yarn,
   27 oz off white (A)
   27 oz burgundy (B)

Note: *Photographed model made with Red Heart® Super Saver® #316 Soft White (A) and Red Heart® Fiesta™ #6915. Burgundy (B)*

Size I (5.5mm) crochet hook
   (or size required for gauge)

GAUGE
14 dc = 4"

Panel = 6" wide

INSTRUCTIONS

Panel (make 8)

Foundation Row: With A, ch 6; CL in 4th ch from hook; (ch 5, CL in 4th ch from hook) 39 times: 40 CL.

Rnd 1 (right side): Ch 5, 3 dc in 4th ch from hook, ch 1; working around post of last tr of each CL, (4 dc in next CL, ch 1) 40 times, skip next ch, in next ch work (4 dc, ch 1) twice; on opposite side of foundation row, working in ch sps of each CL, (4 dc in next ch-sp, ch 1) 40 times; 4 dc in same ch as first 3 dc, ch 1; join with sl st in 5th ch of beg ch-5, changing to B: 336 dc. Finish off A.

Rnd 2: With B, ch 1, sc in same ch as joining and in next 3 dc; Ldc in ch between CLs of Foundation Row, skip next ch-1 sp on working rnd, sc in next 4 dc, (Ldc in next unused ch of Foundation Row, skip next ch-1 sp on working rnd, sc in next 4 dc) 39 times; Ldc in next unused ch of Foundation Row, skip next ch-1 sp on working rnd, sc in next 4 dc, (Ldc in same ch as last Ldc made, skip next ch-1 sp on working rnd, sc in next 4 dc) twice; (Ldc in same ch as Ldc across panel, skip next ch-1 sp on working rnd, sc in next 4 dc) 39 times; Ldc in same ch as first Ldc worked, skip next ch-1 sp on working rnd, sc in next 4 dc, Ldc in same ch as last Ldc worked, skip next ch-1 sp on working rnd; join with sl st in back lp of first sc: 84 Ldc and 336 sc.

Rnd 3: Ch 3, dc in same back lp, working in back lps around, 2 dc in each of next 3 sc and in next Ldc; working in each Ldc and in each sc, dc in next 199 sts, 2 dc in each of next 5 sts, dc in next Ldc, 2 dc in each of next 5 sts; dc in next 199 sts, 2 dc in each of next 5 sts, dc in next Ldc; join with sl st in 3rd ch of beg ch-3, changing to A: 440 dc. Finish off B.

Rnd 4: With A, ch 3, dc in back lp of each dc around; join with sl st in 3rd ch of beg ch-3. Finish off and weave in ends.

Rnd 5: Join B with sc in first dc to the left of joining, sc in next dc; working in unused lps on Rnd 3, skip lp under beg ch-3 and next 3 lps, *tr in next lp, ch 1, on working rnd skip next dc, sc in next dc, ch 1, tr in same lp as last tr made: triangle made **; on working rnd, skip next dc, sc in next 2 dc, skip next 4 unused lps on Rnd 3; rep from * around, end at **; join with sl st in first sc: 88 triangles. Finish off and weave in ends.

Rnd 6: Join A with sl st in first skipped dc on Rnd 4 to left of joining (behind first tr of Rnd 5); ch 3, 2 dc in same dc; working behind triangles and in each skipped dc on Rnd 4 only, 3 dc in next dc, ch 1, [(2 dc in next dc) twice, ch 1] 41 times; [(3 dc in next dc) twice, ch 1] 3 times, [(2 dc in next dc) twice, ch 1] 41 times; [(3 dc in next dc) twice, ch 1] twice; join with sl st in 3rd ch of beg ch-3. Finish off and weave in ends.

FINISHING

Skipping four ch-1 sps and six 3-dc groups on each end, whip stitch long edges of 2-dc groups on panels together. Weave in ends.

#58 LOVELY LACE

Designed by Janie Herrin

SIZE
42" x 49" before border

MATERIALS
Worsted weight yarn,
  24 oz rose
  18 oz pink

Note: Photographed model made with Caron Simply Soft #9719 Victorian Rose and #9719 Soft Pink

Size H (5mm) crochet hook
  (or size required for gauge)

GAUGE
7 dc = 2"

Square = 7" x 7"

INSTRUCTIONS

Square (make 42)

With rose, ch 5, join with sl st to form a ring.

Rnd 1: Ch 3 (counts as a dc), 2 dc in ring, (ch 2, 3 dc) in ring 3 times, ch 2, sl st in 3rd ch of beg ch-3: 12 dc; sl st in next 2 dc and into ch-2 sp.

Rnd 2: Ch 1, in same sp work (sc, ch 3, sc), ch 3; * (sc, ch 3, sc) in next corner sp, ch 3; rep from * 2 times more, sl st in beg sc: 8 ch-3 lps; sl st into next corner sp.

Rnd 3: Ch 1, in same sp work (sc, ch 3, sc); * † ch 3, sc in next lp, ch 3, † in next corner lp, work (sc, ch 3, sc); rep from * 2 times more, then rep from † to † once, sl st in beg sc; sl st into next corner sp.

Rnd 4: Ch 1, in same sp work (sc, ch 3, sc); * † ch 3, (sc in next lp, ch 3) twice, † in next corner lp, work (sc, ch 3, sc); rep from * 2 times more, then rep from † to † once, sl st in beg sc; sl st into next corner sp.

Rnd 5: Ch 1, in same sp work (sc, ch 3, sc); * † ch 3, (sc in next lp, ch 3) 3 times †, in next corner lp work (sc, ch 3, sc); rep from * 2 times more, then rep from † to † once, sl st in beg sc: 20 ch-3 sps; sl st into next corner sp.

Rnds 6 and 7: Work in established pattern: 28 sps at end of Rnd 7; finish off rose yarn.

Rnd 8: Join pink yarn with sl st in any corner sp, ch 3 (counts as a dc), work (dc, ch 2, 2 dc) in same sp; * † (2 dc in next lp, 3 dc in next lp) 3 times †; in next corner sp work (2 dc, ch 2, 2 dc); rep from * 2 times more, then rep from † to † once, join in 3rd ch of beg ch-3.

Rnd 9: Sl st in next dc and into ch-2 sp; in sp work 3 sc; sc in next 19 sts; *in next corner sp work 3 sc, sc in next 19 sts; rep from * 2 times; join with slip st in beg sc; finish off.

Joining

To join squares, hold two squares with right sides tog and sew with overcast st with pink yarn along one side, carefully matching sts and corners; then join squares in same manner in 7 rows of 6 squares each.

Border

Rnd 1: Hold afghan with right side facing you and one short edge at top; join pink yarn with sc in top right corner st, 2 sc in same st; work sc evenly around afghan edge, adjusting sts to keep work flat, and working 3 sc in each outer corner sp; join with sc in beg sc.

Rnd 2: Ch 2, sc in same sc, sk next sc; *(sc, ch 2, sc) in next sc, sk next sc; rep from * around, sl st in beg sc.

Rnd 3: Sc in next ch-2 sp, ch 3, sc in same sp; *(sc, ch 3, sc) in next ch-2 sp; rep from * around, sl st in beg sc.

Rnd 4: Sc in next ch-3 sp, ch 4, sc in same sp; *(sc, ch 4, sc) in next ch-3 sp; rep from * around, sl st in beg sc.

Rnd 5: Sc in next ch-4 sp, ch 5, sc in same sp; *(sc, ch 5, sc) in next ch-4 sp; rep from * around, sc in beg sc.

Rnd 6: *In next ch-5 lp work (sc, ch 3, dc, ch 3, sc); rep from * around, join, finish off.

#59 RENAISSANCE BEAUTY

Designed by Carol Alexander for Coats and Clark

SIZE
52" x 65"

MATERIALS
Worsted weight yarn,
  45 oz blue

Note: *Photographed model made with Red Heart® Super Saver® #382 Country Blue*

Size I (5.5mm) crochet hook
  (or size required for gauge)

GAUGE
Rnd 1 = 2 3/4" across

Square = 6 1/4" x 6 1/4"

INSTRUCTIONS

First Square

Note: *After the first square, all other squares are joined while working Rnd 5.*

Ch 5; join with sl st in first ch to form a ring.

Rnd 1: Work beg CL in ring; ch 4; * CL in ring; ch 4; rep from * 6 times more; join with sl st in top of beg CL.

Rnd 2: Ch 1, sc in beg CL, (2 sc, picot, 2 sc) in next ch-4 sp, sc in next CL; *ch 9, turn; skip last 5 sc made, sl st in next sc, turn; ch 1, 16 sc in ch-9 1p**, [(2 sc, picot, 2 sc) in next ch-4 sp, sc in next CL] twice; rep from * to last sp, end at **; (2 sc, picot, 2 sc) in last sp; join with sl st in first ch-1.

Rnd 3: Sl st in first sc worked in ch-9 1p, ch 7 (counts as dc and ch-4); *skip next 5 sc, sc in next 2 sc, ch 2, sc in next 2 sc; ch 4, skip next 5 sc, dc in last sc worked in ch-9

1p, ch 4**; dc in first sc worked in next ch-9 1p, ch 4; rep from * around, end at **; join with sl st in 3rd ch of ch-7.

Rnd 4: Ch 1, sc in same ch as joining; *3 sc in ch-4 sp, sc in next 2 sc, 3 sc in corner ch-2 sp, sc in next 2 sc; [3 sc in next ch-4 sp, sc in next dc] twice; rep from * around omitting last sc in last rep; join with sl st in first sc.

Rnd 5: *Ch 1, skip next sc; V-st in next sc; ch 1, skip next sc, sl st in next sc, ch 1, skip next 2 sc; (2 dc, ch 3, 2 dc) in next (corner) sc, ch 1, skip next 2 sc; [sl st in next sc, ch 1, skip next sc, V-st in next sc, ch 1, skip next sc] twice, sl st in next sc; rep from * around working last sl st in joining sl st of Rnd 4. Finish off and weave in ends.

Second Square

Rnds 1 through 4: Work same as Rnds 1 through 4 on First Square.

Rnd 5 (joining rnd): Ch 1, skip next sc, V-st in next sc, ch 1, skip next sc, sl st in next sc, ch 1, skip next 2 sc, 2 dc in next (corner) sc, ch 1; with wrong sides together, sl st in corresponding ch-3 sp of completed square, ch 1, 2 dc in same (corner) sc on square in progress, ch 1, skip next 2 sc, [sl st in next sc, ch 1, skip next sc, dc in next sc, sl st in next ch-1 sp on completed square, dc in

same sc on square in progress, ch 1, skip next sc] 3 times; sl st in next sc, ch 1, skip next 2 sc, 2 dc in next (corner) sc, ch 1, sl st in corner sp of completed square, ch 1, 2 dc in same (corner) sc on square in progress: one side joined; *ch 1, skip next 2 sc, [sl st in next sc, ch 1, skip next sc, V-st in next sc, ch 1, skip next sc] 3 times, sl st in next sc, ch 1, skip next 2 sc, (2 dc, ch 3, 2 dc) in next sc; rep from * around working sts in brackets 2 times instead of 3 times at end of rnd; join with sl st in joining sl st of Rnd 4. Finish off and weave in ends.

Join 78 more squares in this manner, 8 squares wide and 10 squares long.

Note: *When joining a corner to previously joined corners, sl st into the center of the previous joining sl st.*

Edging

With right side facing, join with sl st in corner ch-3 sp; ch 4, [dc, (ch 1, dc) 5 times] in same sp, ch 2, *[sc in next sl st, ch 1, (dc, ch 1, dc, ch 1, dc) in ch-1 sp of next V-st, ch 1] 3 times, sc in next sl st**; ch 1, (dc, ch 1, dc, ch 1, dc) in next dc of corner shell, ch 1, skip next dc, sc in corner joining sl st, ch 1, skip next dc of next corner shell, (dc, ch 1, dc, ch 1, dc) in next dc, ch 1; rep from * to next corner, end at **; ch 2, [dc, (ch 1, dc) 6 times] in corner sp, ch 2; rep from * around, end at **; ch 2; join with sl st in 3rd ch of beg ch-4. Finish off and weave in ends.

#60 CLUSTER WHEEL

Designed by Janie Herrin

SIZE
42" x 49" before border

MATERIALS
Worsted weight yarn,
  8 oz beige
  16 oz dk brown
  19 oz cream

Note: *Photographed model made with Red Heart® Super Saver® #0336 Warm Brown (beige), #365 Coffee (dk brown), and 1103 Eggshell (cream)*

Size H (5mm) crochet hook
  (or size required for gauge)

GAUGE
7 dc = 2"

Square = 7" x 7"

INSTRUCTIONS

Square (make 42)

With beige, ch 5, join with sl st to a form ring.

Rnd 1: Ch 3 (equals first dc), 11 dc in ring, join with sl st in 3rd ch of beg ch-3: 12 dc.

Rnd 2: Ch 1, sc in same st, ch 2; *sc in next st, ch 2, rep from * around, join in beg sc: 12 ch-2 lps; finish off.

Rnd 3: Join dk brown with sl st in any ch-2 lp, ch 2; begCL in same lp; ch 3, CL in next lp, ch 3; *CL in next lp, ch 3; rep from * around, join with sl st in top of begCL, finish off: 12 CL and 12 ch-3 sps.

Rnd 4: Join beige with sl st in any ch-3 sp, ch 3, 6 dc in same sp (beg shell made); *(ch 3, sc in next sp) twice, ch 3, ** 7 dc in next sp (shell made); rep from * 2 times more then rep from * to ** once, join in 3rd ch of beg ch-3: 4 shells, 12 ch-3 sps.

Rnd 5: Ch 1, sc in same st; *ch 3, skip 2 dc, in next dc work (sc, ch 5, sc); ch 3, skip 2 dc, sc in next dc; (ch 2, sc in next sp) 3 times, ch 2, sc in next dc; rep from * around, ending with sl st in beg sc, finish off.

Rnd 6: Join cream with sl st in any corner ch-5 lp, ch 3, in same lp work (2 dc, ch 2, 3 dc); *(ch 2, sc in next lp) 6 times, ch 2, in ch-5 lp work (3 dc, ch 2, 3 dc); rep from * around ending with sl st in 3rd ch beg ch-3.

Rnd 7: Ch 1, sc in same st, sc in each of next 2 dc; *3 sc in ch-2 sp, sc in each of next 3 dc, 2 sc in lp, (ch 2, sc in next lp) 5 times, ch 2, 2 sc in next lp, sc in each of next 3 dc; rep from * around, ending with sl st in beg sc, finish off.

Rnd 8: Join dk brown with sc in center sc of any 3-sc corner group, 2 sc in same st; *sc in each of next 6 sc, sc in next sp, 2 dc in each of next 4 sps, sc in next sp, sc in each of next 6 sc, 3 sc in next sc; rep from * around ending with sl st in beg sc, finish off.

Rnd 9: Join cream with sc in center sc of any 3-sc corner group, *ch 1, skip next sc, sc in next 5 sc, sc in sp between next 2 sc, 2 hdc in next sp, 2 hdc in each of 4 sps between 2-dc pairs, 2 hdc in sp between last dc and sc, skip this sc, sc in next 5 sc, ch 1, skip first sc at corner, sc in next sc; rep from * around, ending last rep with ch 1, join in beg sc; finish off. Weave in ends.

Joining

Hold two squares with right sides tog and with cream, sew tog with overcast st along one side edge, carefully matching sts and corners. Join in 7 rows of 6 squares each.

Border

Rnd 1: Hold piece with right side facing you; join cream in upper right corner, work 3 sc in same st; sc in each st around, adjusting sts as needed to keep work flat, and working 3 sc in each rem outer corner; join with sc in beg sc.

Rnd 2: *Ch 3,'sk 2 sc, sc in next sc; rep from * around, join with sl st in beg sc.

Rnd 3: Sl st into first ch-3 sp; in same sp work (ch 3, dc, ch 3, 2 dc); *sc in next sc, (2 dc, ch 3, 2 dc) in next ch-3 sp; rep from * around, join with sl st in beg sc. Finish off.

#61 CHOO-CHOO

Designed by Janie Herrin

SIZE

38" square.

MATERIALS

Worsted weight yarn,
  4 oz light grey
  6 oz black
  8 oz red
  8 oz white

Note: *Photographed model made with Red Heart® Classic® #412 Silver; #12 Black; #902 Jockey Red and #1 White*

Crochet hook size I (5.5mm)
  or size required for gauge

Six yarn bobbins

GAUGE

9 dc sts and 5 dc rows = 3"

INSTRUCTIONS

Center

With grey, ch 52.

Row 1 (right side): Dc in 4th ch from hook and in each rem ch, ch 3 (counts as first dc of next row throughout), turn: 50 dc.

Row 2: Dc each dc, changing to black in last st at end of Row 4; ch 3, turn.

From here on, work following chart on page 133, starting with Row 3 of chart. Do not carry unused colors across more than four sts; instead wind yarn on bobbins and use where needed. At end of last row of chart, work 2 more rows dc with grey. Do not finish off.

Border

Rnd 1: Continuing with grey, ch 1, turn; work 3 sc in same st (corner made); *sc in each st across to last dc, work corner in last dc, work 48 sc evenly spaced across side, work corner as before; rep from * once ending with slip st in beg sc: 204 sc. Finish off.

Rnd 2: With right side facing, join red with sl st in any corner sc, ch 3, (2 dc, ch 2, 3 dc) in same st (beg corner made); *(skip next 2 sc, 3 dc in next sc) 16 times, skip next 2 sc, in next sc work (3 dc, ch 2, 3 dc): corner made; rep from * around, ending with sl st in beg dc.

Rnd 3: Sl st to ch-2 corner sp, ch 3, work beg corner; *(3 dc in next sp between 3-dc groups) across, work corner in corner; rep from * around, ending with sl st in beg dc; finish off red.

Rep Rnds 2 and 3 in following color sequence, working two rows of each color:

*white

black

white

red

Rep from * once more working only 1 rnd for last red stripe. At end of last rnd, do not finish off.

Edging

Rnd 1: Ch 1, sc in same st as joining, sc in each dc around, working 3 sc in each ch-2 corner sp. join with sl st in beg sc.

Rnd 2: Ch 1, sc in same st as joining, sc in each sc around, working 3 sc in center sc of each 3-sc corner group, join, finish off; weave in ends.

Each square on chart = 1 dc

KEY

☐ = Grey

■ = Black

Read odd-numbered rows from right to left, and even-numbered rows from left to right; chart begins with Row 3 of afghan.

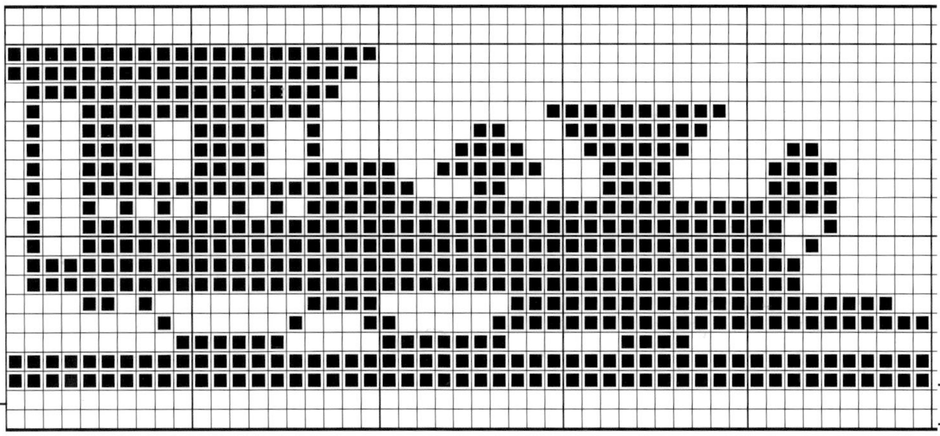

Row 2 —

— Row 3

— Row 1

#62 BOLD PLAID

Designed by Patons Design Staff

SIZE
43" x 56"

MATERIALS
Worsted weight yarn,
   21 oz dk blue (MC)
   10 1/2 oz dk orange (A)
   10 1/2 oz yellow (B)

Note: *Photographed model made with Patons® Canadiana #32 Bright Royal Blue (MC) #72 Deep Orange (A) and #432 School Bus Yellow (B)*

Size 8 (5.5mm) knitting needles (or size required for gauge)

36" Size 8 (5.5mm) circular knitting needle (for border)

GAUGE
14 sts = 4" in patt

44 rows = 4"

INSTRUCTIONS

Strip 1 (make 3)

With MC, cast on 21 sts.

Row 1 (wrong side): Knit.

Row 2: K1, *K1B, K1; rep from * to end of row.

Row 3: Knit.

Row 4: K2, *K1B, K1; rep from * to last st, Kl.

Rows 5 through 44: Rep Rows 1 through 4.

Row 45: With MC, knit.

Row 46: With A, rep Row 2.

Row 47: With A, knit.

Row 48: With MC, rep Row 4.

Rows 49 through 88: Rep Rows 45 through 48.

Row 89: With MC, knit.

Row 90: With B, rep Row 2.

Row 91: With B, knit.

Row 92: With MC, rep Row 4.

Rows 93 through 132: Rep Rows 89 through 92.

Rep last 132 rows twice more ending by working a right-side row. BO as to knit.

Strip 2 (make 2)

With MC, cast on 21 sts,

Row 1 (wrong side): Knit.

Row 2: With A, K1, *K1B, K1, rep from * to end of row.

Row 3: With A, knit.

Row 4: With MC, K2, *K1B, K1, rep from * to last st, K1.

Rows 5 through 44: Rep Rows 1 through 4.

Row 45: With A, knit.

Row 46: With A, rep Row 2.

Row 47: With A, knit.

Row 48: With A, rep Row 4.

Rows 49 through 88: Rep Rows 45 through 48.

Row 89: With A, knit.

Row 90: With B, rep Row 2.

Row 91: With B, knit.

Row 92: With A, rep Row 4.

Rows 93 through 132: Rep Rows 80 through 92.

Rep last 132 rows twice more ending by working a right-side row. BO as to knit.

Continued on next page.

Strip 3 (make 2)

With MC, cast on 21 sts,

Row 1 (wrong side): Knit.

Row 2: With B, K1, *K1B, K1; rep from * to end of row.

Row 3: With B, knit.

Row 4: With MC, K2, *K1B, K1; rep from * to last st, K1.

Rows 5 through 44: Rep Rows 1 through 4.

Row 45: With B, knit.

Row 46: With A, rep Row 2.

Row 47: With A, knit.

Row 48: With B, rep Row 4.

Rows 49 through 88: Rep Rows 45 through 48.

Row 89: With B, knit.

Row 90: With B, rep Row 2.

Row 91: With B, knit.

Row 92: With B, rep Row 4.

Rows 93 through 132: Rep Rows 89 through 92.

Rep last 132 rows twice more ending by working a right-side row. BO as to knit.

Sew strips tog as shown in Strip Diagram,

Side Edgings

With right side of work facing, circular needle and MC, pick up and knit 198 sts along one side edge of afghan.

Row 1 (wrong side): Knit.

Row 2: With B, rep Row 2 of Stripe 1.

Row 3: With B, knit.

Row 4: With MC, knit.

BO as to knit (wrong side). Rep on opposite side edge.

Top Edging

With right side of work facing, circular needle and MC, pick up and knit 159 sts along top edge of Afghan.

Rep Rows 1 through 4 of Side Edging.

Bottom Edging

Rep Top Edging along bottom

Strip Diagram

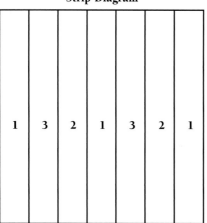

| 1 | 3 | 2 | 1 | 3 | 2 | 1 |

INSTRUCTIONS

With white, ch 164.

Row 1: Sc in 2nd ch from hook and in each rem ch: 163 sc; ch 3 (counts as first dc of next row), turn.

Row 2: Skip first 3 sc, (3 dc in next sc, skip next 2 sc) 3 times; in next sc work shell of (3 dc, ch 3, 3 dc); *(skip next 2 sc, 3 dc in next sc) twice, skip 2 sc; CL in next sc, skip 4 sc, CL in next sc; (skip 2 sc, 3 dc in next sc) twice, skip 2 sc, in next sc work shell of (3 dc, ch 3, 3 dc); rep from * to last 12 sc, skip 2 sc, (3 dc in next sc, sk 2 sc) 3 times, dc in last sc; ch 2, turn.

Note: To work in space (sp) on following rows, work between CLs or 3-dc groups.

Row 3: Skip first sp (between turning ch and next 3-dc group), 3 dc in each of next 3 sps; in next ch-3 sp work shell; *3 dc in each of next 2 sps, CL in next sp, skip sp between CLs, CL in next sp; 3 dc in each of next 2 sps, in next ch-3 sp work shell; rep from * across to last 4 sps; 3 dc in each of next 3 sps, dc in last sp (between last 3-dc group and turning ch-2); ch 2, turn.

Rep Row 3 once more with white, changing to blue in last st.

Rep Row 3 for pattern, working in this color sequence:

3 rows blue

3 rows red

3 rows white

Work until piece measures about 50" long, ending with 3 white rows. Finish off, weave in ends.

Side Edgings

First Edging
Hold afghan with one long edge at top; join blue with sc in edge of row at upper right; sc along edge, working in sides of rows, adjusting sts as needed to keep work flat; finish off.

Second Edging
Hold afghan with other long edge at top; join blue and work as for First Edging.

#66 CATHEDRAL WINDOWS

Designed by Elena Malo for Coats and Clark

SIZE
45" x 70"

MATERIALS
Worsted weight yarn,
   16 oz navy (A)
   14 oz red (B)
   12 oz green (C)
   7 oz gold (D)

Note: *Photographed model made with Red Heart Super Saver #387 Soft Navy (A), #319 Cherry Red (B), #368 Paddy Green (C) and #321 Gold (D)*

Size J (6mm) crochet hook (or size required for gauge)

GAUGE
12 sc = 4"
4 sc rows = 1 ¹/₄" in patt

INSTRUCTIONS

Panel (make 4)
With A, ch 191.

Row 1 (right side): Sc in 2nd ch from hook and in each rem ch: 190 sc; ch 1, turn.

Row 2: Sc in each sc, changing to B in last sc; ch 3, turn. Drop A, do not cut.

Row 3: With B, skip first sc, dc in next sc; *hdc in next sc, sc in next sc, ch 2, skip next 2 sc, sc in next sc, hdc in next sc, dc in next 2 sc**, tr in next 2 sc, dc in next 2 sc; rep from * across, end at **; ch 3, turn.

Row 4: Skip first dc, dc in next dc; *hdc in next hdc, sc in next sc, ch 2, sc in next sc, hdc in next hdc**, dc in next 2 dc, tr in next 2 tr, dc in next 2 dc; rep from * to last 2 sts, end at **; dc in next dc, dc in 3rd ch of ch-3, pick up A in last st; ch 1, turn. Finish off B.

Row 5: With A, sc in first 4 sts; *(Lsc) twice; sc in next 10 sts; rep from * to last 6 sts; (Lsc) twice, sc in next 3 sts, sc in 3rd ch of ch-3; ch 1, turn.

Row 6: Sc in each sc across changing to C in last st: 190 sc; ch 1, turn. Drop A, do not cut.

Row 7: With C, sc in first sc; *hdc in next sc, dc in next 2 sc, tr in next 2 sc, dc in next 2 sc, hdc in next sc, sc in next sc**, ch 2, skip next 2 sc, sc in next sc; rep from * across, end at **; ch 1, turn.

Row 8: Sc in first sc; *hdc in next hdc, dc in next 2 dc, tr in next 2 tr, dc in next 2 dc, hdc in next hdc, sc in next sc**, ch 2, skip 2 chs, sc in next sc; rep from * across, end at **, pick up A in last st; ch 1, turn. Finish off C.

Row 9: With A, sc in first 10 sts, *(Lsc) twice, sc in next 10 sts; rep from * across; ch 1, turn.

Row 10: Rep Row 2.

Rows 11 through 18: Rep Rows 3 through 10.

Rows 19 through 21: Rep Rows 3 through 5.

Row 22: Sc in each sc across. Finish off and weave in ends.

With right side facing, join A with sl st in a corner on a short side edge. Ch 1, work 22 sc evenly across short side; ch 1, turn. Work one more row sc across. Finish off and weave in ends.

With right side facing, join A with sl st in a corner on opposite side edge. Ch 1, work 22 sc evenly across short side; ch 1, turn. Work one more row sc across; ch 1, turn; do not finish off. Work 2 rnds sc around entire panel, joining and turning each rnd and working 3 sc in each corner, being careful to have the same number of sc on each opposing side between corner sc. Finish off and weave in ends.

With right side facing, join D with sl st in any sc, ch 1, work 1 rnd sc; join with sl st in first sc. Finish off and weave in ends.

With right sides facing, sew panels tog on long sides.

Border

With wrong side facing, join D with sl st in any outer corner, work 1 rnd sc; join with sl st in first sc. Finish off and weave in ends. With right side facing, join A with sl st in any sc. Ch 1, work 4 rnds sc, joining and turning each rnd as before, ch 1; work 1 rnd Rev Sc; join with sl st in first st. Finish off and weave in ends.

#67 IMPRESSIONS

Adapted from a Trish Kristoffersen design for Coats and Clark

SIZE

52" x 78"

MATERIALS

Worsted weight yarn,
  5 oz tan (A)
  6 oz dk brown (B)
  11 oz jade (C)
  3 oz pink (D)
  7 oz copper (E)
  11 oz lt purple (F)
  17 oz black (G)

Note: Photographed model made with TLC® Essentials™ #2335 Taupe (A), #2368 Dark Brown (B), #2112 Black (G), TLC® Lustre™ #5507 Bright Jade (C), #5587 Light Purple (F), Red Heart® Kids™ #2734 Pink (D) and Red Heart® Classic™ #289 Copper (E)

Size I (5.5mm) crochet hook (or size required for gauge)

GAUGE

Rnds 1 through 7 of center square = 5 1/2" x 5 1/2"

Each panel = 13" wide

Triple crochet (tr): YO twice, insert hook in specified st, YO and draw up a lp, (YO and draw through 2 lps on hook) 3 times: tr made.

Front post tr (FPtr): YO twice, insert hook from front to back to front around post of specified st, YO and draw up a lp, (YO and draw through 2 lps on hook) 3 times, skip next st: FPtr made.

Front post dc (FPdc): YO, insert hook from front to back to front around post of specified st, YO and draw up a lp, (YO and draw through 2 lps on hook) 2 times, skip next st: FPdc made.

2-Tr decrease (2-tr dec): *YO twice, insert hook in specified st, YO and draw up a lp, (YO and draw through 2 lps on hook) twice; rep from * once; YO and draw through all 3 lps on hook: 2-tr dec made.

3-Tr decrease (3-tr dec): *YO twice, insert hook in specified st, YO and draw up a lp, (YO and draw through 2 lps on hook) twice; rep from * 2 more times; YO and draw through all 4 lps on hook: 3-tr dec made.

Sc decrease (sc dec): (Insert hook in specified st, YO and draw up a lp) twice, YO and draw through all 3 lps on hook: sc dec made.

To change color: Work st until 2 lps rem on hook, drop old color, pick up new color and draw through both lps on hook, cut dropped color.

INSTRUCTIONS

Block 1 (make 12)

Center Square

With A ch 4, join with sl st to form a ring.

Rnd 1: Ch 5 (counts as a tr and ch 1), (tr, ch 1) 11 times in ring: 12 tr and 12 ch-1 sps; join with sl st in 4th ch of ch-5. Finish off and weave in ends.

Rnd 2: Join B with sl st in any ch-1 sp, ch 1; *(sc, ch 3, sc) in ch-1 sp, (sc in next tr, sc in next ch-1 sp) twice, sc in next tr; rep from * around: 28 sc and 4 ch-3 sps; join with sl st in first sc. Finish off and weave in ends.

Rnd 3: Join C with sl st in any corner ch-3 sp, ch 3 (counts as a dc), (dc, ch 2, 2 dc) in same corner ch-3 sp; *ch 1, (FPtr around post of next tr on Rnd 1, ch 1) 3 times**, (2 dc, ch 2, 2 dc) in next corner ch-3 sp; rep from * around, ending at **: 16 dc, 12 FPtr, 16 ch-1 sps and 4 ch-2 sps; join with sl st in 3rd ch of ch-3. Finish off and weave in ends.

Rnd 4: Join D with sl st in any corner ch-2 sp, ch 1;*(sc, ch 2, sc) in corner ch-2 sp, sc in next dc, (sc in next st, sc in next ch-1 sp) 4 times, sc in next 2 dc; rep from * around: 52 sc and 4 ch-2 sps; join with sl st in first sc. Finish off and weave in ends.

Rnd 5: Join E with sl st in any corner ch-2 sp, ch 1; *(sc, ch 2, sc) in corner ch-2 sp, sc in next sc, FPdc around post of next dc on Rnd 3, sc in next sc; (sc in next sc, FPdc around post of next tr on Rnd 3) 3 times, sc in next 2 sc, skip next dc on Rnd 3, FPdc around post of next dc on Rnd 3, sc in next sc; rep from * around: 20 FPdc, 40 sc and 4 ch-2 sps; join as before. Finish off and weave in ends.

Rnd 6: Join F with sl st in any corner ch-2 sp, ch 1; *(sc, ch 2, sc) in corner ch-2 sp, sc in next 15 sts; rep from * around: 68 sc and 4 ch-2 sps; join. Finish off and weave in ends.

Rnd 7: Join C with sl st in any corner ch-2 sp, ch 1; *3 sc in corner ch-2 sp, sc in next 17 sc; rep from * around: 80 sc; join. Finish off and weave in ends. Center Square is now completed.

Continued on next page.

Corner

Row 1: With right side facing, join G with sl st in 3rd sc of any corner 3-sc group, ch 1, sc dec in same st as joining and in next sc, sc in next 15 sc; sc dec in next 2 sc: 17 sts; ch 1, turn.

Row 2: Sc dec in first 2 sts, sc in each sc to last 2 sts, sc dec in last 2 sts: 15 sts; ch 1, turn.

Rows 3 through 8: Rep Row 2 six times more: 3 sts at end of Row 8.

Row 9: Sc dec in first 2 sts, ch 2, sc dec in last st used and in next st, sl st in last st used. Finish off and weave in ends.

Rep Rows 1 through 9 on each of the rem 3 corners of square.

Edging

Rnd 1: With right side facing, join C with sl st in any corner ch-2 sp, ch 1; *(sc, ch 2, sc) in corner ch-2 sp, work 21 sc evenly across to next corner ch-2 sp; rep from * around: 92 sc and 4 ch-2 sps; join with sl st in first sc.

Rnd 2: Ch 1, sc in same st as joining, [(sc, ch 2, sc) in corner ch-2 sp, sc in next 23 sc] 3 times, (sc, ch 2, sc) in corner ch-2 sp, sc in next 22 sc: 100 sc and 4 ch-2 sps; join as before. Finish off and weave in ends.

Top Border

Row 1: With right side facing, join A with sl st in any corner ch-2 sp, ch 1, sc in same sp, sc in next 25 sc, sc in next ch-2 sp: 27 sc. Finish off and weave in ends.

Row 2: With right side facing, join B with sl st in first sc of last row, ch 1, sc in first 2 sc; *hdc in next sc, dc in next sc, 3 tr in next sc, dc in next sc, hdc in next sc, sc in next sc; rep from * to last sc; sc in last sc; ch 1, turn.

Row 3: Sc in first 2 sc; *skip next st, sc in next 2 sts, 3 sc in next st, sc in next 2 sts, skip next st, sc in next st; rep from * to last sc; sc in last sc** changing to D; ch 1, turn. Finish off B and weave in ends.

Row 4: With D, rep Row 3 to **. Finish off and weave in ends.

Row 5: With right side facing, join F with sl st in first sc of last row, ch 4, 2-tr dec in next 2 sc; *dc in next sc, hdc in next sc, sc in next sc, hdc in next sc, dc in next sc**; 3-tr dec in next 3 sc; rep from * to last 3 sc, end at **; 2-tr dec in next 2 sc, tr again in last sc; ch 1, turn.

Row 6: Sc in each st across, sc in 4th ch of ch-4 changing to B; ch 1, turn. Finish off F and weave in ends.

Row 7: With B, sc in each sc across. Finish off and weave in ends.

Bottom Border

Work same as Top Border across opposite side of square, except work color sequence as follows:

Row 1: B.

Rows 2 and 3: A.

Row 4: C.

Rows 5 and 6: E.

Row 7: A.

Block 2 (make 12)

Work same as Block 1 except work color sequence as follows on Center Square:

Rnd 1: B.

Rnd 2: A.

Rnd 3: F.

Rnd 4: D.

Rnd 5: E.

Rnd 6: C.

Rnd 7: F.

Work corners same as for Block 1. Work Edging rnds with F. Work Top and Bottom Borders same as for Block 1.

Strips

Assemble 4 strips of 6 completed Blocks (3 each of Block 1 and Block 2). Alternate blocks in each strip having 1st and 3rd strips starting with Block 1 at top and 2nd and 4th strips starting with Block 2 at top. Join bottom border of one block to top border of next block . Holding squares with right sides tog, sew or sl st together through back lps only.

Right Long Band

Row 1: With right side facing, join D with sl st in lower right-hand corner of bottom border of strip, ch 1, 8 sc across border, 27 sc across square, 8 sc across border, sc in seam, (8 sc across border, 27 sc across square, 8 sc across border, 2 sc in seam) 4 times; 8 sc across border, 27 sc across square, 8 sc across border: 267 sc. Finish off and weave in ends.

Rows 2 through 7: Work same as top border except work color sequence as follows:

Rows 2 and 3: G.

Row 4: F.

Rows 5 and 6: C.

Row 7: E.

Left Long Band

Row 1: With right side facing, join B with sl st on opposite side of strip in upper left-hand corner, ch 1, (8 sc across border, 27 sc across square, 8 sc across border, 2 sc in seam) 4 times, 8 sc across border, 27 sc across square, 8 sc across border, sc in seam, 8 sc across border, 27 sc across block, 8 sc across border: 267 sc. Finish off and weave in ends.

Rows 2 through 7: Work same as Top Border except work color sequence as follows:

Rows 2 and 3: G.

Row 4: E.

Rows 5 and 6: F.

Row 7: C.

Finishing

Arrange 4 completed strips, aligning top edges and alternating top squares. Whip stitch long edges of strips tog with strip 1 on the left and strip 4 on the right.

Edging

With right side facing and G, work one rnd sc evenly around entire afghan; join. Finish off and weave in ends.

#68 CAPTAIN'S WHEEL

Designed by Janie Herrin

SIZE
36" x 48" before border

MATERIALS
Worsted weight yarn,
  11 oz gold
  11 oz brown
  18 oz off white

Note: Photographed model made with Red Heart® Classic™ #645 Honey Gold, #339 Medium Brown, #111 Eggshell

Size H (5mm) crochet hook or
  size required for gauge

GAUGE
7 dc=2"

Square = 6" x 6"

INSTRUCTIONS

Square (make 48)

With gold, ch 4, join with sl st to form a ring.

Rnd 1: Ch 1, in ring work (sc, ch 7) 8 times, join with sl st to beg sc: 8 ch-7 lps; finish off gold.

Rnd 2: Join brown with sl st in any sc between lps, ch 5 (equals first dc plus ch 2), dc in same sp leaving ch-7 lps unworked; (dc, ch 2, dc) in each sc around, join with sl st in 3rd ch of beg ch-5.

Rnd 3: * Sc in next ch-2 sp, ch 7, sc in same sp; work sc by inserting hook through ch-7 lp from Rnd 1 *and* in sp between next 2 dc of Rnd 2 to draw up lp, YO and complete this sc; rep from * around, join with sl st in beg sc: 24 sc and 8 ch-7 lps. Finish off brown.

Rnd 4: Join off white with sl st in center sc of any 3-sc group between lps, ch 3, in same st work (dc, ch 3, 2 dc); *working between next 2 lps, (2 dc, ch 3, 2 dc) in center sc; rep from * around, join with sl st in beg ch-3.

Rnd 5: Sl st to next ch-3 sp, ch 3, (2 dc, ch 2, 3 dc) in same sp;* † ch 1, skip 2 dc, dc by inserting hook in next ch-7 lp of Rnd 3 *and* in sp before next dc to work st; ch 1, 2 sc in next ch-3 sp, ch 1, skip next 2 dc, dc by working in next lp and in sp before next dc, ch 1; † in next ch-3 sp, work (3 dc, ch 2, 3 dc); rep from * 2 times more, then rep from † to † once, join with sl st in beg ch-3.

Rnd 6: Ch 3, dc in next 2 dc; * in next corner sp, work (2 dc, ch 2, 2 dc), dc in next dc and in each st across; rep from * around ending with sl st in beg ch-3, finish off white.

Rnd 7: Join brown with sc in any ch-2 corner sp, 2 sc in same sp; sc in each dc around, working 3 sc in each rem ch-2 corner sp. Finish off brown.

Rnd 8: Join gold in center sc of any 3-sc corner group, 3 sc in same sc; sc in each sc around, working 3 sc in center sc of each rem 3-sc corner group. Finish off.

Joining

To join, hold two squares with right sides tog and with gold, sew with overcast st along one side edge, carefully matching sts and corners. In same manner, continue joining squares into 8 rows of 6 squares each.

Border

Rnd 1: Hold piece with right side facing you. Join gold with sc in sp at upper right outer corner, 3 sc in same sp; sc in each st around, adjusting sts to keep work flat, and working 3 sc in each rem outer corner sp. Finish off gold.

Rnd 2: Join off white in center sc of any 3-sc corner group, 3 sc in same sc; sc in each sc around, working 3 sc in each corner sc; finish off white.

Rnd 3: With brown, rep Rnd 2. Finish off.

Fringe

Following Fringe Instructions on page 221, cut strands 20" long from each of the three colors; work double knot fringe across each short end of afghan, spacing knots every third st.

#69 MERRY SUNSHINE

Designed by Jean Leinhauser

SIZE
36" square before border

MATERIALS
Sport weight yarn,
  21 oz yellow

Note: *Photographed model made with Patons Astra #02943 Maize*

Size F (3.75mm) crochet hook
  (or size required for gauge)

GAUGE
Square = 4 $^1/_2$" x 4 $^1/_2$"

INSTRUCTIONS

Square (make 64)

Ch 2.

Rnd 1: 8 sc in 2nd ch from hook; join with a sl st in beg ch.

Rnd 2: Ch 1, sc in same st as joining; (ch 5, sc in next sc) 7 times; ch 5, join with a sl st in beg sc: 8 ch-5 lps.

Rnd 3: Sl st into first ch-5 sp, ch 1, (2 sc, ch 3, 2 sc) in same sp; (2 sc, ch 3, 2 sc) in each rem ch-5 sp; join in beg sc.

Rnd 4: Sl st in next sc; *ch 1, in next ch-3 sp work (sc, ch 3, sc), ch 1; in next ch-3 sp work (2 dc, ch 3, 2 dc); rep from * around, ch 1, join in beg sc.

Rnd 5: Sl st into next ch-3 sp, ch 5 (counts as a dtr), in same sp work (3 tr, 1 dtr, ch 3, 1 dtr, 3 tr, 1 dtr): corner made; in next ch-3 sp work (hdc, sc, hdc);* in next ch-3 sp work (1 dtr, 3 trc, 1 dtr, ch 3, 1 dtr, 3 tr, 1 dtr): corner made; (hdc, sc, hdc) in next ch-3 sp for side; rep from * two times more, join in top of beg ch-5.

Rnd 6: Ch 1, sc in joining; sc in each st around, working 3 sc in each ch-3 corner sp; join, finish off.

Joining

To join, hold 2 squares with right sides tog. Carefully matching sts, sew tog along one side through both lps, beg in center sc of one corner and ending in center sc of next corner. Join squares in 8 rows of 8 squares each.

Border

Rnd 1: Hold piece with right side facing. Join yarn in any center corner sc, work 3 sc in same st. Sc in each st around, working 3 sc in each center corner st; join in beg sc.

Rnd 2: Ch 3 (counts as a dc), dc in same sc;* (3 dc in next sc, 2 dc in next sc), rep from * around, join in 3rd ch of beg ch-3.

Rnd 3: Ch 3, dc in each dc around, join with sc in 3rd ch of beg ch-3.

Rnd 4: *Ch 4, sk next dc, sc in next dc; rep from * around; join, finish off. Weave in all ends.

#70 SHIP AHOY

Designed by Michele Thompson for Coats and Clark

SIZE
44 1/2" x 44 1/2"

MATERIALS
Worsted weight yarn,
  16 oz red (A)
  17 oz white (B)
  7 oz blue (C)

Note: Photographed model made with Red Heart® Super Saver® #390 Hot Red (A), #311 White (B), and #387 Soft Navy (C)

Size J (6mm) crochet hook (or size required for gauge)

Size H (5mm) crochet hook

Size I (5.5mm) crochet hook

Yarn needle

GAUGE
12 sc = 4" with J hook

14 sc rows = 4"

To change color: Work st until 2 lps rem on hook, drop old color, pick up new color and draw through both lps on hook; do not cut dropped color, but carry it loosely up side of work.

INSTRUCTIONS

With A and J hook, ch 121.

Row 1 (right side): Sc in 2nd ch from hook and in each rem ch: 120 sc; ch 1, turn.

Row 2: Sc in each; ch 1, turn.

Row 3: Rep Row 2.

Row 4: Sc in each sc, changing to B in last sc; ch 1, turn.

Rows 5 through 7: Rep Row 2 three times more.

Row 8: Sc in each sc, changing to A in last sc: ch 1, turn.

Work even in sc, alternating 4 rows A with 4 rows B for stripe sequence until 40" from beg (about 35 stripes or 140 rows). Finish off and weave in ends.

Edging

With right side facing and I hook, join C with sl st in top right-hand corner and work 1 rnd sc evenly around, working 3 sc in each corner; join with sl st in first sc; ch 1, turn. Work 7 more rnds in sc, joining and turning each rnd and inc in corners as before. Finish off and weave in ends.

Stars (make 56)

Rnd 1: With B and H hook, ch 2; 5 sc in 2nd ch from hook; join with sl st in first sc.

Rnd 2: (Ch 2, sc in 2nd ch from hook, sl st in next sc) 4 times, ch 2, sc in 2nd ch from hook, join with sl st in joining sl st of Rnd 1. Finish off, leaving a long yarn end for sewing.

Sew one star to each corner and 13 stars evenly spaced between corners along edging as shown in photograph.

#71 JACOB'S LADDER

Designed by Janie Herrin

SIZE
42" x 42" before border

MATERIALS
Worsted weight yarn,
   24 oz off white
   36 oz rose

Note: Photographed model made with Caron Simply Soft Color #9702 Fisherman and #9721 Soft Victorian Rose

Size H (5mm) crochet hook or
   size required for gauge

GAUGE
7 dc = 2"

Square = 6" x 6"

INSTRUCTIONS

Square (make 49)
Beginning with rose, ch 5, join with sl st to form a ring.

Rnd 1: Ch 3, 2 dc in ring, (ch 2, 3 dc in ring) 3 times, ch 2, join with sl st in 3rd ch of beg ch-3: 12 dc.

Rnd 2: Ch 1, sc in joining; * † ch 3, sc in next ch-2 sp, ch 3, † sc in same sp; rep from * 2 times more, then rep from † to † once, sl st in beg sc: 8 ch-3 lps.

Rnd 3: Ch 1, sc in same st; ch 3, sc in next sc; * † ch 3, sc in next corner sp, † (ch 3, sc in next sc) twice; rep from * 2 times more, then rep from † to † once, ch 3, sl st in beg sc: 12 ch-3 lps.

Rnd 4: Ch 1, sc in same st, (ch 3, sc in next sc) twice; * † ch 3, sc in same st as last sc, † (ch 3, sc in next sc) 3 times; rep from * 2 times more, then rep from † to † once, ch 3, join with sl st in beg sc: 16 ch-3 lps

Rnd 5: Ch 1, sc in same st, (ch 3, sc in next sc) twice; * † ch 3, sc in next corner ch-3 sp, † (ch 3, sc in next sc) 4 times; rep from * 2 times more, then rep from † to † once, ch 3, sc in next sc, ch 3, sl st in beg sc: 20 lps.

Rnd 6: Ch 1, sc in same st, (ch 3, sc in next sc) 3 times; * † ch 3, sc in same st as last sc, † (ch 3, sc in next sc) 5 times; rep from * 2 times more, then rep from † to † once, ch 3, sc in next sc, ch 3, sl st in beg sc: 24 lps.

Rnd 7: Ch 1, sc in same st, (ch 3, sc in next sc) 3 times; * † ch 3, sc in next corner ch-3 sp, † (ch 3, sc in next sc) 6 times; rep from * 2 times more, then rep from † to † once, ch 3, (sc in next sc, ch 3) twice, sl st in beg sc: 28 lps.

Rnd 8: Ch 1, sc in same st, (ch 3, sc in next sc) 4 times; * † ch 3, sc in same st as last sc, † (ch 3, sc in next sc) 7 times; rep from * 2 times more, then rep from † to † once, (ch 3, sc in next sc) twice, ch 3, sl st in beg sc: 32 lps; finish off rose.

Rnd 9: Join off white with sl st in any corner and counting beg ch-3 as first dc, work * (3 dc, ch 2, 3 dc) in corner sp, (2 dc in next sp) 3 times, 3 dc in next sp, (2 dc in next sp) 3 times; rep from * around, join in 3rd ch of beg ch-3: 84 dc.

Rnd 10: Ch 1, sc in same st, sc in next 2 sts, * 3 sc in corner sp, sc in next 21 sts; rep from * around, ending with sc in last 18 sts, join beg sc. finish off. Weave in ends.

Joining
To join, hold two squares with right sides tog and with white, sew tog along one side with overcast st, sewing through outer lps only. Join in 7 rows of 7 squares each.

Border
Hold piece with right side facing you and join off white with sl st in outer corner sp at top right.

Rnd 1: Ch 4 (counts as a dc and ch-1 sp), dc in same st; *(dc, ch 1, dc) in next sc; rep from * around, join in 3rd ch of beg ch-4.

Rnd 2: Sl st in next ch-1 sp, in same sp work [ch 5 (counts as a dc and ch-2 sp), dc]; * in next ch-1 sp work (dc, ch 2, dc); rep from * around, join with sl st in 3rd ch of beg ch-5.

Rnd 3: Sl st in next ch-2 sp, in same sp work [ch 6 (counts as a dc and ch-3 sp), dc];* in next ch-2 sp work (dc, ch 3, dc); rep from * around, join with sl st in 3rd ch of beg ch-6.

Rnd 4: Sl st in next ch-3 sp, in same sp work (ch 7, dc); * in next ch-3 sp work (dc, ch 4, dc); rep from * around, join with sl st in 3rd ch of beg ch-7. Finish off.

#72 COUNTRY HEARTS

Designed by Janie Herrin

SIZE
30" x 40" before border

MATERIALS
Worsted weight yarn,
  4 oz medium blue
  4 oz medium pink
  7 oz ombre
  7 oz off white

Note: *Photographed model made with Red Heart® Classic™ #882 Country Blue, #755 Pale Rose, #972 Wedgwood ombre and #3 Off White*

Size H (5mm) crochet hook
  (or size required for gauge)
Size G (4mm) crochet hook

GAUGE
7 dc = 2" with larger hook
One block = 10"

INSTRUCTIONS

Block (make 12)

Center of Block (make 6 with med pink and 6 with med blue)

Row 1: With larger hook, ch 23, dc in 3rd ch from hook and in each ch across: 21 dc; ch 3 (counts as first dc of following row), turn.

Row 2: Dc in each dc and in 3rd ch of beg ch-3; ch 3, turn.

Rep Row 2 until piece measures 7"; at end of last row, ch 1, turn.

Edging Rnd (right side): 3 sc in first dc for corner; * evenly space 19 sc across to last st, 3 sc in last st for corner; working across ends of rows, evenly space 19 sc across to next corner; *3 sc in next corner; rep from * to * once more, join with sl st in beg sc, finish off, weave in ends.

Border

Hold one Center with right side facing you and join ombre with larger hook with sl st in center sc of any 3-sc corner group.

Rnd 1: (Ch 3, dc, ch 2, 2 dc) in same st for corner; dc in each sc around, working (2 dc, ch 2, 2 dc) in center sc of each 3-sc corner group; join to beg sc.

Rnd 2: Sl st in next dc and into ch-2 sp, (ch 3, dc, ch 2, 2 dc) in same sp; * dc in each dc across to next ch-2 sp, (2 dc, ch 2, 2 dc) in ch-2 sp; rep from * two times more, dc in each dc to beg dc, join with sl st, finish off ombre.

Rnd 3: Join white with sc in any ch-2 corner sp, 2 sc in same sp; sc in each dc around, working 3 sc in each ch-2 corner sp; join, finish off. Weave in all ends.

Heart Applique (make 6)

Row 1: With white and smaller size hook, starting at bottom point, ch 2, sc in 2nd ch from hook, ch 1, turn.

Row 2: 3 sc in sc, ch 1, turn.

Rows 3 through 5: Work 2 sc in first sc, sc across to last sc, 2 sc in last sc: 9 sc at end of Rnd 5; ch 1, turn.

Rows 6 through 8: Sc in each sc, ch 1 turn.

Row 9 (right side): Sc in next 4 sc, ch 1 turn.

Row 10: Sc in each sc: 4 sc; ch 1, turn.

Row 11: *(Insert hook in next sc and draw up a lp) twice, YO and draw through all 3 lps on hook: dec made; rep from * once more: 2 sc; ch 1, turn.

Row 12: Skip first sc, sc in next sc; finish off.

Hold heart with wrong side facing you and join yarn with sc in first sc at right of Row 9; sc in next 3 sc, ch 1, turn (center sc is left unworked. Rep Rows 10 through 12; at end of last row, do not finish off.

Continued on next page.

Edging

Rnd 1: Work sc evenly around outer edge of heart, working into skipped center sc at top and working 3 sc in point at bottom; join with sc.

Rnd 2: *Ch 2, sk next sc, sc in next sc; rep from * around, join with sl st, finish off.

Sew one heart in center of each pink block.

Joining

To join blocks, hold two blocks with right sides tog and with white, sew with overcast st along one side edge, carefully matching sts and corners. Then join in same manner in 4 rows of 3 blocks each, as follows:

Working from left to right:

Row 1: Pink block, blue block, pink block

Row 2: Blue block, pink block. blue block

Row 3: Rep Row 1

Row 4: Rep Row 2

Ruffle

Hold piece with right side facing you. Use larger hook to join white with sc in center sc of 3-sc corner group at upper right.

Rnd 1: Sc in each sc around, working 3 sc in center sc of each 3-sc corner group; join with sl st to beg sc.

Rnd 2: Sl st in next sc; (ch 3, 3 dc in same sc); 3 dc in each dc around, working 4 dc in center sc of each 3-sc corner group; join with sc in 3rd ch at beg of rnd.

Rnd 3: *Ch 3, sk 2 dc, sc in next dc; rep from * around; join, finish off, weave in ends.

#73 STAINED GLASS

Designed by Susan Lowman

SIZE
40" x 56"

MATERIALS
Worsted weight yarn,
  15 oz black
  9 oz dark color(s)
  8 oz medium color(s)
  10 oz light color(s)
Size G (4mm) crochet hook
  (or size required for gauge)

GAUGE
Square motif Rnds 1 through
  4 = 3 1/2" square
Rnds 1 through 7 = 5 1/2"
  square

STITCH GUIDE
Tr decrease (tr dec): *YO twice, insert hook in specified st, YO and draw up a lp, (YO and draw through 2 lps on hook) twice; rep from * once; YO and draw through all 3 lps on hook: tr dec made.

INSTRUCTIONS

Square Motif (Make 59)
With dark color, ch 5, join with sl st to form a ring.

Rnd 1 (right side): Ch 3, 2 dc in ring, (ch 3, 3 dc in ring) 3 times, ch 3; join with sl st in 3rd ch of beg ch-3.

Rnd 2: Sl st in next 2 dc and in next ch-3 sp, ch 3, (2 dc, ch 3, 3 dc) in same sp; *ch 1, (3 dc, ch 3, 3 dc) in next ch-3 sp; rep from * 2 times more; ch 1; join with sl st in 3rd ch of beg ch-3. Finish off and weave in ends.

Continued on next page.

Rnd 3: With wrong side facing, join medium color with sl st in any ch-3 sp on Rnd 2, ch 3, dc in same sp, ch 1, 3 dc in next ch-1 sp, ch 1, (3 dc, ch 3, 3 dc) in next ch-3 sp, ch 1, 3 dc in next ch-1 sp, ch 1, 2 dc in next ch-3 sp; turn.

Rnd 4: Ch 3, (3 dc in next ch-1 sp, ch 1) 2 times, (3 dc, ch 3, 3 dc) in next ch-3 sp, (ch 1, 3 dc in next ch-1 sp) 2 times, dc in 3rd ch of beg ch-3. Finish off and weave in ends.

Rnd 5: With wrong side facing, join light color with sl st in sp between last dc and previous 3 dc on Rnd 4, ch 3, dc in same sp, (ch 1, 3 dc in next ch-1 sp) 2 times, ch 1, (3 dc, ch 3, 3 dc) in next ch-3 sp, (ch 1, 3 dc in next ch-1 sp) 2 times, ch 1, 2 dc in beg ch-3 sp; turn.

Rnd 6: Ch 3, (3 dc in next ch-1 sp, ch 1) 3 times, (3 dc, ch 3, 3 dc) in next ch-3 sp, (ch 1, 3 dc in next ch-1 sp) 3 times, dc in 3rd ch of beg ch-3. Finish off and weave in ends.

Rnd 7: With right side facing, join black with sl st in beg ch-3 sp on Rnd 6, ch 3, 2 dc in same sp, (ch 1, 3 dc in next ch-1 sp) 3 times, ch 1, (3 dc, ch 3, 3 dc) in next ch-3 sp; *(ch 1, 3 dc in next ch-1 sp) 3 times, ch 1, 3 dc in sp between last dc and previous 3 dc on Rnd 6, ch 3, 3 dc around post (vertical bar) of last dc on Rnd 6, ch 1, 3 dc around post of last dc on Rnd 4, ch 1, 3 dc in next ch-3 sp on Rnd 2*, ch 1, 3 dc in next ch-1 sp, ch 1, (3 dc, ch 3, 3 dc) in next ch-3 sp, ch 1, 3 dc in next ch-1 sp, ch 1, 3 dc in next ch-3 sp, ch 1, 3 dc in beg ch-3 sp on Rnd 4, ch 1, 3 dc in beg ch-3 sp on Rnd 6, ch 3; join with sl st in 3rd ch of beg ch-3. Finish off, leaving an 18" end.

Left Half of Square (make 6)

With dark color, ch 4, join with sl st to form a ring.

Rnd 1 (wrong side): Ch 4, (3 dc, ch 3, 3 dc) in ring, ch 1, dc in ring; turn.

Rnd 2 (right side): Ch 4, 3 dc in next ch-1 sp, ch 1, (3 dc, ch 3, 3 dc) in next ch-3 sp, ch 1, 3 dc in beg ch-4 sp on Rnd 1, ch 1, dc in same sp. Finish off and weave in ends.

Rnd 3: With wrong side facing, join medium color with sl st in corner ch-3 sp on Rnd 2, ch 3, dc in same sp, ch 1, 3 dc in next ch-1 sp, ch 1, 3 dc in beg ch-4 sp on Rnd 2, ch 1, dc in same sp; turn.

Rnd 4: Ch 4, (3 dc in next ch-1 sp, ch 1) 2 times, 3 dc in next ch-1 sp, dc in 3rd ch of beg ch-3. Finish off and weave in ends.

Rnd 5: With wrong side facing, join light color with sl st in sp between last dc and previous 3 dc on Rnd 4, ch 3, dc in same sp, (ch 1, 3 dc in next ch-1 sp) 2 times, ch 1, 3 dc in beg ch-4 sp on Rnd 4, ch 1, dc in same sp; turn.

Rnd 6: Ch 4, (3 dc in next ch-1 sp, ch 1) 3 times, 3 dc in next ch-1 sp, dc in 3rd ch of beg ch-3. Finish off and weave in ends.

Rnd 7: With right side facing, join black with sl st in beg ch-4 sp on Rnd 6, ch 3, 2 dc in same sp; rep from * to * on Rnd 7 of Square Motif; (ch 1, 3 dc in next ch-1 sp) 2 times, ch 4, 4 dc around post of last dc on Rnd 2, ch 1, 4 dc in ring, ch 1, 4 dc in beg ch-4 sp on Rnd 2, ch 1, 4 dc in beg ch-4 sp on Rnd 4, ch 1, 4 dc in beg ch-4 sp on Rnd 6, ch 4; join with sl st in 3rd ch of beg ch-3. Finish off, leaving 18" end.

Right Half of Square (make 6)

With dark color, ch 4, join with sl st to form a ring.

Rnds 1 and 2: Rep Rnds 1 and 2 on Left Half of Square.

Rnd 3: With wrong side facing, join medium color with sl st in last ch-1 sp on Rnd 2, ch 4, 3 dc in same sp, ch 1, 3 dc in next ch-1 sp, ch 1, 2 dc in next ch-3 sp; turn.

Rnd 4: Ch 3, (3 dc in next ch-1 sp, ch 1) 2 times, 3 dc in beg ch-4 sp on Rnd 3, ch 1, dc in same sp. Finish off and weave in ends.

Rnd 5: With wrong side facing, join light color with sl st in last ch-1 sp on Rnd 4, ch 4, 3 dc in same sp, (ch 1, 3 dc in next ch-1 sp) 2 times, ch 1, 2 dc in beg ch-3 sp on Rnd 4; turn.

Rnd 6: Ch 3, (3 dc in next ch-1 sp, ch 1) 3 times, 3 dc in beg ch-4 sp on Rnd 5, ch 1, dc in same sp. Finish off and weave in ends.

Rnd 7: With right side facing, join black with sl st in beg ch-3 sp on Rnd 6, ch 3, 2 dc in same sp, (ch 1, 3 dc in next ch-1 sp) 4 times, ch 4, 4 dc around post of last dc on Rnd 6, ch 1, 4 dc around post of last dc on Rnd 4, ch 1, 4 dc around post of last dc on Rnd 2, ch 1, 4 dc in ring, ch 1, 4 dc in beg ch-4 sp on Rnd 2, ch 4, 3 dc in same ch-4 sp, ch 1, 3 dc in next ch-1 sp, ch 1, 3 dc in next ch-3 sp on Rnd 2, ch 1, 3 dc in beg ch-3 sp on Rnd 4, ch 1, 3 dc in beg ch-3 sp on Rnd 6, ch 3; join with sl st in 3rd ch of beg ch-3. Finish off, leaving 18" end.

Joining

Arrange motifs on point in 13 rows with 5 square motifs in the odd-numbered rows and 4 square motifs plus one right half of square and one left half of square in the even numbered rows. Whip stitch motifs together diagonally.

Edging

With right side facing, join black with sl st in ch-3 sp at right corner of top right motif, ch 3, 2 dc in same sp; ***ch 1, [*(3 dc in next ch-1 sp, ch 1) 4 times, (3 dc, ch 3, 3 dc) in next ch-3 sp, (ch 1, 3 dc in next ch-1 sp) 4 times*, tr dec in next ch-3 sp on same motif and in next ch-3 sp on next motif] 4 times; rep from * to * once; ch 1, 3 dc in next ch-3 sp, ch 1, 4 dc in next ch-4 sp on next motif [**(ch 1, 4 dc in next ch-1 sp) 4 times**, (ch 1, 3 tr in next ch-4 sp) 2 times] 5 times; rep from ** to ** once; ch 1, 4 dc in next ch-4 sp, ch 1***, 3 dc in next ch-3 sp on next motif; rep from *** to *** once; join with sl st in 3rd ch of beg ch-3. Finish off and weave in ends.

#74 RAINBOW RIB

Designed by Patons Design Staff

SIZE
46 " x 61"

MATERIALS
Worsted weight yarn,
- 35 oz blue (MC)
- 7 oz red (A)
- 7 oz orange (B)
- 7 oz yellow (C)
- 3 1/2 oz Variegated (D)

Note: Photographed model made with Patons® Canadiana #33 Royal Blue, #5 Cardinal (A), #72 Deep Orange (B), #432 School Bus Yellow(C) and #438 Rainbow Variegated (D)

36" Size 8 (5mm) circular knitting needle (or size required for gauge)

36" Size 7 (4.5mm) circular knitting needle

GAUGE
20 1/2 sts = 4" with larger needle in rib patt

24 rows = 4"

INSTRUCTIONS

With MC and smaller needle, CO 220 sts; do not join, work back and forth in rows.

Bottom Border
Rows 1 through 4: Knit

Row 5: Knit, increasing 30 sts evenly spaced across row: 250 sts.

Body
Note: Sl all sl sts as to purl.

Change to larger needle.

Row 1 (right side): Kl, *Kl, P1; rep from * to last st, K1.

Rows 2 and 3: Rep Row 1.

Row 4: K1, *Pl, PW; rep from * to last st, K1.

Row 5: With A, K1, * sl 1 (dropping extra lp), K1; rep from * to last st, K1.

Row 6: K1, *Pl, sl 1; rep from * to last st, Kl.

Row 7: K1, *KW, K1; rep from * to last st, K1.

Row 8: With B, Kl, *Pl, sl 1 (dropping extra lp); rep from * to last st, K1.

Row 9: With B, K1, * sl 1, K1; rep from * to last st, K1.

Row 10: With B, rep Row 4.

Rows 11 through 13: With C, rep Rows 5 through 7.

Rows 14 through 16: With D, rep Rows 8 through 10.

Rows 17 through 19: With C, rep Rows 5 through 7.

Rows 20 through 22: With B, rep Rows 8 through 10.

Rows 23 through 25: With A, rep Rows 5 through 7.

Rows 26 through 28: With MC, rep Rows 8 through 10.

Row 29: K1, * sl 1 (dropping extra lp), P1; rep from * to last st, K1.

Rows 30 through 32: With MC, K1, *K1, P1; rep from * to last st, K1.

Rows 33 through 36: K1, *Pl, K1; rep from * to last st, K1.

Rows 37 through 40: K1, *K1, P1; rep from * to last st, K1.

Rows 41 through 44: K1, *Pl, Kl; rep from * to last st, K1.

Rows 45 through 60: Rep Rows 37 through 44 twice more.

Rep Rows 1 through 60 four times more, then rep Rows 1 through 32 once more.

Top Border

Change to smaller needle.

Row 1: Knit, decreasing 30 sts evenly spaced across row: 230 sts.

Rows 2 through 5: Knit. At end of last row, BO as to knit. Weave in all yarn ends.

Side Edgings

With right side of work facing, with smaller needle and MC, pick up and knit 234 sts along one side edge. Knit 4 more rows,

BO as to knit.

Rep edging on opposite side.

Fringe

Following Fringe instructions on page 221, cut 16" lengths of yarn in all colors. Use 7 strands of one color in each knot; tie knots across each CO and BO edge, in following color sequence: *A, B, C, D, MC; rep from * across, trim fringe evenly.

#75 RIPPLE AT DAWN

SIZE
50" x 65"

MATERIALS
Worsted weight yarn,
  16 oz dark red (A)
  13 oz rose (B)
  13 oz peach (C)
  13 oz off-white (D)

Note: Photographed model made with TLC® Lustre™ #5915 Claret (A). #5730 Coral Rose (B), #5247 Peach (C), and #5017 Natural (D)

36" Size 9 (5.5mm) circular
  knitting needle (or size
  required for gauge)

GAUGE
22 sts= 4 ³/₄" in patt

12 rows = 2 ¹/₄" in patt

INSTRUCTIONS

With A, CO 233 sts. Do not join, work back and forth in rows.

Row 1 (right side): Knit.

Row 2: Knit.

Row 3: K1; *(K2tog) twice, (YO, K1) 3 times, YO, (SSK) twice; rep from * to last st; K1.

Row 4: Purl.

Rows 5 through 10: Rep Rows 3 and 4 three times more.

Rows 11 and 12: Knit. At end of Row 12, cut A, join B.

Rows 13 through 24: With B, rep Rows 1 through 12. At end of Row 24, cut B, join C.

Rows 25 through 36: With C, rep Rows 1 through 12. At end of Row 36, cut C, join D.

Rows 37 through 48: With D, rep Rows 1 through 12. At end of Row 48, cut D.

Rep Rows 1 through 48 six more times; then rep Rows 1 through 12 once more with A. Knit 1 row.

BO in knit.

#76 BABY CLOUDS

Designed by Janie Herrin

SIZE
33" x 47"

MATERIALS
Super bulky weight yarn,
  30 oz multi-color

Worsted weight yarn,
  7 oz pink

Note: *Photographed model made with Red Heart® Baby Clouds #9008 Cotton Candy and Red Heart® Super Saver® #373 Petal Pink*

Size N (10mm) crochet hook
  (or size required for gauge)

Large-eyed yarn needle

GAUGE
10 sc = 5"

INSTRUCTIONS

With bulky yarn, ch 96. (**Note:** *Afghan is worked lengthwise*)

Foundation Row (right side): Sc in 2nd ch from hook and in each ch across: 95 sc; ch 1, turn.

Row 1: Sc in first sc and in each sc across, ch 1, turn.

Rows 2 through 4: Rep Row 1.

Row 5: Sc in each sc, ch 4 (counts as first dc and ch-1 sp of next row), turn.

Row 6 (eyelet row): Sk first 2 sc, dc in next sc, ch 1; *skip next sc, dc in next sc, ch 1; rep from * across to last 2 sc, skip next sc, dc in last sc: 47 ch-1 sps; ch 1, turn.

Row 7: Sc in first dc, sc in each ch-1 sp and in each dc across, ending with sc in last sp, sc in 3rd ch of ch-4: 95 sc; ch 1, turn.

Rep Rows 2 through 7 six times more, then rep Rows 1 through 5 once; at end of last row finish off; weave in ends.

Finishing

Now you will weave strands of pink worsted weight yarn through each eyelet row.

First Eyelet Row

Cut 8 strands of worsted weight yarn, each about 60" yds long and thread 4 strands into a yarn needle. Beginning at top edge, with right side facing, insert needle *under* post (vertical bar) of first dc. Keeping work straight so as not to ruffle, weave strands over and under each post across keeping equal lengths free at each end for fringe.

Thread remaining 4 strands into yarn needle, and beginning at same edge on same eyelet row, weave strands over and under each post across, inserting needle *over* post of first dc, again leaving equal lengths free at each end.

Holding all 8 strands tog, make lp close to top edge, insert ends through lp and tighten for overhand knot; rep at bottom edge.

Rep across for each eyelet row. Trim fringe evenly.

#77 TWILIGHT WAVE

SIZE
52" x 66"

MATERIALS
Worsted weight yarn,
   14 oz navy (A)
   12 oz dk blue (B)
   12 oz med blue (C)
   12 oz lt blue (D)

Note: Photographed model made with Red Heart® Super Saver® #387 Soft Navy (A), #885 Delft Blue (C), Classic #848 Skipper Blue (B) and #815 Pale Blue (D)

Size I (5.5mm) crochet hook
   (or size required for gauge)

GAUGE
One rep of 19 sts = 4" in patt
8 rows = 4" in patt

INSTRUCTIONS

With A, ch 248.

Foundation Row (wrong side): Sc in 2nd ch from hook and in each ch across: 247 sc; ch 3, turn.

Row 1 (right side): 5 dc in first sc; *(skip next sc, dc in next sc) 3 times, skip next sc, dec; (skip next sc, dc in next sc) 3 times, skip next sc**, (6 dc in next sc) twice; rep from * to last sc, end at **; 6 dc in last sc; ch 1, turn.

Row 2: Sc in each st across and in 3rd ch of ch-3; ch 3, turn.

Rows 3 and 4: Rep Rows 1 and 2, changing to B in last sc on Row 4. Finish off A and weave in ends.

Rows 5 through 8: With B, rep Rows 1 through 4, changing to C in last sc on Row 8. Finish off B and weave in ends.

Rows 9 through 12: With C, rep Rows 1 through 4, changing to D in last sc on Row 12. Finish off C and weave in ends.

Rows 13 through 16: With D, rep Rows 1 through 4, changing to A in last sc on Row 16. Finish off D and weave in ends.

Rep Rows 1 through 16 seven times more, then rep Rows 1 through 4 once more. Finish off and weave in ends.

#78 GARDEN PATH

Designed by Janie Herrin

SIZE
49" x 63" before border

MATERIALS
Worsted weight yarn,
   18 oz rose (A)
   30 oz off white (B)
   18 oz sage green (C)

Note: Photographed model made with Caron® Simply Soft® #9721 Victorian Rose (A), #9715 Fisherman (B) and #9705 Sage (C)

Size H (5mm) crochet hook
   (or size required for gauge)

GAUGE:
7 dc = 2"

7 round square = 7" x 7"

INSTRUCTIONS

Square (make 63)
With Color A, ch 5, join with sl st to form a ring.

Rnd 1 (right side): Ch 1, *in ring work (sc, ch 3, 2 tr, ch 3, sc, ch 2); rep from * 3 times more, join to beg sc; finish off: 4 petals made.

Beginning V-st: Ch 4 (equals first dc plus ch 1), dc in same st: beg V-st made.

V-st: (dc, ch 1, dc) in st or sp indicated: V-st made.

Rnd 2: Join Color B with sc in any ch-2 sp between petals; *ch 4, sc between trs of next petal, ch 4, sc in next ch-2 sp; rep from * around ending with sl st in beg sc.

Rnd 3: Work beg V-st in same sc; *ch 2, sc in next ch-4 lp, ch 2, sc in next sc, ch 2, sc in next ch-4 lp, ch 2, work V-st in next sc; rep from * around, ending with ch 2, sl st in 3rd ch of beg ch 4: 4 V-sts, 16 ch-2 sps; finish off Color B.

Rnd 4: Join Color C with sl st in ch-1 sp of any V-st, in same sp work (beg V-st, ch 2, V-st), *ch 1, skip next ch-2 sp, (3 hdc in next ch-2 sp, ch 1) twice, skip next ch-2 sp, in ch-1 sp of next V-st work (V-st, ch 2, V-st); rep from * around ending with sl st in 3rd ch of beg ch 4: 8 V-sts, 24 hdc.

Rnd 5: Turn, working this round on wrong side, sl st in ch-1 sp, in same sp work beg V-st; *ch 1, (skip 3 hdc, V-st in next ch-1 sp, ch 1) twice, skip next V-st, in ch-2 corner sp work (V-st, ch 2, V-st), ch 1, skip next V-st, V-st in next ch-1 sp; rep from * around ending with last ch-1, join in 3rd ch of beg ch-4; finish off Color C, turn.

Rnd 6: With right side facing, join Color B with sc in any ch-2 corner sp, 2 sc in same sp; *2 sc in ch-1 sp of next V-st, working behind next ch-1, 2 tr in ch-1 sp of V-st 2 rows below, 2 sc in sp of next V-st on Row 5; (working behind ch-1, skip next hdc, tr in each of next 2 hdc 2 rows below, 2 sc in sp of next V-st on Row 5) twice, working behind ch-1, 2 tr in sp of V-st 2 rows

below, 2 sc in sp of V-st on Row 5, 3 sc in ch-2 corner sp; rep from * around: 52 sc, 32 tr; join in beg sc; finish off Color B.

Rnd 7: Join Color A with sl st in center sc of any 3-sc corner group, ch 1 (does not count as a st), 3 hdc in same st, hdc in each st around working 3 hdc in rem corners, join to beg hdc; finish off Color A.

Rnd 8: Join Color B with sc in center hdc of any 3-hdc corner group, 2 more sc in same hdc; hdc in each hdc around, working 3 sc in center hdc of each corner group; join in beg sc, finish off Color B. Weave in all ends.

Joining

To join, hold two squares with right sides tog and sew together with overcast st through outer lps, along one side edge, carefully matching sts and corners. Join squares in 9 rows of 7 squares each.

Border

Rnd 1: Hold piece with right side facing and join Color A with sl st in center sc of 3-sc group at upper right corner; ch 1, 3 hdc in center st, hdc in each st around, working 3 hdc in each center sc of 3-sc corner groups; join in beg hdc.

Rnd 2: Sc in next hdc; *ch 4, sk next hdc, sc in next hdc; rep from * around, join; finish off, weave in all ends.

#79 CURLY O'S

Designed by Janie Herrin

SIZE
30" x 37 ¹/₂" before border

MATERIALS
Worsted weight yarn,
  12 oz multicolor
  8 oz bright orange

Note: Photographed model made with Red Heart® Kids™ #2935 Sherbert and Red Heart® Super Saver® #254 Pumpkin

Size H (5mm) crochet hook or
  size required for gauge

GAUGE
7 dc = 1 "

Square = 7 ¹/₂" x 7 ¹/₂"

INSTRUCTIONS

Square (make 20)
With orange, ch 5, join with sl st to a form ring.

Rnd 1: Ch 3 (equals first dc), 15 dc in ring, join with sl st in 3rd ch of beg ch-3: 16 dc.

Rnd 2: Ch 4 (equals first dc plus ch 1); *dc in next dc, ch 1; rep from * around, join in 3rd ch of beg ch 4.

Rnd 3: Ch 3, 2 dc in next ch-1 sp; *dc in next dc, 2 dc in next ch-1 sp; rep from * around, join: 48 dc.

Rnd 4: Ch 4, dc in next dc, ch 1; *skip next dc, work (dc in next dc, ch 1) twice; rep from * around, join in 3rd ch of beg ch 4.

Rnd 5: Ch 3, working in each dc and in each ch-1 sp, dc in each of next 15 sts; *ch 5, dc in each of next 16 sts; rep from * around, ch 5, join.

Rnd 6: Ch 3, dc in each of next 2 dc; *hdc in each of next 3 dc, sc in each of next 4 dc, hdc in each of next 3 dc, dc in each of next 3 dc; in next sp work (3 dc, ch 2, 3 dc), dc in each of next 3 dc; rep from *around ending with sl st in beg dc, finish off.

Rnd 7: Join multicolor yarn with sc in any corner sp, 2 sc in same sp, sc in each st around, working 3 sc in each rem corner; join in beg sc, finish off. Weave in ends.

Ruffles

First Ruffle

With right side facing you, join multicolor yarn with sc around post (vertical bar) of any dc on Rnd 2; (ch 2, sc) twice around same post; *ch 2, working from right to left, sc around next post on same rnd, (ch 2, sc) twice same post; rep from * around, working around each rem post of Rnd 2; join with sl st in beg ch-2. Finish off.

Second Ruffle

Working on Rnd 4, rep First Ruffle.

Joining

To join, hold two squares with right sides tog and with multicolor yarn, sew squares tog along one side with overcast stitches, working through outer lps only of each square. Join squares in 5 rows of 4 squares each.

Border

Rnd 1: Join multicolor yarn with sc in center sc of any 3-sc corner group, 2 sc in same st, sc in each st around working sc in joining between squares and 3 sc in rem corner sts, join in beg sc; finish off.

Rnd 2: Join orange with sc in any corner sc, ch 3, sc in same st, (ch 3, skip 2 sts, sc in next st) around working (sc, ch 3, sc) in rem corner sts, end with sl st in beg sc. (**Note:** *You may have to alter the number of skipped sts in order to work corners in corner sps.*)

Rnd 3: Sl st in next ch-3 lp, ch 1, (sc, ch 3, sc) in same lp, (ch 3, sc in next lp) around, working (sc, ch 3, sc) in rem corner lps, end with sl st in beg sc.

Rnd 4: Sl st in next lp, ch 3 (equals first dc), 6 dc in same sp; * ch 1, sc in next lp, ch 1, 5 dc in next lp; rep from * around working 7 dc in rem corner lps, end with sl st in beg dc, finish off, weave in ends.

#8 SWEET HEARTS

Designed by Diana Owen for Coats and Clark

SIZE
37" x 41" before fringe

MATERIALS
Sport weight yarn,
   25 oz lt pink

Note: *Photographed model made with Red Heart® Baby Sport Econo #1722 Light Pink*

Size F (3.75mm) crochet hook
   (or size required for gauge)

GAUGE
16 sc = 4"; 15 sc rows = 4"

INSTRUCTIONS

Square (make 48)

With green, ch 5, join with sl st to form a ring.

Rnd 1: Ch 3, 2 dc in ring, (ch 2, 3 dc in ring) 3 times, ch 2, join with sl st in 3rd ch of beg ch-3: 4 ch-2 sps.

Rnd 2: Ch 3, dc in next 2 dc; *5 dc in corner ch-2 sp, dc in next 3 dc; rep from * around ending with 5 dc in last ch-2 corner sp, join with sl st in 3rd ch of beg ch-3.

Rnd 3: Ch 3, dc in next 4 dc; * (dc, ch 2, dc) in next dc, dc in next 7 dc; rep from * around, ending with dc in last 2 dc, join as before.

Rnd 4: Ch 3, dc in next 5 dc; *5 dc in ch-2 corner sp, dc in next 9 dc; rep from * around ending with dc in last 3 dc, join, finish off.

Note: In following rnd you will work a Triple Post Cluster (TrPC) stitch that is worked in five steps, working around sts in rows below. As you work these sts, draw them up to the height of your working row, so that you do not distort the shape of the square. The TrPC really isn't so difficult as it appears in the instructions!

Rnd 5: Join white with sl st in 3rd dc of any corner 5-dc group, ch 1, 3 sc in same st, sc in next 6 dc; work Triple Post Cluster (TrPC) as follows: YO twice, insert hook from front to back around post of 3rd dc from corner on round 3, YO, pull yarn through: (4 lps on hook); (YO, draw through first 2 lps) twice; YO twice, insert hook as before around post of 5th dc of 5-dc group on Rnd 2, YO, pull yarn through: (5 lps on hook); (YO, draw through first 2 lps) twice; YO twice, insert hook as before around center dc of Rnd 1, YO, pull yarn through: (6 loops on hook); (YO, draw through first 2 lps) twice: (4 lps on hook); YO once, insert hook as before around last dc before 5-dc group on Rnd 2, YO, pull yarn through; (YO, draw through first 2 lps) twice: (4 lps on hook); YO once, insert hook as before around 3rd dc from next corner on Rnd 3, YO, pull yarn through; (YO, draw through first 2 lps) twice; YO and draw through all 4 lps on hook (TrPC made); ch 1, skip dc behind TrPC; *sc in next 6 dc, 3 sc in next dc, sc in next 6 dc; TrPC as before, skip dc behind cluster; rep from * around ending with sc in last 6 dc, join with sl st in beg sc.

Rnd 6: Ch 3; * in next st, work (2 dc, ch 2, 2 dc), dc in next 15 sts, (do not work in ch-1 sp that follows the TrPC); rep from * around, ending with dc in last 14 sts, join with sl st in 3rd ch of beg ch-3; finish off.

Continued on next page.

Rnd 7: Join green with sc in any ch-2 corner sp, 2 sc in same sp; *sc in next 19 dc, 3 sc in next corner ch-2 sp; rep from * around, join with sl st in beg sc.

Rnd 8: Ch 1, sc in same sc; * 3 sc in next sc, sc in 21 sc; rep from * around, ending with sc in last 20 sc, join with sl st in beg sc; finish off.

Joining

To join, hold two squares with right sides tog and with green sew with overcast st along one edge through back lps only, carefully matching sts and corners. In same manner join squares in 8 rows of 6 squares each.

Border

Rnd 1: Hold afghan with right side facing you; join green with sc in upper right corner, 2 sc in same sp; sc evenly around outer edges, adjusting sts as needed to keep work flat, and working 3 sc in each rem outer corner sp; join with sl st in beg sc. Finish off green.

Rnd 2: Join white with sc in center sc of any 3-sc corner group; *ch 2, sk 2 sc, sc in next sc; rep from * around, ending ch 2, sl st in beg ch-2 sp.

Rnd 3: Ch 3 (counts as first dc of rnd), 4 dc in same sp; *sc in next sc, 5 dc in next ch-2 sp; rep from * around, ending with sc in last sp, join in 3rd ch of beg ch-3.

Rnd 4: Ch 3, dc in next dc, 3 dc in next dc, dc in next 2 dc; *sc in next sc, dc in next 2 dc, 3 dc in next dc, dc in next 2 dc; rep from * around, join in 3rd ch of beg ch-3. Finish off white.

Rnd 5: Join green with sl st in last st; ch 3, sc in next 7 dc, dc in next sc; *sc in next 7 dc, dc in next sc; rep from * around, join, finish off. Weave in all ends.

#8 ROSE GARDEN

Designed by Rita Weiss for Coats and Clark

SIZE
52" x 65" before border

MATERIALS
Worsted weight yarn,
  68 oz red

Note: *Photographed model made with Red Heart® Plush™ #9907 Red*

Size G (4mm) crochet hook,
  or size required for gauge

GAUGE
Square = 6 1/2" x 6 1/2"

Back post single crochet (BPsc): Insert hook from back to front to back around post of stitch indicated, draw up a lp, YO and draw through 2 lps on hook: BPsc made.

INSTRUCTIONS

Square A (make 40)

Ch 4, join with a sl st to form a ring.

Rnd 1 (right side): Ch 3 (counts as a dc on this and following rnds), 11 dc in ring; join in 3rd ch of beg ch-3: 12 dc.

Rnd 2: Ch 2 (counts as a hdc), hdc in same ch as joining; 2 hdc in each dc, join in 2nd ch of beg ch-2: 24 hdc.

Rnd 3: Ch 1, sc in same ch as joining; (ch 5, skip next 2 hdc, sc in next hdc) 7 times, ch 5, join in beg sc: 8 ch-5 sps.

Rnd 4: Sl st in next ch-5 sp, ch 1, in same sp work (sc, hdc, 5 dc, hdc, sc): petal made; in each rem ch-5 sp work (sc, hdc, 5 dc, hdc, sc); join in back lp of first sc: 8 petals.

Rnd 5: Ch 5, working behind petals of prev rnd, BPsc around next sc on Rnd 3; (ch 5, BPsc around next sc on Rnd 3) 6 times, ch 5, do not join: 8 ch-5 sps.

Rnd 6: Sl st in next ch-5 sp, ch 1; in same sp work (sc, hdc, 7dc, hdc, sc): 7-dc petal made; in each rem ch-5 sp work (sc, hdc, 7dc, hdc, sc); join in back lp of first sc: 8 petals.

Rnd 7: Ch 7, working behind petals of prev rnd, BPsc around next sc on Rnd 5; (ch 7, BPsc around next sc on Rnd 5) 6 times, ch 7, do not join: 8 ch-7 sps.

Rnd 8: Sl st in next ch-7 sp, ch 1, in same sp work (sc, hdc, 9dc, hdc, sc): 9-dc petal made; in each rem ch-7 sp work (sc, hdc, 9dc, hdc, sc); join in first sc.

Rnd 9: Ch 7 (counts as a dc and a ch-4 sp), skip next 5 sts, in next dc work (dc, ch 4, dc): corner made; * † ch 4, skip next 6 sts, dc in next sc, ch 4, skip next 5 sts, sc in next dc, ch 4 †; skip next 6 sts, dc in next sc, ch 4, skip next 5 sts, in next dc work (dc, ch 4, dc); rep from * twice more, then rep from † to † once; join in 3rd ch of beg ch-7.

Rnd 10: Sl st in next ch-4 sp, ch 3 (counts as a dc), 3 dc in same sp; ch 1, in next corner ch-4 sp work (2 dc, ch 3, 2 dc): corner made; * † ch 1, 4 dc in next ch-4 sp; ch 1, (3 hdc in next ch-4 sp, ch 1) twice †; 4 dc in next ch-4 sp; ch 1, in next corner ch-4 sp work (2 dc, ch 3, 2 dc); rep from * twice more, then rep from † to † once; join in 3rd ch of beg ch-3.

Rnd 11: Ch 1, sc in same ch as joining, sc in next 3 dc, sc in next ch-1 sp and in next 2 dc; * 5 sc in next corner ch-3 sp: sc corner made; sc in each st and in each ch-1 sp to next corner ch-3 sp; rep from * twice more; 5 sc in next corner ch-3 sp; sc in each st and in each ch-1 sp to first sc; join in first sc.

Finish off and weave in ends.

Square B (make 40)

Ch 4, join with a sl st to form a ring.

Rnds 1 and 2: Work same as Square A.

Rnd 3: Ch 1, sc in same ch as joining; (ch 7, skip next 2 sc, sc in next sc) 7 times, ch 7, do not join: 8 ch-7 sps.

Rnds 4 through 7: Rep Rnds 8 through 11 of Square A.

Note: Although Square B has 4 fewer rnds than Square A, it is actually the same size; the added rnds on Square A are the lps in which the petals are formed, and do not add to the size.

Finish off and weave in ends.

Joining

Beginning with Square A, and alternating Squares A and B, arrange squares in 10 rows of 8 squares. To join squares, hold 2 squares with right sides tog. Carefully matching sts and corners, sew with overcast st through both lps of each square across one side, beginning and ending with one corner st. Join squares in rows; then sew rows together in same manner, alternating beginning squares to form a checkerboard pattern, being sure that all four corner junctions are firmly joined.

Edging

Rnd 1: With right side facing, join yarn in 3rd sc of any outer corner; *3 sc in center corner st, sc in each sc along sides to next outer corner; rep from * around, adjusting sts as needed to keep work flat; join with sl in beg sc.

Rnd 2: Ch 3, skip 1 st, sc in next st; rep from * around, join, finish off.

#84 SOFT SHADES

Designed by Patons Design Staff

SIZE
44" x 63"

MATERIALS
Worsted weight yarn,
   31 $^1/_2$ oz variegated (MC)
   and
   31 $^1/_2$ oz lavender (A)

Note: Photographed model made with Patons® Décor #16230 First Spring (MC) and #1625 Pale Aubergine (A)

36" Size 10 $^1/_2$ (6.5mm) circular knitting needle (or size required for gauge)

GAUGE
14 sts = 4" with two strands
   held tog in stockinette st
   (knit one row, purl one row)

20 rows = 4" with two strands
   held tog in stockinette st

INSTRUCTIONS

With with one strand of each color held tog, CO 143 sts; do not join, work back and forth in rows.

Bottom Border

Rows 1 through 6: Knit

Row 7: Knit, increasing 6 sts evenly spaced across row: 149 sts.

Body

Row 1 (right side): K3, *K1, (Pl, K11, K1) 5 times, P1; rep from * to last 14 sts, K14.

Row 2: K3, *P11, (K1, P1) 5 times, K1; rep from * to last 14 sts. P11, K3.

Row 3: K3, *P12, (K1, P1) 5 times; rep from * to last 14 sts, P11, K3.

Row 4: Rep Row 2.

Row 5: Rep Row 1.

Row 6: K3; *K12, (P1, K1) 5 times; rep from * to last 14 sts, K14.

Rows 7 through 12: Rep Rows 1 through 6.

Rows 13 and 14: Rep Rows 1 and 2.

Row 15: K3, *(P1, K1) 5 times, P1, K11; rep from * to last 14 sts, (P1, K1) 5 times, P1, K3.

Row 16: K3, *(K1, P1) 5 times, K1, P11; rep from * to last 14 sts, (K1, P1) 5 times, K4.

Row 17: K3, *(P1, K1) 5 times, P12; rep from * to last 14 sts, (P1, K1) 5 times, P1, K3.

Row 18: Rep Row 16.

Row 19: Rep Row 15.

Row 20: K3, *(K1, P1) 5 times, K12; rep from * to last 14 sts, (K1, P1) 5 times, K4.

Rows 21 through 26: Rep Rows 15 through 20.

Rows 27 and 28: Rep Rows 15 and 16.

These 28 rows form patt.

Rep Rows 1 through 28 until piece measures about 63", ending by working either a Row 14 or Row 28.

Top Border

Row 1: Knit, dec 6 sts evenly spaced across row: 143 sts.

Rows 2 through 7: Knit. BO as to knit.

#85 BLUE IS FOR BOYS

Designed by Janie Herrin

SIZE
30" x 42"

MATERIALS
Worsted weight yarn,
  6 oz navy
  12 oz lt blue

Note: *Photographed model made with Caron Simply Soft #9711 Dk Country Blue (navy) #99712 Soft Blue (lt blue)*

Size H (5mm) crochet hook
  (or size required for gauge)

GAUGE
7 dc = 2"

Square = 6" x 6"

INSTRUCTIONS

Square (make 35)

For center block, with navy, ch 14, dc in 8th ch from hook; (ch 2, skip 2 chs, dc in next ch) twice, ch 5, turn; * (dc in next dc, ch 2) twice, skip 2 chs, dc in next ch; ** ch 5, turn; rep from * to **: 9 sps.

Rnd 1 (right side): Ch 1, turn; working around outer edges of center block, 5 sc in first sp, (4 sc in next sp, 9 sc in next sp) 3 times; (4 sc in next sp) twice, join in beg sc: 52 sc.

Rnd 2: Ch 1, in same st work (sc, ch 3, sc): first corner made; *ch 3, skip 4 sc, sc in each of next 4 sc, ch 3, skip 4 sc, in next sc work (sc, ch 3, sc); rep from * around ending with ch 3, skip last 4 sc, join in beg sc, finish off navy.

Rnd 3: Join lt blue with slip st in any corner ch-3 sp, ch 5, dc in same sp; ch 2, V-st in same sp; *3 dc in ch-3 sp, ch 3, sk 4 sc, 3 dc in next ch-3 sp, in corner ch-3 sp work (V-st, ch 2, V-st); rep from * around, ending with sl st in 3rd ch of beg ch-5; finish off lt blue.

Rnd 4: Join navy with sc in any corner ch-2 sp, ch 3, sc in same sp; *2 sc in ch-2 sp of V-st, sk next dc, sc in next 3 dc; working in front of ch-3 sp, dc in each of 4 sc 2 rows below, sc in next 3 dc, 2 sc in sp of next V-st; in corner ch-2 sp work (sc, ch 3, sc); rep from * around, ending with sl st in beg sc. Finish off navy.

Rnd 5: Join lt blue with sl st in any ch-3 corner sp; ch 6 (counts as a dc and ch-3 sp), dc in same sp; *sk next sc, dc in next 5 sc; FPdc around each of next 4 dc on row below, dc in next 5 sc; sk next sc, (dc, ch 3, dc) in next ch-3 corner sp; rep from * around, ending join with sl st in 3rd ch of beg ch-6.

Rnd 6: 3 sc in ch-3 sp, sc in each dc around, working 3 sc in each ch-3 corner sp; finish off, weave in ends.

Joining

To join squares, hold two squares with right sides tog and with lt blue sew tog with overcast st across one side, carefully matching sts and corners. Then join in same manner in 7 rows of 5 squares each

Border

Rnd 1: Hold afghan with right side facing you; join navy yarn with sc in ch sp at upper right corner, 2 sc in same sp; work sc evenly around outer edge, adjusting sts to keep work flat, and work 3 sc in each outer corner sp; join with sl st to beg sc, finish off navy.

Rnd 2: Join lt blue yarn with sl st in center sc of beg 3-sc corner group; ch 2, 3 hdc in same sc; hdc in each sc around, and work 3 hdc in center sc of each 3-sc corner sp, finish off lt blue.

Rnd 3: Join navy yarn with sc in center hdc of beg corner group, 2 sc in same hdc; complete rnd as for Rnd 1. Weave in ends.

#86 SOPHISTICATED SUMMER

SIZE
53" x 66"

MATERIALS
Worsted weight yarn,
26 oz off white (A)
26 oz black (B)

Note: Photographed model made with Red Heart® Super Saver® #313 Aran (A) and #312 Black (B)

Size H (5mm) crochet hook (or size required for gauge)

GAUGE
13 sts = 4" in patt

16 rows = 4" in patt

To change color: Work st until 2 lps rem on hook, drop old color, pick up new color and draw through both lps on hook, cut dropped color.

INSTRUCTIONS

With A, ch 173.

Row 1 (right side): Sc in 2nd ch from hook and in next 3 chs; *dc in next 4 chs, sc in next 4 chs; rep from * across: 172 sts; ch 1, turn.

Row 2: Sc in first 4 sc; *dc in next 4 dc, sc in next 4 sc; rep from * across, changing to B in last sc; ch 3, turn. Finish off A and weave in ends.

Row 3: With B, skip first sc, dc in next 3 sc; *sc in next 4 dc, dc in next 4 sc; rep from * across; ch 3, turn.

Row 4: Skip first dc, dc in next 3 dc; *sc in next 4 sc, dc in next 4 dc; rep from * across working last dc in 3rd ch of ch-3 and changing to A; ch 1, turn. Finish off B and weave in ends.

Row 5: With A, sc in first 4 dc; *dc in next 4 sc, sc in next 4 dc; rep from * across working last sc in 3rd ch of ch-3; ch 1, turn.

Rep Rows 2 through 5 until piece measures about 66" long, ending by working a Row 5.

Last Row: Sc in first 4 sc; *dc in next 4 dc, sc in next 4 sc; rep from * across. Finish off; weave in ends.

Fringe

Following Single Knot Fringe instructions on page 221, cut strands of A and B 14" long. Knot 3 strands of A in each dc and 3 strands of B in each sc across top and bottom edges of afghan.

#87 FLOWER POWER

Designed by Janie Herrin

SIZE
42" x 56" before border

MATERIALS
Worsted weight yarn,
   3 oz red (A)
   9 oz green (B)
   9 oz off white (C)

Note: Photographed model made with Caron Simply Soft #9729 Red (A), #9705 Sage(B),and #9715 Fisherman (C)

Size H (5mm) crochet hook
   (or size required for gauge)

GAUGE
7 dc =2"

Square = 7" x 7"

INSTRUCTIONS

Square (make 48)

With Color A, ch 5, join with a sl st to form a ring.

Rnd 1: Ch 2 (does not count as a st), 16 hdc in ring, join with sl st in beg hdc: 16 hdc.

Rnd 2: Ch 1, for petal work (sc, ch 2, dc, ch 2, sc) in same st; *sk next hdc, in next hdc work (sc, ch 2, dc, ch 2, sc); rep from * around, join with sl st in beg sc: 8 petals made; finish off Color A.

Rnd 3: Working behind petals, join Color B with sl st in back of any hdc on Rnd 1, ch 3 (equals first dc), dc in same st, 2 dc in back of each rem hdc (worked and unworked), join in 3rd ch of beg ch-3: 32 dc.

Rnd 4: Ch 3, in same st work (2 dc, ch 2, 3 dc): beg corner made; *sk 3 dc, 3 dc in next dc, 3 dc; in next dc work (3 dc, ch 2, 3 dc): corner made; rep from * around ending sk 3 dc, dc in last 3 dc, join; finish off Color B.

Rnd 5: Join Color C with sl st in any corner ch-2 sp, ch 3, (2 dc, ch 2, 3 dc) in same sp; *(3 dc in sp between next 3-dc groups) twice, in next ch sp work corner as in Rnd 4; rep from * around, join to beg ch-3: 48 dc.

Rnd 6: Sl st in next 2 dc and into ch-2 lp, ch 1, (sc, ch 3, sc) in same lp; *(ch 3, sc in sp between next 3-dc groups) 3 times, ch 3, in corner sp work (sc, ch 3, sc); rep from * around, ending with sc in last sp before corner, ch 3, join; ch 3, pull up a lp and drop yarn, do not cut: 20 ch-3 lps.

Rnd 7: Join Color B with sl st in any corner lp, work beg corner as on Rnd 4; *(3 dc in next ch-3 lp) 4 times, work corner in corner ch-3 lp; rep from * around, ending with sl st in beg dc: 72 dc; finish off Color B.

Rnd 8: Pick up Color C lp from Rnd 6, sl st in nearest dc, ch 2, hdc in each dc around, working (2 hdc, ch 2, 2 hdc) in corner sps; at end of rnd, join; finish off. Weave in ends.

Joining

To join squares, hold two squares with right sides tog and with Color C, sew tog along one side, carefully matching sts and corners; join into rows in same manner, having 8 rows of 6 squares each.

Border

Rnd 1: Hold piece with right side facing you and one short end at top. Join Color B with a sl st in outer corner ch-2 sp at upper right. Work 3 sc in ch-2 sp; sc evenly around, working 3 sc in each outer corner and adjusting sts to keep work flat. At end, join with sl st in first sc.

Rnd 2: * Ch 3, sk next sc, sc in next sc; rep from * around; join, finish off.

#88 A WALK IN THE WOODS

SIZE
35" x 49" before border

MATERIALS
Worsted weight yarn,
  21 oz off white (A)
  9 oz brown (B)
  9 oz green (C)

Note: Photographed model made with Lion Brand® Wool-Ease® #099 Fisherman(A), #127 Mink (B), and #177 Loden (C)

Size I (5.5mm) crochet hook
  (or size required for gauge)

GAUGE
Square = 7" x 7"

INSTRUCTIONS

Square (make 35)

With A, ch 3; join with a sl st to form a ring.

Rnd 1: Ch 3 (counts as first dc), 2 dc in ring, ch 1, (3 dc in ring, ch 1) 3 times; join with sl st in 3rd ch of beg ch-3; finish off A.

Rnd 2: Join B in any ch-1 sp; ch 3, (2 dc, ch 1, 3 dc) in same sp: beg corner made, ch 1; *(3 dc, ch 1, 3 dc) in next sp for corner, ch 1; rep from * twice more: 4 corners made; join as before.

Rnd 3: Sl st to first ch-1 corner sp, work beg corner in same sp; *ch 1, 3 dc in next ch-1 sp, ch 1, work corner in next corner ch-1 sp; rep from * around ending ch 1, 3 dc in next ch-1 sp, ch 1, join; finish off B.

Rnd 4: Join A in any ch-1 corner sp; work beg corner in same sp; *ch 1, (3 dc in next ch-1 sp, ch 1) to next corner, corner in corner; rep from * around, work last side in same manner, join, finish off A.

Rnd 5: Join C in any corner sp; *work beg corner, ch 1, work (3 dc, ch 1) in each ch-1 sp to next corner sp; repeat from * around, work last side in same manner, join; finish off C.

Rnd 6: Join A in any corner sp; work same as Rnd 5, join, finish off and weave in all ends.

Joining

Hold two squares tog and join along one side with overcast st and A, sewing through BLO of each square, carefully matching sts and corners. Then join in 7 rows of 5 squares each.

Border

Rnd 1: Hold piece with right side facing and join A with a sl st in ch-1 sp at any outer corner; in same sp work beg corner; † * ch 1, (3 dc, ch 1) in each ch-1 sp to next corner of same square, dc in corner sp of same square, dc in joining, dc in corner sp of next square (3-dc group made at joining); rep from * to next afghan corner, (3 dc, ch 1, 3 dc) in corner ch-1 sp; rep from † around, work last side in same manner; join; finish off off A.

Rnd 2: Join C in any ch-1 corner sp, work beg corner in same sp; *ch 1, (3-dc, ch 1) in each sp to next corner, corner in corner; rep from * around, work last side in same manner, join; finish off C.

Rnd 3: Join A in any ch-1 corner sp; work as for Rnd 2, join, finish off, weave in all ends.

#89 DAISIES WON'T TELL LAPGHAN

SIZE
30" x 30"

MATERIALS
Worsted weight yarn,
  7 oz natural
  11 oz pale green
  7 oz med green

Note: Photographed model made with Bernat® Berella® "4" #01010, Soft Heather (natural), #01244 Soft Forest Green (pale green), and #01235 Soft Green (med green

Size G (4mm) crochet hook
  (or size required for gauge)

GAUGE
Square = 4" x 4"

INSTRUCTIONS

Square (make 49)

With natural, ch 4, join with a sl st to form a ring.

Rnd 1: Ch 1, 8 sc in ring, join with sl st in first sc.

Rnd 2: Draw lp on hook up to 1" high, (YO, insert hook in same sc and draw up a 1" lp) 3 times, YO and draw through all 7 lps on hook: beg petal made; *ch 3, (YO, insert hook in next sc and draw up a 1" lp) 3 times, YO and draw through all 7 lps on hook: petal made; rep from * 6 times more, ch 3, join with sl st in top of beg petal: 8 petals made; finish off.

Rnd 3: Join med green with sl st in any ch-3 sp, ch 3 (counts as a dc), 4 dc in same sp: first corner made; *4 dc in next ch-3 sp, 5 dc in next ch-3 sp: corner made; rep from * twice more, 4 dc in last ch-3 lp, join with sl st in 3rd ch of beg ch-3. Finish off.

Rnd 4: Join pale green with sl st in center dc of any 5-dc group, ch 3, 4 dc in same dc; *dc in each dc to center dc of next 5-dc corner group, 5 dc in center dc; rep from * around, ending last rep with dc in rem dc, join in 3rd ch of beg ch-3; finish off.

Joining

To join, hold two squares with right sides tog and with pale green sew through outer lps only of each st, carefully matching sts and corner spaces. Join squares in 7 rows of 7 squares each.

Edging

Row 1: Hold piece with right side facing you and join pale green in upper right corner with sc; 2 sc in same sp; sc evenly around afghan, adjusting sts as needed to keep work flat, and working 3 sc in rem outer corner sps; join in beg sc, finish off.

Row 2: Join natural in any sc; *ch 3, sk next 2 sc, sc in next sc; rep from * around, ending ch 3, join in beg sc; finish off.

#90 MESH'IN AROUND

Designed by Janie Herrin

SIZE
50 3/4" x 65 1/4" before border

MATERIALS
Worsted weight yarn,
  12 oz orange (A)
  20 oz medium brown (B)
  20 oz dk brown (C)

Note: Photographed model made with Red Heart® Super Saver® #354 Vibrant Orange A), #336 Warm Brown (B), and #365 Coffee (C)

Size H (5mm) crochet hook
  (or size required for gauge)

GAUGE
7 dc = 2"

Square = 7 1/4" x 7 1/4"

INSTRUCTIONS

Square (make 63 squares)

With Color A, ch 6, join with sl st to form a ring.

Rnd 1: Ch 3 (equals first dc), 15 dc in ring, join: with sl st in 3rd ch of beg ch-3: 16 dc.

Rnd 2: Ch 1, sc in same st; *ch 2, sc in next dc, rep from * around, ending ch 2, join in beg sc: 16 ch-2 sps.

Rnd 3: Sl st in next sp, ch 1, sc in same sp; *ch 2, sc in next sp; rep from * around, ending ch 2, join in beg sc.

Rnd 4: Sl st in next sp, ch 1, sc in same sp; *ch 3, sc in next sp; rep from * around, ending ch 3, join in beg sc: 16 ch-3 sps; finish off Color A

Rnd 5: Join Color B with sc in any ch-3 sp; *ch 4, sc in next sp; rep from * around, ending ch 4, join in beg sc: 16 ch-4 sps.

Rnd 6: Sl st in next sp, ch 3 (equals first dc), (2 dc, ch 2, 3 dc) in same sp; *ch 1, 3 hdc in next sp, ch 1, 3 sc in next sp, ch 1, 3 hdc in next sp, ch 1; in next sp work (3 dc, ch 2, 3 dc); rep from * around ending with sl st in beg dc: 24 dc, 24 hdc, 12 sc.

Rnd 7: Ch 3, dc in each of next 2 dc; *in corner ch-2 sp work (2 dc, ch 3, 2 dc); dc in each of next 3 dc, dc in ch-1 sp, (ch 3, skip 3 sts, dc in next ch-1 sp) 3 times, dc in each of next 3 dc; rep from *around, ending with sl st in beg ch-3: 56 dc, 16 ch-3 sps; finish off Color B.

Rnd 8: Join Color C with sl st in any corner ch-3 sp, ch 2, (hdc, ch 2, 2 hdc) in same sp; *hdc in each of next 6 dc; (2 hdc in next sp, hdc in dc) twice, 2 hdc in next sp, hdc in each of next 6 dc; in corner sp work (2 hdc, ch 2, 2 hdc); rep from * around ending with sl st in beg hdc.

Rnd 9: Sl st in next hdc and into ch-2 corner sp; 3 sc in same sp; sc in each st around, working 3 sc in each rem corner sp, join in beg sc; finish off Color C. Weave in ends.

Joining

To join, hold two squares with right sides tog and sew together with overcast st through outer lps, along one side edge, carefully matching sts and corners. Join squares in 9 rows of 7 squares each.

Border

Rnd 1: Hold piece with right side facing you; join Color A in center sc of 3-sc group in upper right corner; ch 1, 3 sc in same st; sc in each st around, working 3 sc in each outer corner; join to beg sc; finish off Color A.

Rnd 2: Join Color B in center sc of any 3-sc corner group; ch 1, 3 sc in same sc; sc in each sc around, working 3 sc in center sc of each outer corner; finish off Color B.

Rnd 3: Join Color C with sc in center sc of any 3-sc corner group, 2 sc in same sc; sc in each sc around, working 3 sc in center sc of each outer corner; finish off Color C, weave in ends.

#91 CABLED CLASSIC

SIZE
46" x 60"

MATERIALS
Worsted weight yarn,
  48 oz off white

Note: Photographed model made with Red Heart® Super Saver® #313 Aran

29" Size 10 1/2 (6.5 mm) circular knitting needle

Cable needle

GAUGE
20 sts = 4" in Cable Patt

37 rows = 8"

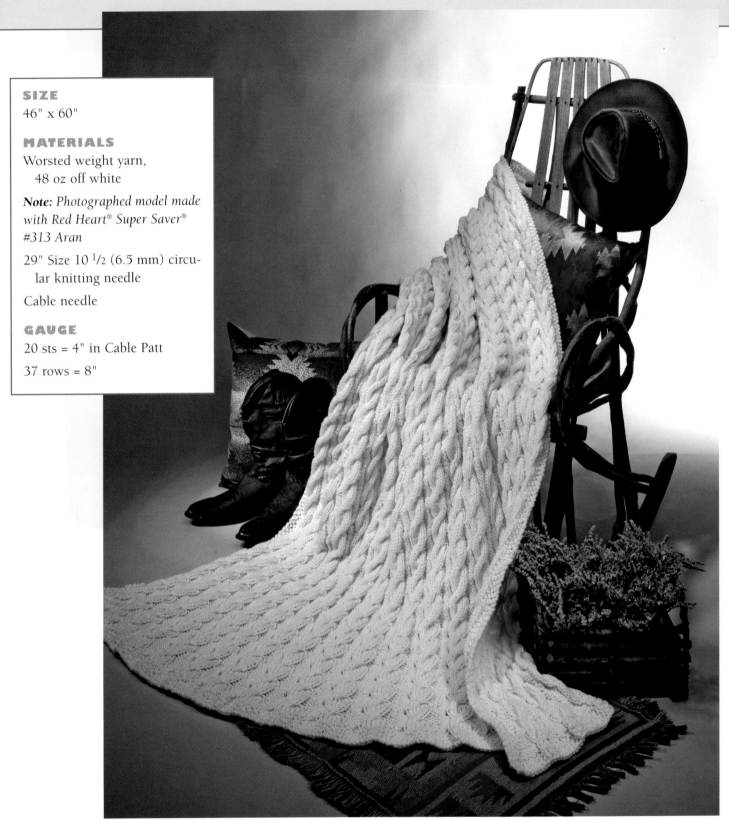

C6B: Sl next 3 sts onto a cable needle and leave at back of work, K3, then K3 from cable needle: C6B made.

INSTRUCTIONS

CO 230 sts; do not join; work back and forth in rows.

Row 1 (right side): *K1, P1; rep from * across.

Row 2: *P1, K1; rep from * across.

Rows 3 and 5: Rep Row 1.

Rows 4 and 6: Rep Row 2.

Row 7: (K1, P1) twice, K6; * P6, K6; rep from * to last 4 sts; (K1, P1) twice.

Row 8: (P1, K1) twice, P6; * K6, P6; rep from * to last 4 sts; (P1, K1) twice.

Row 9: (K1, P1) twice; C6B; * P6, C6B; rep from *to last 4 sts; (K1, P1) twice.

Rows 10 and 12: Rep Row 8.

Rows 11 and 13: Rep Row 7.

Row 14: (Pl, K1) twice, P6; * C6B, P6; rep from * to last 4 sts; (P1, K1) twice.

Row 15: Rep Row 7.

Row 16: Rep Row 8.

Rep Rows 7 through 16 until piece measures about 59" from beg, ending by working a Row 15.

Border

Row 1: Rep Row 2.

Rows 2 and 4: Rep Row 1.

Row 3 and 5: Rep Row 2.

Row 6: Rep Row 1.

Finish off, weave in ends.

#92 EMBOSSED FLORAL

Designed by Janie Herrin

SIZE
35" x 49" before border

MATERIALS
Worsted weight yarn,
  31 /2 oz gold
  7 oz medium rose
  25 oz light rose
  14 oz dark green

Note: Photographed model made with Bernat® Berella® "4 " #08886 Light Tapestry Gold, #08816 Med Antique Rose, #08814 Pale Antique Rose, and #01243 Forest Green

Size H (5mm) crochet hook
  (or size required for gauge)

GAUGE
7 dc = 2"

Square = 7" x 7"

INSTRUCTIONS

Square (make 35)

With gold, ch 5, join with sl st to form a ring.

Rnd 1: Ch 3 (equals first dc), in ring, work 2 dc, (ch 1, 3 dc) 3 times, ch 1, join with sl st in 3rd ch of beg ch-3: 12 dc and 4 ch-1 corner sps, finish off.

Rnd 2: Join medium rose with sc in center dc of any 3-dc group, *ch 5, sc in next ch-1 sp, ch 5, skip next dc, sc in next dc; rep from * around ending with sl st in beg sc: 8 ch-5 lps.

Rnd 3: Sl st in next ch-5 lp, ch 1, 7 sc in same lp; 7 sc in each rem lp around, join in beg sc, finish off.

Rnd 4: Join lt rose with sc in center sc of any 7-sc group, ch 7; *sc in center sc of next 7-sc group, ch 7; rep from * around, join in beg sc.

Rnd 5: Sl st in next ch-7 lp, ch 3, in same lp work (4 dc, ch 2, 5 dc); 7 sc in next lp; *in next lp work (5 dc, ch 2, 5 dc), 7 sc in next lp; rep from * around, join.

Rnd 6: Sl st in next dc, ch 4 (equals first dc plus ch 1), skip next dc, dc in next dc; *ch 1, (3 dc, ch 2, 3 dc) in next lp, (ch 1, skip next st, dc in next st) 8 times; rep from * around ending with (ch 1, skip next st, dc in next st) 6 times, ch 1, join, finish off.

Rnd 7: Join green with slip st in any corner sp, ch 2, in same sp work (hdc, ch 2, 2 hdc), *hdc in each of next 3 dc, (2 hdc in sp, hdc in next sp) 4 times, 2 hdc in next sp, hdc in each of next 3 dc, in corner sp work (2 hdc, ch 2, 2 hdc); rep from * around ending with sl st in 2nd ch of beg ch-2.

Rnd 8: Ch 1, sc in next hdc, 3 sc in ch-2 sp; sc in each st around, working 3 sc in each rem outer ch-2 sp; join, finish off.

Joining

To join, hold two squares with right sides tog and with green sew with overcast st through outer lps only along one side, carefully matching sts and corners. In same manner, continue joining in 7 rows of 5 squares each.

Border

Rnd 1: Hold afghan with right side facing you and join green with sl st in any outer corner center sc, 3 sc in same sc; sc in each st and joining around, adjusting sts to keep work flat, and working 3 sc in each rem out corner center sc; finish off green.

Rnd 2: Join lt rose in center sc of 3-sc group in any outer corner sp; 3 sc in same sp; sc in each sc around, working 3 sc in each rem outer corner sp; join in beg sc.

Rnd 3: Sl st in next sc; (ch 3, 3 dc, ch 3, 4 dc) in same sc; *sk next 2 sc, 4 dc in next sc; rep from * to next corner 3-sc group, in center sc work (4 dc, ch 3, 4 dc); rep from * around, join in 3rd ch of beg ch-3.

Rnd 4: Sl st in next dc, (ch 4, dc) in same dc; *(dc, ch 1, dc) in next dc; rep from * around, working (dc, ch 1, dc) twice in each ch-3 corner sp; join in 3rd ch of beg ch-4.

Rnd 5: *Sc in next ch-1 sp, ch 5, sc in next ch-1 sp, ch 10; rep from * around, join in beg sc. Finish off, weave in ends.

#9B SUMMER NIGHT PATCHWORK

Designed by Pattons Design Staff

SIZE
53" x 67"

MATERIALS
Worsted weight yarn,
   17 $^1/_2$ oz variegated (MC)
   21 oz med blue (A)
   21 oz pale blue (B)

Note: *Photographed model made with Pattons® Décor #16220 Cape Cod Variegated (MC), #1622 Rich Country Blue (A) and #1620 Pale Country Blue (B)*

14" Size 7 (4.5mm) knitting needles (or size required for gauge)

36" Size 7 (4.5mm) circular knitting needle

Cable needle

GAUGE
20 sts = 4" in stockinette st (knit 1 row, purl 1 row)

26 rows = 4" in stockinette st

INSTRUCTIONS

Note: Afghan is made of 7 strips, each worked vertically. Each strip includes three different pattern stitches: Color Box Patttern A, Color Box Patttern B, and Slip Stitch Patttern. Strips are sewn together, then side, top and bottom edgings are added.

Strip 1 (make 2)
Color Box Patttern A

With B, cast on 18 sts, with A, cast on 18 sts: 36 sts.

**Row 1 (right side): With A, K18, with B, K18.

Row 2: With B, P18, with A, P18.

Rows 3 through 24: Rep Rows 1 and 2 in sequence.

Row 25: With MC, K18, with A, K18.

Row 26: With A, P18, with MC, P18.

Rows 27 through 48: Rep Rows 25 and 26 in sequence 11 times more.

These 48 rows form Color Box Patt A.

Slip Stitch Patttern

Note: Sl all sl sts as to purl.

Row 1 (right side): With B, K4, (M1, K4) 8 times: 44 sts; cut color B.

Row 2: With MC, P1, PW, P4, *(PW) twice, P4; rep from * to last 2 sts, PW, P1; cut MC.

Row 3: With B, K1, sl 1, drop extra lp, K4; *(sl 1, drop extra lp) twice, K4; rep from * to last 2 sts, sl 1, drop extra lp, K1.

Row 4: P1, sl 1, P4; *(sl 1) twice, P4; rep from * to last 2 sts, sl 1, P1.

Row 5: K1, sl 1, K4, *(sl 1) twice, K4; rep from * to last 2 sts, sl 1, K1.

Row 6: Rep Row 4.

Row 7: K1, *C3F, C3B; rep from * to last st, K1; finish off B.

Rep Rows 2 through 7 six times more.

Next row: With B, P4, (P2tog, P3) 8 times: 36 sts; finish off B.

Color Box Patttern B

Row 1 (right side): With A, K18, with B, K18.

Row 2: With B, P18, with A, P18.

Rows 3 through 24: Rep Rows 1 and 2 in sequence 11 times more.

Row 25 (right side): With B, K18, with MC, K18.

Row 26: With MC, P18, with B, P18.

Rows 27 through 48: Rep Rows 25 and 26 in sequence 11 times more.

These 48 rows form Color Patt B.

Next Row: With A, K4, (M1, K4) 8 times: 44 sts; finish off color A.

Rep Rows 2 through 7 of Slip Stitch Patt 7 times, substituting A for B.

Continued on next page.

Next row: With A, P4, (P2tog, P3) 8 times: 36 sts; finish off A.**

Rep from ** (Row 1 of Color Box Patttern A) to ** once more.

Work 48 rows of Color Box Patt A, BO. Weave in all ends.

Strip I is now completed.

Strip II (make 2)

With B, cast on 36 sts

***Row 1 (right side):** K4, (M1, K4) 8 times: 44 sts; finish off B.

Rep Rows 2 through 7 of Slip Stitch Patt 7 times.

Next Row: With B, P4, (P2tog, P3) 8 times: 36 sts; finish off B.

Work 48 rows of Color Box Patt A.

Next Row (right side): With A, K4, (Ml, K4} 8 times: 44 sts; finish off A.

Rep Rows 2 through 7 of Slip Stitch Patt 7 times, substituting A for B.

Next Row (wrong side): With A, P4, (P2tog, P3) 8 times: 36 sts; finish off A.

Work 48 rows of Color Box Patt B.***

Rep from ***(Row 1 of Strip II) to *** once more.

Next Row (right side): With A, K4, (M1, K4) 8 times: 44 sts; finish off A.

Rep Rows 2 through 7 of Slip Stitch Patt 7 times substituting A for B.

Next Row: With A, P4, (P2tog, P3) 8 times: 36 sts; BO, weave in ends.

Strip II is now completed.

Strip III (make 2)

With B, cast on 18 sts, with A, cast on 18 sts: 36 sts.

†Work 48 rows of Color Box Patt B.

Next Row: With A, K4, (M1, K4) 8 times: 44 sts; finish off A.

Rep Rows 2 though 7 of Slip Stitch Patt 7 times, substituting A for B.

Next Row: With A, P4, (P2tog, P3) 8 times: 36 sts; finish off A.

Work 48 rows of Color Box Patt A.

Next Row (right side): With B, K4, (Ml, K4) 8 times: 44 sts; finish off B.

Rep Rows 2 through 7 of Slip Stitch Patt 7 times.

Next row (wrong side): With B, P4, (P2tog, P3) 8 times: 36 sts; finsh off B. †

Rep from † to † once more.

Work 48 rows of Color Box Patttern B; BO, weave in all ends.

Strip III is now completed.

Strip IV (make 1)
With A, cast on 36 sts.

††**Next Row (right side):** With A, K4, (M1, K4) 8 times: 44 sts; finish off A.

Rep Rows 2 through 7 of Slip Stitch Patt 7 times, substituting A for B.

Next Row (wrong side): With A, P4, (P2tog, P3) 8 times: 36 sts; finish off A.

Work 48 rows of Color Box Patt B.

Next Row (right side): With B, K4, (M1, K4) 8 times: 44 sts; finish off B.

Rep Rows 2 through 7 of Slip Stitch Patt 7 times.

Next Row (wrong side): With B, P4, (P2tog, P3) 8 times: 36 sts; finish off B.

Work 48 rows of Color Box A. ††

Rep from †† to †† once more.

Next Row (right side): With A, K4, (M1, K4) 8 times: 44 sts; finish off A.

Rep Rows 2 through 7 of Slip Stitch Patt 7 times, substituting A for B.

Next Row (wrong side): With A, P4, (P2tog, P3) 8 times: 36 sts; BO, weave in all yarn ends.

Strip IV is now completed

Joining
Sew strips tog from left to right in following sequence: I, II, III, IV, I, II and III.

Side Edgings
With right side of work facing, with MC and circular needle, pick up and knit 286 sts along one side edge of afghan.

With MC, knit 3 rows.

With A, knit 4 rows.

With B, knit 2 rows.

With A, knit 4 rows.

With MC, knit 3 rows. BO as to knit.

Work opposite side edge the same.

Top and Bottom Edgings

Top Edging
With MC and circular needle, pick up and knit 251 sts across Top (last row worked) of afghan. Work as for Side Edgings.

Bottom Edging
Work as for Top Edging across opposite end.

#94 SOFT AND SWEET

Designed by Janie Herrin

SIZE

48" X 56" before border

MATERIALS

Worsted weight yarn,
  24 oz off white
  12 oz pink
  18 oz green

Note: Photographed model made with Caron Simply Soft #9715, Fisherman, #9719 Soft Pink, and #9705 Soft Sage

Size H (5mm) crochet hook
  (or size required for gauge)

GAUGE

7 dc = 2"

Square = 8" x 8"

INSTRUCTIONS

Square (make 42)

With off white, ch 6, join to form a ring.

Rnd 1: Ch 3; in ring work dc, ch 1, (2 dc, ch 1) 7 times, join with sl st in 3rd ch of beg ch-3: 8 ch-1 sps.

Rnd 2: Sl st in next dc and into first ch-1 sp, ch 3 (counts as first dc of rnd); in same sp work (dc, ch 1, 2 dc); * in next ch-1 sp work (2 dc, ch 1, 2 dc); rep from * around, join in 3rd ch of beg ch-3.

Rnd 3: Sl st in next dc and into next ch-1 sp; ch 3, in same sp work (dc, ch 2, 2 dc): beg shell made, ch 1; * in next ch-1 sp work (2 dc, ch 2, 2 dc): shell made, ch 1; rep from * around, join as before: 8 shells.

Rnd 4: Sl st in next dc and into ch-2 sp; ch 3, in same sp work (2 dc, ch 2, 3 dc), ch 3; * sk next ch-1 sp, in next ch-2 sp work (3 dc, ch 2, 3 dc) rep from * around, join, finish off. *ch3;*

Rnd 5: Join pink with sc in ch-2 sp of any shell, 2 sc in same sp; *sc in next 3 dc, ch 1; working in front of ch-3, sc in ch-1 sp on Rnd 3, ch 1; sc in next 3 dc, 3 sc in ch-2 sp of next shell; rep from * around, ending with sl st in beg sc, finish off.

Rnd 6: Join green with sc in center sc of any 3-sc point group, ch 3, sc in same st; *ch 3, sk next sc, sc in next sc; ch 5, sk next 5 sc, sc in next sc; ch 3, sk next sc, (sc, ch 3, sc) in center sc of next 3-sc group; rep from * around ending ch 3, join in beg sc.

Rnd 7: Sl st in next ch-3 sp, ch 3 (counts as a dc), (2 dc, ch 2, 3 dc) in same sp: corner made; * 2 dc in next ch-3 sp, 5 dc in ch-5 lp, 2 hdc in next ch-3 sp; sc in next ch -3 sp, 2 hdc in next ch-3 sp; 5 dc in ch-5 lp; 2 dc in ch-3 sp, (3 dc, ch 2, 3 dc) in next ch-3 sp for corner; rep from * around two times more; 2 dc in next ch-3 sp, 5 dc in ch-5 lp, 2 hdc in next ch-3 sp, sc in next ch-3 sp, 2 hdc in next ch-3 sp, 5 dc in ch-5 lp, 2 dc in last ch-3 lp, join with sl st in 3rd ch of beg ch-3; finish off.

Rnd 8: Join pink with sc in same st as joining; sc in next 2 dc, 3 sc in ch-2 corner sp; sc in each rem st around, working 3 sc in each rem ch-2 corner sp; join with sl st in beg sc, finish off.

Rnd 9: Join off white with sc in joining and work as for Rnd 8, working 3 sc in center st of each corner sp; finish off, weave in ends.

Joining

To join, hold two squares with right sides together; with off white yarn, sew tog along one side, carefully matching sts and corners, working through outer lps only. Join squares in 7 rows of 6 squares.

Border

Rnd 1: Hold afghan with right side facing you and join off white with sc in center st at upper right corner, 2 sc in same st; sc around outer edge, adjusting sts as needed to keep work flat, and working 3 sc in center st of each outer corner; join with sl st in beg sc.

Rnd 2: Sl st in next sc, ch 3 (counts as a dc), in same sc work shell of (dc, ch 2, 2 dc), ch 1, sk 3 sc; *(2 dc, ch 2, 2 dc) in next sc, ch 1, sk 3 sc; rep from * around, on last side sk 2 or sk 4 sc at end as needed to come out even; end ch 1, join in 3rd ch of beg ch-3.

Rnd 3: Sl st in next dc and into ch-2 sp; ch 3, in same sp work shell of (2 dc, ch 2, 3 dc), ch 3; *sk next ch-1 sp, in next ch-2 sp work (3 dc, ch 2, 3 dc), ch 3; rep from * around, join, finish off.

Rnd 4: Join green with sc in ch-2 sp of any shell, 2 sc in same sp; *sc in next 3 dc, ch 1; working in front of ch-3 in rows below, sc in ch-1 sp on Rnd 2; ch 1, sc in next 3 dc, 3 sc in ch-2 sp of next shell; rep from * around, ending with sl st in beg sc, finish off.

#95 LONG STITCH RIPPLE

SIZE
42" x 56"

MATERIALS
Worsted weight yarn,
   24 oz off white (MC)
   8 oz purple (A)
   8 oz grey (B)
   8 oz lt blue (C)

Note: Photographed model made with Red Heart® Super Saver® #313 Aran (MC), #528 Medium Purple (A), #341 Light Grey (B) and #381 Light Blue (C)

Size I (5.5mm) crochet hook
   (or size required for gauge)

3" x 4 1/2" piece of cardboard

GAUGE
6 sts = 2"

2 dc rows and 2 sc rows = 2"

INSTRUCTIONS

With MC, ch 202.

Row 1 (right side): 2-dc dec in 4th ch from hook and in next ch, dc in next 9 chs, (2 dc, ch 2, 2 dc) in next ch, dc in next 9 chs; *2-dc dec in next 2 chs, skip 2 chs, 2-dc dec in next 2 chs, dc in next 9 chs, (2 dc, ch 2, 2 dc) in next ch, dc in next 9 chs; rep from * 6 times more; 3-dc dec in last 3 chs; ch 1, turn.

Row 2: Sc dec in 3-dc dec and in next dc, sc in next 10 dc, 3 sc in ch-2 sp; *sc in next 11 dc, skip next two 2-dc dec, sc in next 11 dc, 3 sc in ch-2 sp; rep from * 6 times more; sc in next 10 dc, sc dec in next dc and in 2-dc dec, changing to A; ch 3, turn. Do not finish off MC.

Row 3: Working in BLO of each st, skip first sc, 2-dc dec in next 2 sc, dc in next 9 sc, (2 dc, ch 2, 2 dc) in next sc; *dc in next 9 sc, 2-dc dec in next 2 sc, skip 2 sc, 2-dc dec in next 2 sc, dc in next 9 sc, (2 dc, ch 2, 2 dc) in next sc; rep from * 6 times more; dc in next 9 sc, 3-dc dec in last 2 sc and in sc dec; ch 1, turn.

Row 4: Rep Row 2, changing to MC in last sc dec; ch 3, turn. Finish off A and weave in ends.

Row 5: Skip first sc; *2-dc dec in next 2 sc, dc in next 5 sc, FPdtr around post of last dc before ch-2 sp 4 rows below, dc in next sc, working behind previous FPdtr, FPdtr around post of same dc 4 rows below; dc in next sc, (2 dc, ch 2, 2 dc) in next sc, dc in next sc, FPdtr around post of first dc after ch-2 sp 4 rows below, dc in next sc; working in front of previous FPdtr, FPdtr around post of same dc 4 rows below, dc in next 5 sc**, 2-dc dec in next 2 sc, skip 2 sc; rep from * 6 times more; rep from * to ** once; 3-dc dec in last 2 sc and in sc dec; ch 1, turn.

Row 6: Sc dec in 3-dc dec and in next dc, sc in next 4 dc, sc in next FPdtr, sc in next dc, sc in next FPdtr, sc in next 3 dc, 3 sc in next ch-2 sp; *sc in next 3 dc, sc in next FPdtr, sc in next dc, sc in next FPdtr; sc in next 5 dc, skip two 2-dc dec, sc in next 5 dc, sc in next FPdtr, sc in next dc, sc in next FPdtr, sc in next 3 dc, 3 sc in ch-2 sp; rep from * 6 times more; sc in next 3 dc, sc in next FPdtr, sc in next dc, sc in next FPdtr, sc in next 4 dc, sc dec in next dc and in 2-dc dec, changing to B; ch 3, turn. Do not finish off MC.

Row 7: Rep Row 3.

Continued on next page.

Row 8: Rep Row 2, changing to MC in last sc dec; ch 3, turn. Finish off B and weave in ends.

Row 9: Rep Row 5.

Row 10: Rep Row 6, changing to C in last sc dec; ch 3, turn. Do not finish off MC.

Row 11: Rep Row 3.

Row 12: Rep Row 2, changing to MC in last sc dec; ch 3, turn. Finish off C and weave in ends.

Row 13: Rep Row 5.

Row 14: Rep Row 6, changing to A in last sc dec; ch 3, turn. Do not finish off MC.

Rows 15 through 98: Rep Rows 3 through 14 seven times more. At end of Row 98, do not ch 3, turn. Finish off and weave in ends.

Edging

With right side facing, join MC with sl st around beg chs on Row 1 at bottom right-hand edge, ch 1, 2 sc around same chs, sc around edge of each sc row, 2 sc around dc post of each dc row across right-hand edge. Finish off and weave in ends. Join MC with sl st around edge of first st on Row 98 at top left-hand edge, ch 1, sc around same st, work sc across left-hand edge same as before. Finish off and weave in ends.

Tassels (make 17)

Cut two cardboard pieces 4 ¹/₂" by 3". Holding cardboard together, place a 12" length of yarn across top of cardboard. Holding A, B and C together, wind 8 times around cardboard. Tie strands together around top with 12" length. Cut yarn at bottom edge between cardboard pieces. Wrap a piece of yarn tightly around strands a few times 1" below top, securing ends with a knot. Trim ends of tassels and attach tassels to points at top and bottom of afghan.

#96 VICTORIAN ROSES

SIZE
47 1/2" x 58"

MATERIALS
Worsted weight yarn,
   30 oz off-white (A)
   18 oz pink (B)
   16 oz green (C)

Note: Photographed model made with Red Heart® Super Saver® #313 Aran (A), #372 Rose Pink (B), and #362 Spruce (C)

Size H (5mm) crochet hook
   (or size required for gauge)

GAUGE
Square = 6 1/4" x 6 1/4"

STITCH GUIDE

Beg popcorn (beg Pc): Ch 3, 3 dc in ring, remove hook from lp, insert hook from the front into 3rd ch of ch-3 and into dropped lp, draw dropped lp through ch: beg Pc made.

Popcorn (PC): 4 dc in ring, remove hook from lp, insert hook from the front into first of 4 dc and into dropped lp, draw dropped lp through first dc: PC made.

Tr decrease (tr dec): *YO twice, insert hook in next sc, YO and draw up a lp, (YO and draw through 2 lps on hook) twice**, skip next 4 sc (2 sc on current leaf and 2 sc on next leaf); rep from * to ** once; YO and draw through all 3 lps on hook: tr dec made over 6 sts.

Dc decrease (dc dec): (YO, insert hook in next st, YO and draw up a lp, YO and draw through 2 lps on hook) twice, YO and draw through all 3 lps on hook: dc dec made.

Crossed dc (Crdc): Skip next sc, dc in next sc, dc in skipped sc: Crdc made over 2 sts.

Picot: Ch 3, sl st in 3rd ch from hook: picot made.

Note: Always join new color with right side of work facing.

INSTRUCTIONS

SQUARE (make 63)

With B, ch 4; join with sl st to form a ring.

Rnd 1 (right side): Beg PC, ch 4; (PC in ring, ch 4) 3 times; join with sl st in top of beg pc: 4 PC.

Rnd 2: Sl st in next ch-4 1p, ch 1, (sc, 4 dc, sc) in same lp, *(sc, 4 dc, sc) in next ch-4 1p; rep from * around; join with sl st in first sc: 4 petals.

Rnd 3: Working behind Rnd 2 in ch-4 1ps and PC on Rnd 1, ch 4, *sc in ch-4 1p between 2nd and 3rd dc of next petal, ch 4, sc in top of next PC**, ch 4; rep from * around, end at **.

Rnd 4: Sl st in next ch-4 1p, ch 1, (sc, 5 dc, sc) in same lp, *(sc, 5 dc, sc) in next ch-4 1p; rep from * around; join with sl st in first sc: 8 petals. Finish off and weave in ends.

Rnd 5: Working behind Rnd 4, join C with sl st in any sc on Rnd 3; *ch 7, sc in 2nd ch from hook, hdc in next 2 chs, dc in last 3 chs, sl st in next sc on Rnd 3; rep from * around, working last sl st in same st as joining: 8 leaves.

Rnd 6: *Working in free lp of chs along unworked side of ch-7 on Rnd 5, skip free lp of next ch, sc in free lp of next 5 chs; 3 sc in next sc, sc in next 2 hdc, sc in next 3 dc; rep from * around; join with sl st in first sc. Finish off and weave in ends.

Rnd 7: Join A with sl st in center sc of 3 sc at point of any leaf; ch 1, 3 sc in same sc, *sc in next sc, hdc in next sc, dc in next sc; work tr dec; dc in next sc, hdc in next sc, sc in next sc**, 3 sc in next sc; rep from * around, end at **; join with sl st in first sc.

Rnd 8: Sl st in next sc, ch 1, sc in same sc, sc in next sc, *ch 1, skip next sc; (dc dec in next 2 sts) 3 times, ch 1, skip next sc, (3 dc, ch 2, 3 dc) in next (corner) sc, ch 1, skip next 2 sc, (dc dec in next 2 sts) 3 times, ch 1, skip next sc**, sc in next 2 sc; rep from * around, end at **; join with sl st in first sc.

Rnd 9: Ch 1, sc in same st as joining, sc in each st and ch-1 sp around, working 3 sc in each corner ch-2 sp; join with sl st in first sc: 84 sc (18 sc between each corner 3-sc group). Finish off and weave in ends.

Joining

Sew squares tog through back lps into 9 strips of 7 squares each.

Edging

Rnd 1: With right side of work facing, join B with sl st in center sc of any 3-sc corner group; ch 3, 4 dc in same sc; **(Crdc in next 2 sc) 10 times, *skip next joining between squares, (Crdc in next 2 sc) 10 times; rep from * to next afghan corner***; 5 dc in next corner sc; rep from ** around, end at ***; join with sl st in 3rd ch of beg ch-3. Finish off and weave in ends.

Rnd 2: Join C with sl st in to center dc of any 5-dc corner group; ch 1, sc in same st as joining; **picot, ch 3, sc in sp before next crossed dc, *picot, ch 3, sc in sp between next 2 crossed dc; rep from * to next corner, picot, ch 3, sc in sp before next corner 5-dc group; picot, ch 3***, sc in center dc of next 5-dc group; rep from ** around, end at ***; join with sl st in first sc. Finish off and weave in ends.

#97 BRIGHT AND BOLD

Designed by Janie Herrin

SIZE
32" x 48"

MATERIALS
Worsted weight yarn,
  8 oz bright blue
  8 oz bright lime
  12 oz bright multicolor

Note: Photographed model made with Red Heart® Kids™ #2854 Blue, #2652 Lime, and #2940 Beach

Size H (5mm) crochet hook,
  or size required for gauge

GAUGE
7 dc = 2"
1 square = 7 1/2" x 7 1/2"

INSTRUCTIONS

Square (make 24)

With blue, ch 5, join with a sl st to form a ring.

Rnd 1: Ch 3 (equals first dc), in ring, work 2 dc, ch 2, (3 dc, ch 2) 3 times, join in 3rd ch of beg ch-3, pull up a lp and drop yarn, do not cut blue.

Rnd 2: Join lime with sc in center dc of any 3-dc group, ch 3, sc in same st; *ch 3, sc in next ch-2 sp, ch 3, skip next dc, in next dc work (sc, ch 3, sc); rep from * around ending ch 3, join in beg sc: 12 ch-3 sps.

Rnd 3: Sl st in next sp, ch 1, 5 sc in same sp; *(3 sc in next sp) twice, 5 sc in next sp; rep from * around ending with sl st in beg sc, ch 4, pull up lp and drop yarn, do cut.

Rnd 4: Pick up blue from Rnd 2, sc in first sc of 5-sc group; *ch 2, skip next sc, in next sc work (sc, ch 2, sc); ch 2, skip next sc, sc in each of next 8 sc; rep from * around, ending with sl st in beg sc.

Rnd 5: Ch 5 (equals first dc plus ch-2); *skip next sp, in next sp work (2 dc, ch 2, 2 dc), ch 2, skip next sp, dc in sc; ch 2, skip 2 sc, dc in each of next 2 sc, ch 2, skip 2 sc, dc in next sc, ch 2; rep from * around ending with last ch 2, slip st in 3rd ch of beg ch 5; ch 3, pull up lp and drop yarn, do cut.

Rnd 6: Pick up lime from Rnd 3, 3 sc in ch-2 sp; *ch 2, skip next 2 dc, 3 sc in corner sp, ch 2, skip 2 dc, (3 sc in next sp) twice, ch 2, skip 2 dc, (3 sc in next sp) twice; rep from * around ending with 3 sc in last sp, join.

Rnd 7: Ch 1, sc in same st and in each of next 2 sc, 2 sc in sp; *sc in next sc, 3 sc in next sc, sc in next sc, 2 sc in sp, (sc in each of next 6 sc, 2 sc in sp) twice; rep from * around ending with sc in last 3 sc, join, finish off.

Rnd 8: Pick up blue from row below, sc in nearest sc (you should have 6 unused sc before next corner st), (ch 1, skip next sc, sc in next sc) twice; *ch 1, skip 2 sc, (sc, ch 3, sc) in next sc, (ch 1, skip next sc, sc in next sc) 10 times; rep from * around ending with last ch 1, join, finish off blue.

Rnd 9: Join multi-color yarn in last st, sl st in next sp, ch 3 (equals first hdc plus ch 1), (hdc in next sp, ch 1) twice; *(2 hdc, ch 2, 2 hdc) in corner sp, (ch 1, hdc in next sp) 11 times, ch 1; rep from * around ending with ch 1, sl st in 2nd ch of beg ch-3.

Rnd 10: Sl st into first sp, ch 1, sc in same sp; sc evenly around, working 3 sc in each ch-2 corner sp; join, finish off.

Joining

To join, hold 2 squares with right sides tog and sew with overcast st along one side, carefully matching sts and corners. Join squares in 6 rows of 4 squares each.

Edging

Rnd 1: Hold afghan with right side facing; join multicolor yarn with sc in corner sp at upper right; 2 sc in same sp; work sc evenly around, adjusting sts as needed to keep work flat, and working 3 sc in each rem outer corner sp; join in beg sc, finish off multicolor.

Top Border

Row 1: Hold afghan with right side facing you and one short end at top; join blue with sc in center sc of 3-sc corner group at right; *ch 20, sk next sc, sc in next sc; rep from * across to last sc of row, sc in last sc, finish off blue, do not turn.

Row 2: Join lime with sc in first skipped sc of prev row; *ch 12, sc in next skipped sc; rep from * across. Finish off.

Bottom Border

At opposite end of afghan, Rep Rows 1 and 2 of Top Border.

#98 BABY STRIPES

SIZE
31" X 36" before border

MATERIALS
Baby weight yarn,
  6 oz green print (MC)
  3 ½ oz pastel green (A)
  3 ½ oz pastel blue (B)

Note: Photographed model made with Lion Brand® Jamie® Pompadour #252 Mint Print; #269 Pastel Green; #206 Pastel Blue

Size J (6mm) crochet hook, or size required for gauge

Size I (5.5mm) crochet hook

GAUGE
13 dc = 4" with larger hook and two strands of yarn tog

9 dc rows = 4" with larger hook and two strands of yarn tog

INSTRUCTIONS

Note: Afghan is worked with two strands of yarn held tog throughout.

With two strands of yarn, larger hook and MC, ch 101.

Row 1: Dc in 4th ch from hook and in each ch across: 99 sts (counting beg skipped chs as a dc); ch 3 (counts as a dc on following row), turn.

Rows 2 and 3: Dc in each dc, ch 3, turn.

Row 4: Dc in each dc, join two strands of A held tog, ch 1, turn; finish off MC.

Row 5: With smaller hook and A, sc in first dc; *in next dc work (sc, CL); skip next dc; rep from * across, ending skip last dc, dc in top of turning ch; ch 1, turn.

Row 6: Sc in first dc; *skip top of CL; in next st, work (sc, CL); rep from * across, ending last rep dc in last st; finish off A, join two strands of B held tog; ch 1, turn.

Rows 7 and 8: With B, rep Rows 5 and 6; change to larger hook and two strands of MC held tog, ch 3, turn.

Row 9: With MC, dc each in top of CL and in next st; rep from * across, ending dc in last sc; ch 3, turn.

Rep Rows 2 through 9 eight times more, then rep Rows 2 through 4 once: 9 CL stripes worked. Finish off, weave in all ends.

Border

Rnd 1: With right side facing, join two strands of MC held tog and with larger hook in upper right corner; ch 1, 2 sc in same st; sc evenly around piece, working 3 sc in each corner and adjusting sts as needed to keep work flat; join in beg sc.

Rnd 2: Sl st in next sc; *ch 1, skip 1 sc, Pst in next st; ch 1, skip next st, sl st in next st; rep from * around, join in beg ch-1.

Rnd 3: *Ch 2, sl st to top of next Pst, ch 2, Pst in next sl st; rep from * around, join; finish off and weave in all ends.

#99 CROSS OVER THROW

Designed by Janie Herrin

SIZE
49" x 49" before border

MATERIALS
Worsted weight yarn,
   32 oz brown
   32 oz gold

Note: Photographed model made with Caron Natura One Pound, #0581 Espresso and #0549 Sunflower

Size H (5mm) crochet hook or
   size required for gauge.

GAUGE
7 dc = 2"

Square = 7" x 7"

INSTRUCTIONS

Square (make 49)

With brown, ch 6, join with sl st to form a ring.

Rnd 1: Ch 3 (equals first dc now and throughout), 15 dc in ring, join with sl st in 3rd ch of beg ch-3:16 dc.

Rnd 2: Work beg V-st, ch 2, V-st in same st; *skip next dc, V-st in next dc, skip next dc; ** in next dc work (V-st, ch 2, V-st); rep from * 2 times more, then rep from * to ** once; join with sl st in 3rd ch of beg ch 5. 12 V-sts, 4 corner ch-2 sps.

Rnd 3: Sl st in ch-2 sp of V-st, ch 1, 3 sc in same sp and in each ch-2 sp around, join in beg sc: 48 sc; finish off brown.

Rnd 4: Join gold with sl st in center sc of any corner 3-sc group, ch 3, in same sp work (2 dc, ch 2, 3 dc); *skip next 2 sc, (dc in each of next 2 sc, working in front of last 2 dc made, tr in last skipped sc, skip next sc) 3 times; in next sc work (3 dc, ch 2, 3 dc); rep from * around, ending with sl st in beg dc: mark joining for stitch placement later.

Rnd 5: Sl st in next dc, ch 3, dc in next st; working in front of last 2 dc made, tr in marked st; * (2 dc, ch 2, 2 dc) in corner sp; (skip next st, dc in each of next 2 sts, tr in skipped st as before) 5 times; rep from * around ending with 4 crossed sts, join, finish off.

Rnd 6: Join brown with sl st in any corner sp, in same sp work (ch 3, dc, ch 2, 2 dc), dc in each st around working (2 dc, ch 2, 2 dc) in each rem corner sp, end with sl st to beg dc.

Rnd 7: Sl st in next dc and into ch-2 corner sp; ch 1, 3 sc in same sp, sc in each st around, working 3 sc rem outer corner ch-2 sps; finish off, weave in ends.

Joining

To join, hold two squares with right sides tog and with brown, sew together with overcast st, carefully matching sts and corners. Then join in same manner in 7 rows of 7 squares each.

Border

Rnd 1: With right side of piece facing you, join brown with sc in center sc of 3-sc corner group at upper right, 2 sc in same st; sc in each st around, adjusting sts to keep work flat and working 3 sc in each rem corner 3-sc group.

Rnd 2: Ch 4, 2 tr in same st; 3 tr in each sc around, join with sc in 4th ch of beg ch-4.

Rnd 3: Ch 4, sk next tr, sc in next tr; *sc in next tr, ch 4, sk next tr, sc in next tr; rep from * around, join with sl st, finish off.

#100 FLORAL ACCENT

DESIGNED BY JANIE HERRIN

SIZE
45 ¹/₂" x 52 " before border

MATERIALS
Worsted weight yarn,
   18 oz mauve
   14 oz green
   18 oz natural

Note: Photographed model made with Bernat® Berella® "4" #01305 Soft Mauve, #01235 Soft Green, and #08949 Natural

Size H (5mm) crochet hook
   (or size required for gauge)

GAUGE
7 dc = 2"
Square = 6 ¹/₂" x 6 ¹/₂"

INSTRUCTIONS

Square (make 56)

With mauve, ch 5, join with sl st to form a ring.

Rnd 1: Ch 4 (equals first dc plus ch 1), in ring work (dc, ch 1) 11 times, join in 3rd ch of beg ch 4: 12 dc.

Rnd 2: Sl st in ch-1 sp, ch 4; (hdc in next sp, ch 2) 11 times, join in 2nd ch of beg ch 4: 12 ch-2 sps.

Rnd 3: Sl st in ch-2 sp, ch 3, 4 dc in same sp; *(ch 2, sc in next sp) twice, ch 2, 5 dc in next sp; rep from * around, ending with ch 2, join in 3rd ch of beg ch-3.

Rnd 4: Ch 1, sc in same st; *hdc in next dc, shell in next dc, hdc in next dc, sc in next dc; ch 1, skip next ch-2 lp, shell in next lp, ch 1; skip next lp, sc in next dc; rep from * around ending with ch 1, sl st in beg sc: 8 shells; finish off.

Rnd 5: Join green with sl st in any ch-2 corner sp, work beg shell; *ch 7, sc in ch-2 sp of next shell, ch 7, work shell in next shell; rep from * around ending ch 7, join to beg dc, ch 3 and drop yarn, do not cut.

Rnd 6: Join natural with sl st in any corner sp, work beg shell; *working behind ch-7 lp, tr in each of next 2 dc on Rnd 4, 3 dc around ch-7 lp; working behind ch-7 lp, tr in each of next 2 dc of shell on Rnd 4, dc in sc; working behind ch-7 lp, tr in each of next 2 dc on Rnd 4, 3 dc around ch-7 lp; working behind ch-7 lp, tr in each of next 2 dc of shell on Rnd 4, work shell in corner sp; rep from * around, ending with sl st in beg dc, finish off.

Rnd 7: Pick up dropped lp from Rnd 5, sc in first dc of shell, sc in next dc, 3 sc in corner sp, sc in each st around, working 3 sc in rem corners, end sl st in beg sc; finish off. Weave in ends.

Joining

To join, hold two squares with right sides tog and with green, sew through outer lps only along one side, carefully matching sts and corners. Join squares in 8 rows of 7 squares.

Border

Rnd 1: Hold piece with right side facing you and join green with sc in upper right corner; 2 sc in same st; sc in each st around, adjusting sts as needed to keep work flat, and working 3 sc in each rem outer corner st; join with sl st; finish off.

Rnd 2: Join mauve in any center sc of any 3-sc corner group, 2 sc in same sp; sc in each sc around, working 3 sc in each corner st; join with sl st, finish off.

Rnd 3: Join natural with sl st in center sc of any corner group; ch 2 (counts as a hdc), 2 hdc in same st; sk next sc; * hdc in each sc to next corner group, skip first sc of group, 3 hdc in next sc, skip next sc of group); rep from *twice more, hdc in each rem sc, join with sl st in beg hdc. Finish off.

Abbreviations and Symbols

Knit and crochet patterns are written in a special shorthand, which is used so that instructions don't take up too much space. They sometimes seem confusing, but once you learn them, you'll have no trouble following them.

These are Standard Abbreviations

BB . . . . bobble
Beg . . . . beginning
BLO . . . . back loop only
BO . . . . bind off
BPdc . . . . Back post double crochet
CL(s) . . . . cluster(s)
CO . . . . cast on
Cont. . . . . continue
Ch(s) . . . . chain(s)
Dc . . . . double crochet
Dec. . . . . decrease
Dtr . . . . double triple crochet
Fig . . . . figure
FPdc . . . . front post double crochet
FPtr . . . . front post triple crochet
Hdc. . . . . half double crochet
Inc. increase(ing)
K . . . . knit
Lp(s) . . . . loop(s)
P . . . . purl
Pat(t) . . . . pattern
PC . . . . popcorn
Prev . . . . previous
PSSO . . . . pass the slipped stitch over
Pst . . . . puff stitch
Rem . . . . remain(ing)
Rep. . . . . repeat(ing)
Rev Sc . . . . reverse single crochet
Rnd(s) . . . . round(s)
Sc. . . . . single crochet
Sk . . . . skip
Sl . . . . slip
Sp(s) . . . . space(s)
SSK . . . . slip, slip, knit
St(s) . . . . stitch(es)
Stock st . . . . stockinette stitch
Tbl . . . . through back loop
Tog . . . . together
Tr . . . . triple crochet
Trtr. . . . . triple triple crocheetss
YB. . . . . . . yarn in back of needle or hook
YF . . . . yarn in front of needle or hook
YO. . . . . Yarn over the needle or hook
YRN . . . . Yarn around needle

These are Standard Symbols

* An asterisk (or double asterisks**) in a pattern row, indicates a portion of instructions to be used more than once. For instance, "rep from * three times" means that after working the instructions once, you must work them again three times for a total of 4 times in all.

† A dagger (or double daggers ††) indicates that those instructions will be repeated again later in the same row or round.

: The number after a colon tells you the number of stitches you will have when you have completed the row or round.

( ) Parentheses enclose instructions which are to be worked the number of times following the parentheses. For instance, "(ch1, sc, ch1) 3 times" means that you will chain one, work one sc, and then chain again three times for a total of six chains and 3cs, or "(K1, P2) 3 times" means that you knit one stitch and then purl two stitches, three times.

Parentheses often set off or clarify a group of stitches to be worked into the same space or stitch. For instance, "(dc, ch2, dc) in corner sp."

[ ] Brackets and ( ) parentheses are also used to give you additional information.

Terms

Front Loop—This is the loop toward you at the top of the crochet stitch.

Back Loop—This is the loop away from you at the top of the crochet stitch.

Post—This is the vertical part of the crochet stitch

Join—This means to join with a sl st unless another stitch is specified.

Finish off—This means to end your piece by pulling the yarn through the last loop remaining on the hook or needle. This will prevent the work from unraveling.

Continue in Pattern as Established—This means to follow the pattern stitch as if has been set up, working any increases or decreases in such a way that the pattern remains the same as it was established.

Work even—This means that the work is continued in the pattern as established without increasing or decreasing.

Gauge

This is probably the most important aspect of knitting and crocheting!

GAUGE simply means the number of stitches per inch, and the numbers of rows per inch that result from a specified yarn worked with hooks or needles in a specified size. But since everyone knits or crochets differently—some loosely, some tightly, some in-between—the measurements of individual work can vary greatly, even when the crocheters or knitters use the same pattern and the same size yarn and hook or needle.

If you don't work to the gauge specified in the pattern, your afghan will never be the correct size, and you may not have enough yarn to finish your project. Hook and needle sizes given in instructions are merely guides, and should never be used without a gauge swatch.

To make a gauge swatch, crochet or knit a swatch that is about 4" square, using the suggested hook or needle and the number of stitches given in the pattern. Measure your swatch. If the number of stitches is fewer than those listed in the pattern, try making another swatch with a smaller hook or needle. If the number of stitches is more than is called for in the pattern, try making another swatch with a larger hook or needle. It is your responsibility to make sure you achieve the gauge specified in the pattern.

The patterns in this book have been written using the knitting and crochet terminology that is used in the United States. Terms which may have different equivalents in other parts of the world are listed below.

United States	International
Double crochet (dc)	treble crochet (tr)
Gauge	tension
Half double crochet (hdc)	half treble crochet (htr)
Single crochet	double crochet
Skip	miss
Slip stitch	single crochet
Triple crochet (tr)	double treble crochet (dtr)
Yarn over (YO)	yarn forward (yfwd)
Yarn around needle (yrn)	yarn over hook (yoh)

Knitting Needles Conversion Chart

U.S.	0	1	2	3	4	5	6	7	8	9	10	10½	11	13	15	17
Metric	2	2.25	2.75	3.25	3.5	3.75	4	4.5	5	5.5	6	6.5	8	9	10	12.75

Crochet Hooks Conversion Chart

U.S.	B-1	C-2	D-3	E-4	F-5	G-6	H-8	I-9	J-10	K-10 12	N	P	Q
Metric	2.25	2.75	3.25	3.5	3.75	4	5	5.5	6	6.5	0	10	15

Fringe

Basic Instructions

Cut a piece of cardboard about 6" wide and half as long as specified in the instructions for strands, plus 1/2" for trimming allowance. Wind the yarn loosely and evenly lengthwise around the cardboard. When the card is filled, cut the yarn across one end. Do this several times; then begin fringing. You can wind additional strands as you need them.

Single Knot Fringe

Hold the specified number of strands for one knot of fringe together, then fold in half.

Hold the project with the right side facing you. Using a crochet hook, draw the folded ends through the space or stitch from right to wrong side.

Pull the loose ends through the folded section.

Draw the knot up firmly.

Space the knots evenly and trim the ends of the fringe.

Double Knot Fringe

Begin by working Single Knot Fringe. With right side facing you and working from left to right, take half the strands of one knot and half the strands in the knot next to it, and knot them together.

Triple Knot Fringe

First work Double Knot Fringe. Then working again on right side from left to right, tie the third row of knots.

ACKNOWLEDGMENTS

Technical Editor: Susan Lowman
Photography: Carol Wilson Mansfield
Book Design: Graphic Solutions, inc-chgo
Produced by: Creative Partners,™ LLC.

All of the afghans in this book were tested to ensure the accuracy and clarity of the instructions. We are grateful to the following pattern testers who made the afghans photographed in this book:

Crystal Babcock, Milford, Connecticut

J. Barrett, Portsmouth, Rhode Island

Denise Black, Oceanside, California

Brenda Bourg, Firestone, Colorado

Sherry Briggs, Memphis, Missouri

Kimberly Britt, Gurnee, Illinois

Kathy Christensen, Oceanside, California.

Cheryl Cole, Youngstown, Ohio

Peggy Cress, Chesterton, Indiana

Carrie Cristiano, Escondido, California

Sarah Fleming Davis, Centralia, Washington

Vinette DePhillipe, Galien, Michigan

Cathy Fogel, Los Angeles, California

Eileen Gaffigan, Silver Springs, Maryland

Toni Gill, Grand Junction, Colorado

Patricia Honaker, East Liverpool, Ohio

Lois Karklus, Tulsa, Oklahoma

Wilma Keith, Sacramento, California

Flora Loobey, Bristol, Tennessee

Jenny Lute, Kingsville, Ohio

Jennifer Marr, Edmond, Oklahoma

Hilary Murphy, Derry, New Hampshire

Joyce Noverr, Auburndale, Massachusetts

Denise Petersen, Evanston, New York

Tracy Pokrzwa, Kalamazoo, Michigan

Kelly Robinson, Anza, California

Marsha Sieber, Sweet Home, Oregon

Lindsay Streem, Chicago, Illinois

Carole Sullivan, Lakeside, Arizona

Gretchen Thorson, Sarasota, Florida

Sue Wagenschwanz, Cumming, Georgia

Alice Wheatley, Des Moines, Iowa

Renee Wissbroecker, Delano, Minnesota

The authors extend their thanks and appreciation to Kathleen Sams and her associates at Coats & Clark, to Catherine Blythe and the design department at Patons Yarns, and to Nancy Thomas of Lion Brand Yarn for sharing many of their most creative designs with us.

Wherever we have used a special yarn, we have given the brand name. If you are unable to find these yarns locally, write to the following manufacturers who will be able to tell you where to purchase their products, or consult their internet sites. We also wish to thank these companies for supplying yarn for this book.

Bernat Yarns
320 Livingston Avenue South
Listowel, Ontario
Canada N4W 3H3
www.bernat.com

Caron International
Customer Service
P. O. Box 222
Washington, North Carolina 27889
www.caron,com

Lion Brand Yarn
34 West 15th Sreet
New York, New York 10011
www.LionBrand.com

Patons Yarns
2700 Dufferin Street
Toronto, Ontario
Canada M6B 4J3
www.patonsyarns.com

Plymouth Yarn Co., Inc.
500 Lafayette Street
P. O. Box 28
Bristol, Pennsylvania 19007-0028
www.plymouthyarn.com

Red Heart Yarns
Coats and Clark
Consumer Services
P. O. Box 12229
Greenville, South Carolina 29612-0229
www.coatsandclark.com

TLC Yarns
Coats and Clark
Consumer Services
P. O, Box 12229
Greenville, South Carolina 29612-0229
www.coatsandclark.com

*Every effort has been made to ensure the accuracy of these instructions.
We cannot, however, be responsible for human error or variations in your work.*

Abbreviations, 220
Afghans in a Jiffy, 137
Americana, 84
Aran Isle, 70
Autumn Glory, 32
Baby Clouds, 164
Baby Stripes, 214
Beautiful Blues, 14
Blue is for Boys, 184
Blueberry Pie, 40
Bold Plaid, 134
Branches & Berries, 50
Bright and Bold, 212
Cabled Classic, 196
Cables & Checks, 10
Captain's Wheel, 146
Cathedral Window, 140
Chevrons & Diamonds, 113

Children's Afghans
Baby Clouds, 164
Baby Stripes, 214
Blue is for Boys, 184
Bright and Bold, 212
Choo-Choo, 132
Cotton Candy, 68
Country Hearts, 154
Curly O's, 170
Fringed for Baby, 54
Just Peachy, 118
Merry Sunshine, 148
Nursery Time, 21
Pretty Plaid, 64
Pretty Puffs, 93
Ship Ahoy, 150
Sweet Hearts, 172
Two Sides to the Story, 96

Choo-Choo, 132
Classic Style, 42,
Cluster Wheel, 130
Coming Up Rosy, 78
Cotton Candy, 68
Country Hearts, 154
Country Roses, 26
Cozy Mile-a-Minute, 124

Crochet Afghans
Afghans in a Jiffy, 137
Americana, 84
Aran Isle, 70
Autumn Glory, 32
Baby Clouds, 164

Baby Stripes, 214
Beautiful Blues, 14
Blue is for Boys, 184
Blueberry Pie, 40
Branches & Berries, 50
Bright and Bold, 212
Cables & Checks, 10
Captain's Wheel, 146
Cathedral Window, 140
Chevrons & Diamonds, 113
Choo-Choo, 132
Classic Style, 42,
Cluster Wheel, 130
Coming Up Rosy, 78
Cotton Candy, 68
Country Hearts, 154
Country Roses, 26
Cozy Mile-a-Minute, 124
Cross Over Throw, 216
Curled Tips Daisy, 22
Curly O's, 170
Daisies Won't Tell Lapghan, 192
Dancing Daisies, 12
Deep Purple, 72
Dream Panels, 106
Embossed Floral, 198
Evening Shadows, 88
Filet Ruffles, 94
Floral Accent, 218
Flower Power, 188
Fringed for Baby, 54
Garden Path, 168
Granny Goes Straight, 138
Impressions, 142
Jacob's Ladder, 152
Just Peachy, 118
Lemonade Skies, 86
Lilac Lace, 16
Long Stitch Ripple, 206
Lovely Lace, 126
Lumberjack, 31
Marvelous Mauve, 116
Merry Sunshine, 148
Mesh'in Around, 194
Monet Pineapple, 36
Nursery Time, 21
Pineapple Throw, 82
Polka Dot Country, 122
Popcorn & Lace, 76
Pretty Plaid, 64
Pretty Puffs, 93
Reflections on the Go, 60
Renaissance Beauty, 128

Ripple Romance, 35
Rose Garden, 179
Rose Ripple, 104
Rosy Ruffles, 108
Sage Wheel, 102
Sailing Along, 66
Sand Castle, 44
Scrap Sensation, 56
Shaded Panels, 46
Ship Ahoy, 150
Singing the Blues, 48
Snow Trees, 176
Soft and Sweet, 204
Sophisticated Summer, 186
Stained Glass, 157
Starry Night, 100
Summer Sunshine, 98
Sweet Hearts, 172
Tiffany Rose, 90
Tropical Daisy, 174
Turtle Shells, 8
Twilight Wave, 166
Two Sides to the Story, 96
Victorian Roses, 209
Vineyard View, 120
Walk in the Woods, A, 190
White Stars, 18

Cross Over Throw, 216
Curled Tips Daisy, 22
Curly O's, 170
Daisies Won't Tell Lapghan, 192
Dancing Daisies, 12
Deep Purple, 72
Double Knot Fringe, 221
Dream Panels, 106
Earth Tones, 28
Embossed Floral, 198
Evening Shadows, 88
Filet Ruffles, 94
Floral Accent, 218
Flower Power, 188
Fringe, 221
Fringed for Baby, 54
Garden Path, 168
Gauge, 220
General Directions, 220
Granny Goes Straight, 138
Impressions, 142
International terms, 221
In the Pink, 62
Jacob's Ladder, 152
Jewel Ripple, 81

Just Peachy, 118

Knit afghans
Bold Plaid, 134
Cabled Classic, 196
Earth Tones, 28
In the Pink, 62
Jewel Ripple, 81
Pretty Lace, 39
Quick Cable, 24
Rainbow Rib, 160
Rich Cables, 110
Ripple at Dawn, 162
Soft Shades, 182
Summer Night Patchwork, 200
Sweet Scallops, 59
Waves, 75

Lemonade Skies, 86
Lilac Lace, 16
Long Stitch Ripple, 206
Lovely Lace, 126
Lumberjack, 31
Marvelous Mauve, 116
Merry Sunshine, 148
Mesh'in Around, 194
Monet Pineapple, 36
Nursery Time, 21
Pineapple Throw, 82
Polka Dot Country, 122
Popcorn & Lace, 76
Pretty Lace, 39
Pretty Plaid, 64
Pretty Puffs, 93
Quick Cable, 24
Rainbow Rib, 160
Reflections on the Go, 60
Renaissance Beauty, 128
Rich Cables, 110

Ripple Afghans
Jewel Ripple, 81
Long Stitch Ripple, 206
Ripple at Dawn, 162
Ripple Romance, 35
Rose Ripple, 104
Singing the Blues, 48
Summer Sunshine, 98
Twilight Wave, 166

Ripple at Dawn, 162
Ripple Romance, 35
Rose Garden, 179

Rose Ripple, 104
Rosy Ruffles, 108
Sage Wheel, 102
Sailing Along, 66
Sand Castle, 44
Scrap Sensation, 56
Shaded Panels, 46
Ship Ahoy, 150
Singing the Blues, 48
Single Knot Fringe, 221
Snow Trees, 176
Soft and Sweet, 204
Soft Shades, 182
Sophisticated Summer, 186
Stained Glass, 157
Starry Night, 100
Summer Night Patchwork, 200
Summer Sunshine, 98
Sweet Hearts, 172
Sweet Scallops, 59
Symbols, 220
Terms, 220
Tiffany Rose, 90
Triple Knot Fringe, 221
Tropical Daisy, 174
Turtle Shells, 8
Twilight Wave, 166
Two Sides to the Story, 96
Victorian Roses, 209
Vineyard View, 120
Walk in the Woods, A, 190
Waves, 75
White Stars, 18